THE EDUCATIONAL SERVICE AGENCY

American Education's Invisible Partner

E. Robert Stephens

William G. Keane

University Press of America,®️ Inc.
Lanham · Boulder · New York · Toronto · Oxford

Copyright © 2005 by
University Press of America,® Inc.
4501 Forbes Boulevard
Suite 200
Lanham, Maryland 20706
UPA Acquisitions Department (301) 459-3366

PO Box 317
Oxford
OX2 9RU, UK

Library of Congress Control Number: 2005921312
ISBN 0-7618-3155-X (paperback : alk. ppr.)

Contents

Chapter 4–Structure and Organization of ESAs: A Commentary   **85**

Chapter 8–Strengthening Schools Through ESA Partnerships
161

List of Figures

List of Tables

Contents

Acknowledgements

This first book in general circulation about educational service agencies would not have happened without the support and assistance of many people too numerous to name here. However, a few people deserve special mention.

Members of the Association of Educational Service Agencies (AESA), a national association representing service agencies primarily in America but with a few members from Europe, were essential to the data-gathering process. Since there is such a paucity of research and writing about educational service agencies, it was necessary to create our own data files. Members of AESA were most gracious in sharing copies of annual reports and other district publications, which were invaluable in identifying agencies that featured programs of the types described herein. Some chief executives also helped with a targeted survey that we distributed nationally. Dr. Brian Talbott, chief executive of the association and Kari Arfstrom, the associate director, facilitated communication with the membership across the country.

Three Ph.D. students in Educational Leadership at Oakland University—Cheryl Peters, William Coale and Nancy Larsen—were responsible for uncovering research on several key topics.

Two highly regarded educational service agency chief executives read the manuscript in draft form and offered valuable ideas about content and presentation of the text. We are indebted to Craig Stanley, executive director of the Greater Lawrence Educational Collaborative in Methuen, Massachusetts and Peter Young, now fiscal agent for AESA and former executive director of ACES, in North Haven, Connecticut, for their editorial suggestions.

Completion of a book about a topic with so shallow a database proved more challenging in the execution than in the contemplation. We are grateful to our spouses, Donna Stephens and Gerry Keane, for their patience, support and understanding throughout the development of this book.

Despite the kindness, encouragement, and suggestions from many, we fully accept responsibility for the content of this book.

E. Robert Stephens
William G. Keane

Introduction
The Invisible Service Agency

America's educational service agencies (henceforth referred to as ESAs, the generic acronym used to identify these entities in federal legislation) are unequivocally the least understood and the worst-documented component of public elementary and secondary education. There are many reasons for this situation.

Service agencies come in many shapes and forms. Some are deliberate creations of the state, either through constitutional mandate, legislative authorization, or state board of education rule-making authority. While some voluntary cooperatives are authorized in state legislation and may have the benefit of a small amount of state funding, others are constantly popping up as a result of voluntary initiatives among a group of local school districts that realize that they can provide low incidence, and therefore expensive, programming and/or services less expensively by pooling resources. There are hundreds, if not thousands, of examples of special schools and sites established by local districts at their own initiative to serve children with low-incidence disabilities, to offer expensive vocational education programs, to create special schools for gifted and talented, and to carry out other program initiatives often beyond the financial capability of one district. When separate organizational structures are established to operate these programs, they often become eligible to seek discretionary funding from state and federal agencies as well as other funding sources; therefore, in this manner they become even more cost-effective.

The state-initiated networks of service agencies and the voluntary collaboratives probably constitute the largest number of service centers in America. Regional offices of the state department of education, in the limited instances where they exist, do provide some services, but these offices are not a major type of service agency. There is a fourth general type of service agency that defies easy description. Many of them are simply regional offices of the state department of education. In a few other cases agencies established for one purpose are evolving into something else. For example, county offices of education in the state of Arizona, established largely to carry out administrative functions on behalf of the state department of education in dealing with local school districts, often small and rural, are evolving into agencies that provide programs and services needed and requested by local school districts (Harmon 2001). Service agencies in Connecticut, originally established to facilitate cooperation among local districts but initially provided with virtually no state funding, are evolving into instruments of state policy, at least in relation to the state's obligation to provide equity among school districts (Saloom 2001). *Chapters 1* and *2* will provide detailed information about the history of educational service agencies as well as the most widely used taxonomy to describe their similarities and differences from state to state.

In order to assure clarity throughout the discussion it is best to start with a widely accepted definition of what is meant by the term "educational service agency." The Association of Educational Service Agencies (AESA), the national professional association representing service agencies throughout America, describes service agencies as "public entities created by statute to provide educational support programs and services to local schools and school districts" (AESA 2000). However, this organization has chosen to represent only those service agencies that provide a range of services to local districts, not those that provide one targeted area of service (special education, for example). Therefore, their definition does not include, nor do they try to serve, all of the ad hoc organizations initiated collaboratively by local school districts that provide a single program or service. The topic of what type of agency is properly described as a service agency will be developed in *Chapter 3*.

State organized networks of service agencies tend to have common purposes in state policy. The state of Texas is quite precise in defining the purposes of its education service centers:

- ◆   assist school districts in improving student performance (TEC § 8.002)
- ◆   enable school districts to operate more efficiently and economically (TEC §8.002)
- ◆   implement initiatives assigned by the legislature or the commissioner (TEC §8.002)
- ◆   (may) offer any service requested and purchased by any school district or campus in the state (TEC § 8.053)
- ◆   (may) provide purchasing and administrative functions in order to achieve efficiencies of operation for any school district when the board of trustees of a school district so determines (TEC § 8.122(d))

The purposes of improving student performance and fostering more efficient and cost-effective performance on the part of local school districts are common in legislation authorizing service agencies in almost all states.

Under the AESA definition of service agency, in the year 2004 there were 42 states that had established or authorized the establishment of service agencies. Earlier data compiled when only 35 states had service agencies showed that approximately 65 million school children in American public schools went to schools in states with multi-function service agencies (AESA 2000). It is probable that voluntarily established service centers exist in virtually all states. Much of the information referenced in this book are generally drawn from the last data compiled by the National Center for Educational Statistics in 2001-2002.

The difficulties involved in gathering reliable data about service agencies can easily be seen. Some states have formally established state networks of service agencies; therefore, state departments of education might reasonably be expected to collect reliable data about these entities. Yet, partially because of the downsizing of many state departments of education in recent years, there may be no office or person who can devote substantial time to managing the affairs of service agencies or to collecting data about their work. Single purpose centers are constantly being organized and disbanded and, though they may exist under the authority of legislation which permits them, they are not a specific concern of the state department; therefore, there is virtually no organized data about them.

Federal efforts to collect data about service agencies inevitably succumb to the weaknesses of state data collection efforts. No one knows for sure how much money is spent in the aggregate even by the state-authorized multi-service agencies, either directly in carrying out their responsibilities or indirectly by serving as a state-approved "flow-through" center for federal and state funds. One estimate of the number of dollars expended by or through service agencies, this one by (AESA n.d.) identifies the figure of 1.5 trillion dollars, though this figure is more an extrapolation of data known about K-12 education than it is a summary of service agency-provided information (AESA). A study of service agencies in the 15 states that have a network of service centers reaching all or nearly all of the pupils in the state showed that ESAs in just six states (Georgia, Michigan, Pennsylvania, Texas, Washington, and Ohio) expended 2.7 billion dollars in one year. The same study showed that the expenditure levels of most of the other states were "not available" (Stephens 2001). Data gathered by the National Center for Educational Statistics depend on state-supplied data. Different states have different capacities to collect their own data, different levels of confidence in the accuracy of the data (Is it supplied directly by the service center or it derived from data at the state department?), and different definitions of what entities should be reported in the category "service agency."

The authors of this publication attempted to gather data from the approximately 500 service agencies that are members of their national association, the Association of Educational Service Agencies (AESA). (Actually it is an international association of service agencies. A discussion of other countries in which service agencies are part of the educational delivery system is beyond the scope of this book.). Two areas of information were the focus of this study for the fiscal year 2001-2002: (1) the number of dollars spent directly by the agency in providing programs and services and the number of state and federal "flow-through" dollars moving to local districts and for which service agencies usually have some accounting responsibility; and, (2) the number of teachers, administrators, non-certificated staff, and "other" personnel who participated in training programs. A response was received from 142 of these agencies. The data are not precise in that some agencies admitted that they did not keep client participation data separate by class of employees or "others" (parents, business people, etc.). Nevertheless these data are probably the most precise yet collected regarding service agencies. These data show that 142 service agencies spent **over $3.5 billion** on the direct delivery of programs and services and managed an additional **$17 billions** of flow-through money. Over **1.1 million** people—teachers, administrators, classified staff, parents and others—were provided education and training through these entities. It cannot be stated with confidence that, because a little over 20% of the service agencies in the nation responded to this study, that a likely total figure for the nation is five times study results. Actually the numbers may be higher since large states like California and New York responded poorly to attempts to gather this data. This kind of extrapolation is dangerously flawed.

The data that were collected are, we would suggest, sufficiently gargan-
tuan to identify education services agencies as major players in the education delivery system. Their "invisibility" needs to end if public policy makers are to
have adequate information to assess whether service agencies should be established in states where they do not exist, enhanced in their scope and number in
states where they already have a presence, and to determine the most effective
number of agencies to most appropriately service the needs of students within
the different geographies of each state.

Despite the data deprivation surrounding the finances of service agencies,
much is known about their history (covered in *Chapters 1 and 2*) and current
programs and services.

The 1960s and 1970s saw rapid growth and expansion in the roles and
functions of county offices of education, which had provided basic administrative services on behalf of local districts, into service agencies providing a wide
variety of programs and services requested by local school districts (Stephens
and Turner 1991). In the 1990s and beyond, service agencies have been pressed
by state leaders to demonstrate the efficacy of their programs and services in
helping underachieving schools and districts (discussed in *Chapters 3 and 4*).
Chapter 5 describes the work of service agencies in facilitating the improvement
of teacher performance and therefore student achievement as well as the current
roles played by ESAs in providing programs and services to children in the general education population.

A number of states first decided on the need to create service agencies
upon the passage of the federal *Education of All Handicapped Act* in 1973.
Whether or not the state had provided mandatory educational services for handicapped students in its own law, serving all handicapped students in the "least restrictive environment" at that time became the law of the land. Legislators soon
realized that it would be prohibitively expensive to try to educate children with
low incidence handicaps separately in every school district. The service center
became a commonly accepted vehicle for serving these students on behalf of local districts. *Chapter 6* looks at the role of service agencies in providing special
education and vocation education, another expensive delivery system, on behalf
of local districts, as well as programs on behalf of other "special populations."
Though not all service agencies are organized to provide training and support for
the cost-efficient delivery of administrative services in local districts (transportation, food service, financial services, etc.), there are enough that are to make it
important to tell this story (*Chapter 7*). From helping to recruit and train school
bus drivers to instructing food service staff how to provide nutritious meals in a
sanitary environment, as well as other administrative services, service agencies
are providing expert help at minimal, if any, cost to local districts. These are
services that all students across America ought to receive.

As public education has moved into the 21st Century, service agencies
have taken on several important new roles. The aphorism that it "takes a village"
to educate a child has been transformed from a book title by the former First
Lady of the United States, now senator from New York (Rodham Clinton 1996)

into state and national policy. Schools have found themselves working with police agencies, health departments, the courts, family service agencies, nonprofit
organizations, business organizations such as Chambers of Commerce and other
entities to avoid duplication of services, pool resources, and share knowledge
and information. Service agencies, which have a constituency across a region,
become the ideal agency to coordinate the work of educators with these other
organizations. These partnerships are discussed in *Chapter 8.*

As these new roles for educational service agencies have been evolving,
many questions have been raised about the willingness of service agencies to accomplish these new tasks and their effectiveness in being a key instrument of
state policy in improving schools. Therefore, many states have recently commissioned studies of the effectiveness of their state-endorsed system of service
agencies. In virtually every case the efficacy of service agencies has been con-
firmed. A number of states have sought to assure the continuing ability of service agencies to make local school districts more effective and efficient by establishing accreditation procedures for service agencies, an effort that is forcing
ESAs to measure not only the satisfaction of users with their programs and services but also to provide hard evidence that student learning is improving because of these very programs and services *(Chapters 9 and 10).*

Some states have asked regional service agencies not only to help districts
improve their programs but also to act on behalf of the state in assuring that state
dollars are being expended for their defined purpose and to monitor whether
various state rules and regulations are being implemented as required. Most service agencies relish their role as confidants, helpers, and supporters. However,
they feel that serving as monitoring and compliance officers on behalf of the
state requires of them what is essentially a conflict of roles.

In recent years private business has taken on an increasingly visible role in
public education. Whether the company is offering to take over and run a school
or, occasionally, a school district, or simply provide a special program such as
foreign language instruction in nonconventional languages, business entities are
seeking o provide many of the services formerly the exclusive province of the
service agency (Flam and Keane 1997).

In addition, some of the fundamental principles of school finance and administration are under attack. It has been proposed that dollars follow each child
to whatever school the parents choose for the child (Solmon and Fox 1998). It
has been argued that schools, not central administrators, should build the budget
for each building (McAdams 2000). Some national and state political figures
have argued that state education dollars should be given to parents (vouchers) to
be invested in whatever public or private school the parent wishes to select
(Chubb and Moe 1990). The option for states to do that very thing was approved
by the U.S. Supreme Court in 2000. Any and all of these changes would under-
cut the basic processes and funding mechanisms whereby service agencies either
use state dollars in the form of state aid or district dollars in the form of purchase
of programs and services for the district. The nature and form of service agencies may well be changed dramatically in an increasingly market-driven educa-

tional environment. *Chapter 11,* in discussing the future of educational service agencies, will explore how these changes may require ESAs to become increasingly entrepreneurial and to form partnerships with the very entities that could become their competitors.

Nothing remains the same indefinitely. Service agencies, narrowly defined, were largely conceived and established just 30-40 years ago. The authors develop three possible scenarios for their future in *Chapter 11.*

One of the many features of educational service agencies that make them difficult for the average citizen to grasp is the different names by which they are known in the various states. In Michigan, where one of the authors served as a service agency superintendent for 14 years, they were generally known as *intermediate school districts* for the first 30 years of their existence since they were perceived to stand at an intermediate point between the state department of education and local districts. While the name may be logically sound, it has been a mixed blessing. When one of the authors of this publication was leaving the superintendency of a local school district to assume the leadership of the intermediate unit, a parent, generally well-versed in school affairs, called to congratulate him on becoming head of all the middle schools in the county! While the majority of service agencies in this state are still known as intermediate school districts (ISDs), some are now called Educational Service Agencies (in line with the name of the national organization). A few others, perhaps to justify the title of "superintendent" for the chief executive, have become ESDs (education service districts). It's hardly a surprise that the average citizen finds it hard to learn more about the nature and purposes of these entities. A list of titles for the comprehensive service agencies that are the subject of this book may be found in *Chapter 3.*

It is the intention of this publication to try to develop a common knowledge base about the least understood component of America's system of public education. Therefore, many examples are given of services, both standard and singular, provided throughout the country. However, it is not the goal of this publication to offer a comprehensive database regarding every service agency in each state. In no case should the reader assume that citation of a service provided by one agency implies that no other agency provides such a service, even in the same state. Identification of one, two or three service agencies with a particular service is intended only to be of assistance to the reader in any personal effort to find out more about how a particular service is provided.

Comprehensive service agencies are often charged in law to meet the special needs of their constituents. Therefore, service agencies serving rural districts tend to provide similar but by no means identical services since each type of community (rural, urban, suburban) has special needs and circumstances. On the other hand, ESAs serving metropolitan areas throughout the county may resemble each other more so than another ESA serving essentially rural area within the same state.

Virtually all citations of services provided by ESAs were drawn from annual reports shared by each agency with the authors. Therefore, no formal citations have been given for each program reference. All comprehensive service agencies throughout the nation have web pages so for further information about referenced programs the reader is encouraged to access the web page of the ESA that provides the program of interest. The offices of the Association of Education Service Agencies (AESA) may also be contacted for further information about an individual agency. It should be noted that the availability and comprehensiveness of the annual reports submitted by each agency somewhat influence the number of examples that could be offered from each state.

REFERENCES

Association of Educational Service Agencies. n.d. *AESA's design for the future: The first look.* Arlington, VA: Author.

Association of Educational Service Agencies. 2000. "Foundation for the Future" campaign prospectus. Arlington, VA: Author.

Chubb, J. E., and Moe, T. M. 1990. *Politics, markets, and America's schools.* Washington, DC: Brookings Institution Press.

Flam, S., and Keane, W. G. 1997. *Public education/private enterprise: What you should know and do about privatization.* Lancaster, PA: Technomic Press.

Harmon, J. 2001. Educational service agencies in Arizona: Changing to meet new needs. *Perspectives,* 7:43-45.

McAdams, D. R. 2000. *Fighting to save our urban schools and winning! Lessons from Houston.* New York: Teachers College Press.

Rodham Clinton, H. 1996. *It takes a village: And other lessons children teach us.* New York: Simon and Schuster.

Saloom, S. 2001. Reducing racial, ethnic, and economic isolation in Connecticut: An essential role for service agencies. *Perspectives,* 7:4-7.

Solmon. L. C., and Fox, M. 1998. Fatally flawed school funding formulas. *Education Week,* 60 (June 17):48.

Stephens, E. R. 2001. *Characteristics of state networks of educational service agencies comparable to the Ohio educational service centers.* Edmond, OK: Institute for Regional and Rural Studies.

Stephens, E. R., and Turner, W. 1991. *Approaching the next millennium: Educational service agencies in the 1990s.* Arlington, VA: American Association of Educational Service Agencies.

Texas Education Code. 1997. § 8.122(d).

Chapter 1

The Evolution of the Educational Service Agency Concept 1930-1960

INTRODUCTION

Educational service agencies are organizations that are created by enactment of special state legislation or administrative rule to provide programs and services to a collection of schools and local school districts, or to serve state interests in other ways. They are now in place in a majority of the 50 state systems. They represent what earlier students of school government in the past (e.g., DeYoung 1942) frequently referred to as the "middle echelon" unit of school government that characterizes the three-tier structure of most state systems of elementary-secondary education. More recent observers of the structure of state school systems have used the term "intermediate unit" in reference organizations that lie between the state and local districts (Knezevich 1984; Campbell, Cunningham, Mystrand and Usdan 1990; Guthrie and Reed 1991) and some of the nation's most important state networks of service agencies still have the term "intermediate" in their official titles (e.g., in the case of the 29 Intermediate Units in Pennsylvania, in the case of most of the 57 Intermediate School Districts in Michigan). It is also true that the two terms—"middle echelon" and "intermediate unit" satisfy two important criteria that ought to be honored in naming an organization; that is, they both have conceptual clarity and descriptive validity. However, the continued use of these terms is only of limited utility at the present time. As will be established below, not all contemporary educational service agencies should be viewed as a highly formalized unit of school government positioned between the state and local districts.

The generic appellation "educational service agency" (ESA) is now commonly used in the professional literature to refer to all these units, irrespective of the specific nomenclature by which they are known in each state, and this expression will be used through the book. For example, the one major national professional association devoted to the interests of professionals who work in educational service agency-type organizations is called the Association of Educational Service Agencies. Moreover, and importantly, a number of recently enacted federal pieces of legislation, such as *Goals 2000: Educate America Act of 1994*, and *No Child Left Behind Act of 2001*, both use the term educational service agency, thus adding further legitimacy to the term in federal policy circles that it had not enjoyed before.

The mission and programming of most of the present day service organizations that are chartered by the state to serve schools and local school district interests, the state interests, or the interests of both has changed fundamentally from earlier "middle echelon" agencies. Indeed, the evolution of the earlier day educational service agency-type organization is arguably one of the most significant developments in school government, especially during the past four decades. Moreover, the development of the contemporary educational service agency is a fascinating story for it in many ways mirrors the struggles faced by local and state interests to address the huge socioeconomic changes that have impacted public education over time, as well as the challenges presented by the rising expectations that have been placed on schools, school districts, and the state. The efforts of ESAs, with their limited resources, to implement policy issues initiated by the state and also serve needs defined by local districts reflect their continuing efforts to strike a meaningful balance in the centralization-decentralization of educational policy.

STAGES IN THE EVOLUTION OF THE SERVICE AGENCY CONCEPT

We have chosen to make use of four stages to trace the gradual progression and advancement of the contemporary concept of educational service agency-type organizations as they currently operate in the states:

Stage 1: The Early Formative Period

Stage 2: The Concept at a Crossroads

Stage 3: The "Golden Age" of Development

Stage 4: The Restructuring Period

The approximate time period covered by each of the stages is shown in Figure 1.1. Also provided is a brief description of the major distinguishing features of each. Brief descriptions are provided regarding the most significant features in the development and advancement of the concept.

We acknowledge that all attempts at the periodization of the type used here are, of course, artificial. However, such efforts are of value in outlining broad trends, the approximate time period when major shifts took place or were discernable in the workings of service agencies, reflecting as these do changing expectations held for them by local and state interests.

Additionally, it is stressed that the four stages described here represent an attempt to convey the unfolding of a concept as it has been and is being implemented across a large number of states. However, not every existing example of an educational service agency-type organization has moved through each of the four stages. Indeed, some states initially sanctioned the use of a type of service agency early in its statehood (e.g., the county office of education), only to subsequently dissolve the office. Moreover, some of the currently operating educational service agency-type organizations do not represent a restructuring of a predecessor agency, but were created whole in Stage 3, the "Golden Age of Development Period."

The rest of this chapter will discuss the first two stages of this evolution. Stage 3 and Stage 4 are discussed in the next chapter.

Figure 1.1
The Four Major Stages in the Development of the
Educational Service Agency Concept

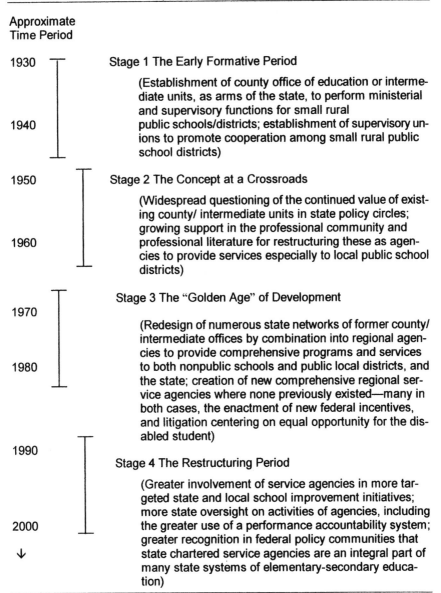

Approximate
Time Period

1930 ─ Stage 1 The Early Formative Period

(Establishment of county office of education or intermediate units, as arms of the state, to perform ministerial
and supervisory functions for small rural
1940 public schools/districts; establishment of supervisory unions to promote cooperation among small rural public
school districts)

1950 Stage 2 The Concept at a Crossroads

(Widespread questioning of the continued value of existing county/ intermediate units in state policy circles;
growing support in the professional community and
1960 professional literature for restructuring these as agencies to provide services especially to local public school
districts)

Stage 3 The "Golden Age" of Development
1970

(Redesign of numerous state networks of former county/
intermediate offices by combination into regional agencies to provide comprehensive programs and services
1980 to both nonpublic schools and public local districts, and
the state; creation of new comprehensive regional service agencies where none previously existed—many in
both cases, the enactment of new federal incentives,
and litigation centering on equal opportunity for the disabled student)

1990

Stage 4 The Restructuring Period

(Greater involvement of service agencies in more targeted state and local school improvement initiatives;
more state oversight on activities of agencies, including
2000 the greater use of a performance accountability system;
greater recognition in federal policy communities that
↓ state chartered service agencies are an integral part of
many state systems of elementary-secondary education)

STAGE 1: THE EARLY FORMATIVE PERIOD

The evolution of the concept of an educational service agency-type organization designed to provide programs and services to schools and school districts

and/or to the state is intricately related to the early history of the development of public education in the nation and how the states originally organized their state system of elementary-secondary education. It is well-established in constitutional, statutory, and judicial decisions that public education is a state function. All state constitutions direct the state legislatures to provide for a state system of public education (Valente 1994). Moreover, the principle is also well-established that the state legislature, subject to both state and federal restrictions, "has authority to pass any act of a legislative nature which may in its option seems wise" (Edwards 1995, p. 27). It follows then that the power of the state over its educational system is plenary; subject only to such limitations as may be imposed by the state and federal constitutions. That is, the state may alter or dissolve that which it has plenary authority to create. In commenting on the pervasive power of the state, Alexander and Alexander (1985) cite a section of a 1962 ruling by an Ohio appellate court case to illustrate the plenary power of the state over education:

> the control of schools, be they public or private, providing elementary and secondary education for the youth of Ohio, reposes in the Legislature of our state. When the General Assembly speaks on matters concerning education it is exercising *plenary* power and its action is subject only to the limitations contained in the constitution. . . . We can, therefore, indulge in generalities and make a broad statement to the effect that the Legislature of Ohio, in passing laws concerning elementary and secondary schools, is restrained only by its own conscience. (Board of Education of Aberdeen—Huntington Local School District v. State Board of Education 1962, pp.85, 86)

Alexander and Alexander also note that the plenary power of the state over education also emanates from a state's police power and that this term "encompasses all the elements vested in state sovereignty" and that these include "those powers necessary to preserve the peace, morals, good order, and well-being of society" (p. 86). These authors are clear in viewing the provision of a state system of education as an exercise of the state's police power to protect the individual and county, a position held by other students of education law, a position shared by many other students of the legal underpinning of education.

Great diversity as well as commonalities in how the states exercised their constitutional responsibility and plenary authority has existed for some time. The most significant early common practice was the establishment of local school districts in all states that were created as instruments through which the state would carry out its mandate to provide a system of education. Many students of school government assert that local school districts were created for administrative convenience as a way to honor the state's constitutional mandate. However, it can be argued that a more accurate position is that their creation seemingly reflects the strong traditions in this nation to decentralize government. The diversity in how states structured their state system of local school districts was also greatly influenced by the political traditions of an individual state. An overview of the nature of these is provided below.

Origins of State Variations

The designs used by the states to create their early system of local school districts clearly were influenced by state traditions relative to the structure of all local governments, of which local school district governments are but one. In an earlier piece on school district reorganization practices, Stephens (1991) stressed that the existing structure of local government in the United States "has its roots in the colonial period and was patterned in many ways after the system of local government used in England" (p. 16). He then cited the position of Wagner (1950), who maintained that four major systems of local government developed in colonial America:

- the New England plan, where the town was the principal local government unit;
- the Virginia plan, where the county was the major unit and where the town or townships were seldom used;
- the New York plan, where both the county and town were both used; and
- the Pennsylvania plan, where both the county and township were established, with the latter subordinate to the former. (pp. 7-8)

The tradition of the significant political support for a system of local government structures to be found in colonial times subsequently greatly influenced regions of the country as the nation expanded. The Advisory Commission on Intergovernmental Relations (1982), when commenting on the great variations to be found in the current structure of local government in the 50 states, provides a useful overview of this process:

> According to a succession of scholars over the past 90 years, the subsequent settlement of the rest of the nation (or at least the contiguous 48 states) was characterized by the transplanting of the East Coast's tripartite system in a manner that generally followed the path of westward-moving settlers. This produced a regional pattern again based mainly on the relative importance of the township and the county, although some observers also have seen evidence of patterned distribution of municipalities and special districts. Under this interpretation, the 48 contiguous states fall into four or five regions: (1) New England, with the town preeminent; (2) the south, the southwest and the far west, all using primarily the familiar county system initiated in the south and carried from there by westward-moving southerners; and (3) and (4), two parts of what is generally known as the Midwestern or midcentral states, divided by the relative influence of the New York or Pennsylvania type of mixed county-township system. (p. 258)

Types of Local School Districts

The states made use of a multiplicity of basic types of local school districts in the formative years of statehood. However, this is not the place for a detailed discussion of these very earliest patterns. Rather we emphasize what was prevalent in the first half of the 20th century. This focus is appropriate for three interrelated reasons.

It was during the early decades of the last century that the need for a more active leadership and service role of some form of state central educational agency became increasingly apparent, a point stressed by Thurston and Roe (1957). It was also during the first part of the last decade that the growing expectations for greater state leadership and service were thwarted in many states by the huge number of local districts, many of them very small, and their distant location from the state capital. Finally, the need to provide more active state leadership and service roles in local affairs was frequently met by the establishment of some form of county or intermediate unit, most typically as an arm of the state, to perform state functions. Actually, a few states (e.g., California in 1858 and Arizona in 1912) called for this office in their original state constitutions.

As stressed previously, great diversity can be seen in how states structured their system of local school districts, a decision which reflected important political traditions in each state. Moreover, some states have made simultaneous use of one or more structural arrangements. Others opted for a particular structure earlier in their history, only to change subsequently.

De Young (1942) made use of four types of prevailing local units in characterizing the structure of local districts in the 48 states in the early 1930s. He argued that these can be "distinguished on the basis of their size and their identity with some units" (p. 72). The predominant type of administrative organization in the several states is presented in Table 1.1. DeYoung also correctly cited that the 26 states making use of the "district system" used a variety of terms to describe these local units (e.g., community, consolidated, non-high school, first or second class).

The National Center for Education Statistics now uses the school year 1937-38 as the starting point for its now comprehensive efforts to describe the public school universe. The *2000 Digest of Education Statistics*, the principal non-fiscal annual report published by the Center, cites the figure 119,001 as the number of local public school districts in the United States in that year (p. 95). These would include those classified by De Young as county systems, township or town systems, and district systems. The number of reported local districts by the Center in 1949-50, the approximate ending of Stage 1 of this review of the development of the education service agency concept, was 83,718 (p. 95).

The Emerging Role of State School Administration
The office of state superintendent, or commissioner of education as this position continues to be called in some states, was in place in the 48 contiguous states at the end of 1912. Some of the most influential early contributors to the development of public education in this nation (e.g., Horace Mann, Massachusetts; John Pierce, Michigan; John Swelt, California) occupied this position. However, with few exceptions, early state school administration was largely underutilized, certainly in a relative sense when compared to the central role the state now plays in setting the direction of education policy, but in absolute terms as well. This early pattern, however, soon changed.

Table 1.1
De Young's Four Types of Local District Structure in the Early 1930s

State System (1)

Delaware (also city of Wilmington and 13 special districts)

County System (12)

Alabama	Louisiana (parish)
	Tennessee
Florida	Maryland
	Utah
Georgia	New Mexico
	Virginia
Kentucky	North Carolina
	West Virginia

Township or Town System (9)

Connecticut	Massachusetts
	Pennsylvania
Indiana	New Hampshire
	Rhode Island
Maine	New Jersey
	Vermont

District System (26)

Arizona	Minnesota
	Oklahoma
Arkansas	Mississippi
	Oregon
California	Missouri
	South Carolina
Colorado	Montana
	South Dakota
Idaho	Nebraska
	Texas
Illinois	Nevada
	Washington
Iowa	New York
	Wisconsin
Kansas	North Dakota
	Wyoming
Michigan	Ohio

Source: Adapted from W. S. Deffenbaugh and T. Covert 1933, pp. 4, 5.

Thurston and Roe's (1957) treatise on the development of state school administration is one of the few early attempts to describe the emerging role of the state. They cite a number of specific factors that they believe contributed to the expanding role of the state in the first half of the last decade (e.g., greater state fiscal support; greater recognition that the state has a responsibility for public education if all school-age children were to be assured an equitable educational opportunity). However, their general comments regarding this process are especially insightful:

> With the advance of technology and the complementary social, economic, and political refinements education became a positive agency for social development and adjustment. Educational opportunities became somewhat synonymous with success. Thus, in the latter half of the nineteenth century and beginning of the twentieth century, people became conscious of the great variations in educational advantages through the country. Much of this variation was due to inequalities in educational opportunities springing from extreme differences in local ability and local desire to support education as well as vast differences in educational leadership. People began to demand a more comprehensive type of education as they realized that education, good or bad, affected the welfare of the whole state and that education in isolation was no longer satisfactory. If these inequities were to be corrected and if education was to perform a function for the state as well as for the individual it soon became apparent that the leadership and service of some type of state central educational agency was indispensable. Education of all the youth was becoming a growing concern for all people, forcing the chief state school officer and the state educational agency gradually to emerge with a new and vital role in American life. (pp. 74-75)

Hansen and Morphet's (1970) treatment of the evolution of the role of the state education agency is also instructive, and reflects the view of many observers of school government. They argue that the history of state education agencies can be characterized as moving through three phases.

1. Prior to the turn of the last century, state departments of education clearly devoted most of their energies to the collection and dissemination of basic statistics on the status of education (e.g., enrollment and financial data).

2. After the turn of the century, and concurrent with the development of state fiscal support for schools, and federal assistance for high school vocational education programs, attention was turned to the need to provide an inspection and regulatory role. State departments became involved in school accreditation, teacher certification, distribution of state aid, and providing assurance that state standards concerning the curriculum, compulsory attendance, facilities, and transportation were being observed. Some even operated schools (e.g., special technical schools, schools for the blind and deaf).

3. In the 1930s, the emphasis tended to be placed on providing leadership in the state system by focusing on the setting of goals and priorities for education, sponsoring research, providing consultative services to local school districts, and assisting in the coordination of federal, state, and local agencies (pp. 37-63).

The Emergence of Early Forms of Service Agencies

Two forms of service agencies were established in the approximate time period used here to cover Stage 1 in the evolution of the conceptualization of this type of organization—the early part of the 19th century to the end of the decade of the 1940s:

♦ the county office of education or intermediate unit, two terms that are used interchangeably in much of the literature in the early development of state systems, with the latter term gaining greater acceptance beginning around the start of World War II;

♦ the supervisory union/supervisory union administrative center.

One of the major distinguishing features of these early forms of service agencies centers on the geographic area served. The county office of education and the earlier versions of the intermediate unit served school districts located within the boundaries of a county. On the other hand, the boundaries of supervisory unions/supervisory union administrative centers had little relationships to the boundaries of the county in which they were located.

County office of education—intermediate unit. Delaware is credited with being the first state to establish a county office of education. This action, first taken in 1829, was later rescinded. Fifty years later, 34 of the existing 38 states had established the office as a county or intermediate unit of school government setting between the state and local districts. Some states established the county office in their original state constitution (e.g., California in 1858, Arizona in 1912). By the end of Stage 1 of this four-part history of service agencies, the same number of states, 34, had some form of county or intermediate office. However, 48 were in existence at the end of the decade of the 1940s. In two of the 14 nonparticipating states, Delaware and Nevada, all administrative and supervisory roles for local school districts were provided by the state. The remaining 12 states had predominately county-wide local school districts (Butterworth and Dawson 1952).

In most states, the county office of education was primarily created as an arm of the state education agency. Cubberley (1934) provides a succinct statement on the evolution of the county superintendency:

> As education began to evolve into a state interest in our country, the need for developing some subordinate form of state control became evident. . . hence a county school officer, known as a county superintendent of education, a county school superintendent, or a county superintendent of public instruction, was gradually provided for, sometimes by amendment of or during a revision of the constitution of the state, and sometimes by statute. Sometimes, too, the office was gradually evolved out of some other county office, such as auditor, or treasurer, or probate judge. . . . The office of county superintendent of schools began about 1835, and by about 1870 was common in most of the older states. In the newer states to the west, the office was frequently created in the territorial period. (pp. 45, 46)

While acknowledging that the functions of the county office—intermediate unit differed widely, the 1955 yearbook of the National Education Association

(NEA), Department of Rural Education, suggested that, in general, these offices were designed to serve the purposes of: (1) maintaining, through the exercise of general supervisory oversight in local districts, the minimum educational standards prescribed by state law; (2) maintaining the essential unity of purpose in the educational programs of local districts without the smothering effects of uniformity; (3) maintaining a two-way flow of information between the local districts and the state department of education; (4) exercising the function of general educational leadership in educational planning and classroom instruction; and, (5) serving as a spokesman for education in the arena of county government (pp. 141-142).

The 1950 Department of Rural Education of the National Education Association (NEA) reported on the number of superintendents and other professional staff members in 27 states having a county as the intermediate unit in 1948: a total of 2,009 superintendents, with several over 100 (Illinois, 102; Kansas, 105; Missouri, 114; Texas 254), and several others in the 90s (Indiana, 92; Iowa, 99; Nebraska, 93). A total of 1,769 other professional staff were employed in these 2,009 units (NEA, pp. 175,176). In only six of 27 states did the number of other professional staff exceed the number of superintendents: California, Mississippi, New Jersey, Oklahoma, Pennsylvania, and South Carolina.

The 1950 yearbook also provided information on the qualifications for the position of superintendent of a county intermediate unit, the methods of selection for the position, and term of office. Diverse qualifications for the position in the 27 states included in the report were noted. Educational requirements were a common feature, but these varied substantially (e.g., two or four years of college), as did the requirement of administrative experience or experience of some type in education. In general, the eligibility requirements for the position were far less stringent than those of the superintendent of a supervisory union that are cited below.

Several different methods of selection were in use, with election by popular vote or on a nonpartisan ballot being the most common method (in 13 and 5 cases, respectively, for a total of 18, or two-thirds of the 27 states included in the report). The term of office varied from one to five years, with a four-year or two-year term being the most common (in 15 and 7 cases, respectively) (pp. 178-180).

The supervisory union-supervisory union administrative center. These types of organizations have been and continue to be largely concentrated in the New England states, and, as noted by Knezevich (1984), this can be attributed to "the relatively weak position of the county as a political unit in these states" (p. 191). Knezevich defined a supervisory union as a collection or federation of town school districts that were initially formed by permissive legislation in Massachusetts (1881), New Hampshire (1895), Maine (1897), Connecticut (1903), Rhode Island (1903), and Vermont (1906). In the beginning, local school district membership was voluntary, but this feature was subsequently amended by a requirement for mandatory membership for districts not employing a superintendent (p. 191).

The 1950 Yearbook of the NEA's Department of Rural Education was devoted exclusively to all forms of the county superintendent of schools' position, those of county local school districts as well as the county superintendent, who served in some administrative capacity for all local districts in a county. The yearbook included information on the number of administrative and professional staff positions in supervisory unions in the six New England states and New York in 1948 (p. 175).

Connecticut	12 superintendents	no other professional staff
Maine	105 superintendents	no other professional staff
Massachusetts	66 superintendents	no other professional staff
New Hampshire	48 superintendents	2 other professional staff
New York	175 superintendents	no other professional staff
Rhode Island	2 superintendents	no other professional staff
Vermont	44 superintendents	105 other professional staff
Total	**452 superintendents**	**107 other professional staff**

As noted, the NEA also classified the early New York Supervising District as an example of a supervisory union and cited the number of superintendents in that state in 1948 as 175, with no other professional staff employed (p. 175). Developments in New York are treated separately below. The qualifications for the position of superintendent of a supervisory union, the methods of selection, and the terms of office are also cited in the yearbook: all states required an occupant of the position to have at least four years of college, teaching experience, and an administrative certificate. The superintendents were appointed by the state board of education or state commissioner in Connecticut and New Hampshire, but in the case of the latter, on nomination by town boards of education that comprised the union. The most popular method of appointment practiced in three states was also by the governing boards of the member districts (Maine, Massachusetts, and Vermont). The term of office was for an indefinite period in a majority of the six states.

In the first of three editions of one of the most popular introductory treatises on the structure and governance of education by Campbell, Cunningham, and McPhee (1965), the authors take issue with the decision to include supervisory unions as an organization similar to a county or intermediate unit. They argued,

> The supervisory unions found in the six New England states have often been treated as intermediate units of school administration. Actually, the supervisory unions serve chiefly as a way of promoting cooperative action among the boards of the local districts (towns). The union is composed of board members, who, in many unions, meet to select a superintendent of schools and attend to other joint business. The superintendent tends to work with each district board instead of an intermediate district capacity. (p. 118)

The concerns of Campbell, Cunningham, and McPhee (1965) are important, but appeared to be only partially correct. There is anecdotal evidence to suggest that in the early part of the 20th century at least some member districts of supervisory unions employed their own superintendent, but also supported the development of a more comprehensive service role for the administrative center of the supervisory union, including the retention of a superintendent. No accurate data on the number of supervisory union administrative centers are available, leaving the issue of whether or not the previously reported counts of supervisory units operating in Stage 1 unsettled.

As will be subsequently discussed, this issue has remained one of the major sources of concern in how states describe the types of educational organizations operating in their state. In the past few years the National Center for Education Statistics (NCES) took the first of several steps to address the apparent ambiguity surrounding the supervisory union-supervisory union administrative center issue. NCES began to ask the states to make use of an education agency code that classifies education agencies within the geographic boundaries of a state according to the "level of administrative and operational control" (*Instructions for Completing the Nonfiscal Surveys, 1994-95*). Three of the seven education agency types in the code clarify some but not all of the issues surrounding NCES's coding system:

Code 2   Local school district component of a supervisory union sharing a superintendent and administrative services with other local school districts.

Code 3   Supervisory union administrative center, or a county superintendent serving the same purposes.

Code 4   Regional education services agency, or county superintendent serving the same purposes. (p. 17)

STAGE 2: THE CONCEPT AT A CROSSROAD

The decade of the 1950s to the early part of the 1960s is the approximate time period used to designate Stage 2 in the evolution of the service agency concept. This was the time when the concept of a service agency designed to provide programs and services to local school districts and/or to the state was under severe criticism in many states, and in the professional community as well. To state that the concept was on trial would probably be an understatement. The voices calling for reform of the earlier county office of education-intermediate unit as it was typically structured in many states clearly accelerated in the decade of the 1950s, and first part of the 1960s. Moreover, the controversy was largely centered on the county office of education-intermediate union-type of service agency, not the supervisory union-supervisory union administrative center type. Especially scorned were county offices—intermediate units that Butterfield and Dawson (1952) categorized as "underdeveloped types" (p. 354), units that generally performed what they acknowledged were important administrative functions in state systems of elementary-secondary education, but these "were more or less routine and require little in the way of . . . educational leadership" (p. 355).

At the beginning of this second stage many states that operated a county office of education-intermediate unit had taken steps to address a number of the early criticisms directed at these organizations. Knezevich (1984) provides a useful summary of the frequent concerns raised in early periods concerning many of the positions: the offices are too political; superintendents lack professional and academic experiences on a par with local school superintendents; the roles and functions are not clear; there is little in the way of support staff; the salary is not competitive; and, the office devotes most of its energy to one-teacher and other small local school districts (p. 192). Knezevich also stated that by the 1940s, progress was being made on many of the earlier criticisms. He correctly stressed that by the end of the 1940s, many county-intermediate superintendents gained professional stature when an increasing number of states began to require administrative preparation and certification as a condition of employment or election (p. 192).

However, other significant factors were at work that caused members of state and local policy circles to question the continued viability and support for the county-intermediate unit as generally organized.

Major Factors Giving Rise to the Controversy

Many forces were in play at the approximate beginnings of Stage 2, some a continuation of events unfolding over the history of the nation, others relatively new. Moreover, the impact of these developments was uneven across the 48 state systems of elementary-secondary education then in existence, especially those states that were predominately organized with only two units of school government, the local school district that was county-wide in area, and the state education agency.

Clearly, the school district reorganization movement that was underway in many states arguably became the single greatest impetus to the debate on the merits of continued support for the county office of education-intermediate unit. If former one-room and small enrollment size schools and districts were now generally reorganized into larger districts that presumably would possess the human and fiscal capacity to offer what at that time was generally accepted as a sound educational program, one of the main rationales for the early support of the county-intermediate unit no longer was sustainable. A summary of the nature of the changes in the structure of the basic unit of school government, the local school districts, follows.

The changing school district. During this period there was an acceleration of the demise of the one- or two-teacher schools that were predominately located in rural, sparsely populated regions and with them went the original raison d'être in the eyes of many state interests who supported the concept of a service agency in the first place.

A publication of the National Education Association (1960) provides two types of data that contribute to an understanding of the vanishing one-teacher school (not school district) in the period 1947-59. As shown in Table 1.2, the number of one-teacher schools experienced a decline of over 50,000 schools during this 11 year period. Simultaneously, there was an acceleration of the reorganization of larger rural small school districts from 83,718 in 1949-50 to

Table 1.2
Changes in the Number, and Percent of One-Teacher Schools,
1947-48 and 1958-59

School Year	Number of One-Teacher Schools	One-Teacher Schools as a Percent of All Schools
1947-48	74,844	44.0
1958-59	23,654	18.2

Source: *One-Teacher Schools Today* 1960, pp. 12 and 15.

31,705 in 1965. Not all of this reduction can be attributed to the smaller number of one-teacher schools that frequently represented a school district in large tracts of nonmetropolitan regions of the nation. State-sponsored school district reorganization initiatives were implemented in a number of states well before the advent of World War II, and again vigorously pressed soon after the conclusion of the war, and then well into the decades of the 1950s, 1960s, and 1970s. The success of the efforts seems indisputable.

There can be little doubt that new state policies aimed at the reorganization of school districts, usually low-enrollment districts located in rural areas, were effective. In the 1970s, Sher and Tompkins (1976) offered the observation that "the most successfully implemented education policy of the past 50 years has been the consolidation of rural schools and school districts" (p. 1). Guthrie (1980) is even more assertive with his comment that the school reorganization movement "reflects one of the most awesome and least publicized governmental changes in the nation during the 20th century" (p. 120).

The school reorganization movement in the first decades following World War II resulted in a nearly 300% reduction of districts in the relatively short time span, 1947-48, when there were 94,817 districts, to 1965-66, when there were 26,783 districts (National Center for Education Statistics 2000, p. 95).

Proposals for Change

Advocacy for the elimination of the county office of education-intermediate unit as it was generally structured and operated in the immediate post-World War II period was widespread. Van Miller's (1965) position was typical of the views of many who questioned the necessity for a middle-echelon educational agency, and advocated the eventual abolishment of units of these types. Van Miller's argument was contingent on one critical development, the continual drastic reduction in the number of local districts. He argued that larger administrative units could then provide most services. Any unmet needs could be provided through branch offices of the state education agency (p. 138-39).

A number of states in the 1950s and 1960s did, in fact, eliminate their county offices of education. However, what clearly stands out as the dominant characteristic of this time period was the search for ways to strengthen, not abolish, the county office of education-intermediate unit and to build on what was perceived as a number of promising examples of successful efforts being made in some states to change these organizations to meet new needs in state systems of education.

There certainly was no shortage of recommended changes proffered by national professional organizations, students of school government, and other observers. Singled out here is what is regarded to be four of the most significant of these proposals.

The Department of Rural Education (NEA) 1950 Yearbook. The Department of Rural Education 1950 yearbook, *The County Superintendent of Schools in the United States,* was clearly focused on rural education, as expected, and described how a revitalizing county office-intermediate unit could contribute to the welfare of the nation's large number of schools in nonmetropolitan areas. An eight-member committee wrote the report that stood as a resounding endorsement of a strengthened county office-intermediate unit. Of interest, the committee membership included: an assistant secretary of the American Association of School Administrators, a representative from both the U. S. Office of Education, one university professor from a leading land-grant institution, a superintendent from one of the largest county offices in the country and one superintendent from a smaller county office from a Midwestern state. Two professors of educational administration served as consultants to the committee: Frank Cyr, Teachers College, Columbia University, and Russell Gregg, University of Wisconsin, Madison. It is important to note the composition of the committee because a number of positions taken in the yearbook greatly influenced much of the debate regarding this unit of school government that characterized the approximate time period used to designate Stage 2.

The central thesis advanced in the report was that a revitalized county office-intermediate unit could, indeed must, provide not only general administrative and supervisory oversight but also a range of educational services as well. Advocacy for this dual role, the provision of selected services for the state, as well as programs and services to local schools, is one of the first, highly visible enunciations of this concept, dual features of many service agencies to this day.

The first example given prominence was the experience of one of the nation's largest county offices, the Los Angeles County Office. The report cited a long list of services to the then 133 local school districts in the county, many of them small, as an illustration of where "the intermediate unit has gone beyond the limited function of providing general administrative oversight for the school districts under its jurisdiction" (p. 123).

The committee acknowledged that the programs and services of a county office-intermediate unit would vary in different areas of a state, but argued that the practices of the Los Angeles County Office of Education demonstrate that:

> The principles that are involved are the pooling of resources from local districts and the sharing of services. The county superintendent's office is the administrative agency that facilitates this cooperative action. Rather than being an agency for destroying local initiative and control it serves the purpose of encouraging and supporting it. The end result is greatly extended and enriched educational opportunities for children in the smaller school

districts. (p. 124)

The second example given prominence by the committee in support of its position that two roles are needed was the description of the evolution of the service agency concept in New York State that culminated with the establishment in 1948 of the Boards of Cooperative Educational Services (BOCES). The major milestones in this evolution cited by the committee include:

> 1910 - Enactment of the Rural School Supervision Act that divided the state into 208 supervisory districts covering all areas of the state except those included in population centers of 4,500 or more.
>
> 1948 - Permissive legislation allowing the formation of intermediate districts to be governed by a five member board with power to appoint a superintendent, and having the responsibility for the following services: administering transportation and attendance in constituent districts; providing instruction in industrial-trade education for adults and for handicapped children; assisting principals and teachers in the improvement of instruction; providing such other educational services assigned to it by the intermediate council made up of members of board of education and school directors in…districts comprising the intermediate district. The program was to be financed in part by state and in part by a tax levied on property in the local districts. (p. 127)

The 1948 permissive legislation was never fully implemented. What was created was a state network of Boards of Cooperative Educational Services that were superimposed over one or more of the supervisory districts, an action that is described in the next chapter. However, many of the design features contained in the 1948 permissive legislation creating intermediate districts are clearly what the committee was anxious to disseminate.

The final portion of the yearbook contained a discussion of what it referred to as a set of a "few principles that are particularly applicable to this development" (of an effective intermediate district) (p. 139). While acknowledging that conditions in various parts of the country will dictate the form that a revitalized county office-intermediate unit will take, the committee offered what should be viewed as five nonnegotiable design principles.

1. A system of state, intermediate, and local administrative units should not be regarded as a hierarchy of administrative controls with authority flowing from top to bottom or moving from the prominent to the obscure. One level is no more important in the total structure of the state school system than another. Each is but a device that has been created by the people to serve their needs. Each is performing its function well when it serves the purpose for which it was created. The power flows from the people—not from the instruments they have created to serve them.

2. Nothing should be done by the intermediate unit that can be equally well done by the local unit. Likewise, no function should be assigned to the state level of administration that can be performed equally as well by the intermediate

district.

3. The intermediate district should be organized and operated in a manner that will secure the participation of lay citizens and school officials in the local units of which it is comprised in forming and shaping educational policy. The further a level of administration is removed from the people, the greater the responsibility on the superintendent becomes for keeping channels of communication open and maintaining participation on an effective basis.

4. The superintendent of the intermediate district should strive to maintain his identity as a local school official rather than as an arm of the state education department.

5. The responsibilities for educational control which are assigned to the intermediate district superintendent should not be thought of merely as being limiting and directive. They should be considered as opportunities for activating the energy of people and giving them assistance and guidance in dealing with educational problems. (p. 139)

Butterworth and Dawson's Treatise. Another early 1950s' statement on the need to revitalize the county office-intermediate unit as a fully functioning service agency that would also be an especially valuable asset for the nation's still large number of rural schools was Butterworth and Dawson's (1952) text. They introduced or emphasized anew a number of important concepts that helped shape the debate regarding how to make the county office-intermediate unit a more effective partner in the state system of elementary-secondary education.

They proposed several major functions for these entities: pupil personnel services, including the administration of special classes for districts with fewer than 750 to 1,000 students; adult education; leadership in curriculum services, including a curriculum-materials library; administration of an area-wide transportation program and a cooperative purchasing program for buses; sponsorship of an area vocational education program; and, assistance to schools in "scientific budget planning . . . and the establishment of an adequate accounting system" (pp. 358,59).

The authors also proffer their seven recommendations of what they regard to be the essential organizational features of a good intermediate district that would be able to assist rural schools with the provision of needed support services.

1. A sufficient pupil enrollment that would make it possible to provide desired programs and services both effectively and economically. What this figure is would depend on local circumstances. Planners were encouraged to avoid a tendency to make the new units too small.

2. Insofar as possible, the intermediate district should represent a community of interests. This can mean that county boundaries would be ignored.

3. There should be a board representing the public with authority to set policy, a board that should usually be small (five, seven or nine members), and serve five-year terms. While members may be selected from geographic areas, they should represent the district as a whole. This suggests that a board member

should not be a member of a local district board, a person who might have divided loyalties. The board should appoint the superintendent.

4. There should be staff attached to the superintendent's office adequate in numbers and qualifications to meet the needs of the local districts.

5. The law establishing the intermediate district should clearly define the functions to be performed in order to minimize potential conflict with local authorities.

6. The intermediate district should exercise leadership rather than mere legal authority. While the unit should have definite responsibilities if it is to be effective, much progress will come as a result of the leadership shown by the board, and staff.

7. The intermediate district must have financial support, but how this is provided will depend on the pattern of financial support in a state. Undoubtedly, the unit must have the authority to levy taxes on the property of its region. Usually some form of state aid for intermediate districts would be desirable for its stimulating and equalizing value (pp. 359-362).

Butterworth and Dawson conclude their discussion of the important role of the intermediate district in assisting rural schools with this plea:

> In those states that accept the intermediate district concept, considerable attention should be given in the immediate future to making it an organization that may do more effectively and more easily what is demanded in our expanding educational program. If this is done there will be less need for the state to extend its influence or for local districts, close to the people, to give up those elements of control that they are competent to manage. (p. 365)

The Department of Rural Education 1954 Yearbook. The Department of Rural Education (NEA) 1954 yearbook, *The Community School and the Intermediate Unit* (Eisenberg) introduced several new and important concepts as well as proposing refinements of others previously cited.

One of the most interesting ideas emphasized in the yearbook centered on the issue of the allocation of the functions to an intermediate unit. The principle argued for was that "a function should be allocated to that unit closest to the people where it can be carried out with completeness, equity, and efficiency" (p. 182). The use of this principle means that the discussion of each function to be performed in a state system of elementary-secondary education should be allotted from the bottom up, not the top down, as is typically the case.

The application of this principle when applied to the role of an intermediate unit would result in the formulation of the principle that "the role of the intermediate unit should be that of assisting the local community schools in developing their own programs" (p. 182). The intermediate unit should not assume any functions which community schools can perform unless it can be demonstrated that it can perform these with greater "completeness, equity, and efficiency." Any existing intermediate unit functions should be returned to local schools once they can carry them out with comparable effectiveness (p. 182).

Other interesting positions taken in the yearbook include those relating to the issue of what specific types of services should be performed by an intermediate unit.

1. The service role of an intermediate district must be a joint concern of the community school, the intermediate district, and the state education agency. This is the best way to determine what is now provided to community schools in the state system, what is needed, how the needed services can be secured, and, then, and only then, which services can best be provided by the community school and which by the intermediate unit (p. 185).

2. In areas where nonschool services (e.g., public health services, mental health services) are being provided by nonschool agencies, the intermediate unit should not attempt to dispel or duplicate their services; rather, their greatest contribution can be as a coordinating, facilitating agency (p. 187).

3. Intermediate units will perform certain services because of statutory requirements. Though these will differ somewhat from one state to another, they are likely to fall into the following areas: (a) Communication: The administration of a system of reports and the compiling, checking, handling, and interpreting of accurate information; (b) Coordination: The establishment by consensus of bases and standards for practice among the local community school units within the intermediate area; (c) Arbitration: The settlement or handling of affairs involving two or more local districts within the intermediate area; (d) Interpretation: The discovery, documentation, and definition of problems peculiar to the local community school units in the area. The interpretation and application of state policies and rulings among the local community school units; and, (e) Representation: The representation of the particular interests of local community school units in the intermediate area in the formulation of state policy through intercession with state school officials and, conversely, representing the interests of the state with local officials (p. 189).

4. A final position taken in the yearbook that warrants mention relates to the need for an intermediate unit to coordinate the governmental service units and other organizations and agencies in their service area that relate to the needs of children and youth (p. 189).

The Department of Rural Education (NEA) 1955 Yearbook. The last of the three early 1950s yearbooks, *Rural Education—A Forward Look*, stresses many of the same points of earlier yearbooks. Of particular importance is the repeated advocacy of the position that an effective intermediate unit has a dual role—assisting local districts in improving the quality of the educational program and assisting the state education agency in the administration of a state system of schools (p. 151).

The sometimes difficult relationships with local school districts is also addressed with this reminder:

> The intermediate unit is not a substitute for local community school districts. Local districts are a necessary part of educational organization if control is to be kept as close as possible to the people served. Modification of present intermediate units to better serve education should in no way weaken local districts or retard efforts to reorganize them into desirable

community districts. Intermediate units function best when local school districts are strong. Experience shows that effective intermediate units strengthen local districts. Local community school districts are not subordinates of an intermediate unit. They are completely autonomous as defined by state law and full partners with the intermediate unit and state education department in providing educational services. (p. 152)

SUMMARY

The evolution of the present-day educational service agencies that are the focus of this book is arguably one of the most significant developments in school government. It is a fascinating story as well in that, in a number of important ways, it reflects how state and local policy makers have wrestled with not only the huge socioeconomic changes that have impacted public education over time, but also the raising expectations that have been placed on public education, particularly during the mid and late decades of the 20th century.

In many states, the first generation of the present-day educational service agency were single county offices of education, initially established to perform coordinating, administrative, and supervisory functions for the state, especially for the large number of one-room and other very small enrollment size districts found in many states from the early years of statehood through the first half of the 20th century.

The successful efforts of the state to greatly reduce the number of one-room and other very small enrollment size districts through enactment of mandatory reorganization requirements caused state and local interests to question the continued viability of the county office of education. However, the prevailing position in the professional community was that a reconstituted middle echelon unit of school government setting between the state and a collection of local districts would greatly strengthen a state system of elementary-secondary education by providing needed support services to local districts, as well as provide services for the state.

REFERENCES

Advisory Commission on Intergovernmental Relations. 1963. *Performance of urban functions: Local and areawide* (Report M-21 revised). September. Washington, DC: Author.

Advisory Commission on Intergovernmental Relations. 1982. *State and local roles in the federal system* (Report A-88). April. Washington, DC: Author.

Alexander, K., and Alexander, M. D. 1985. *American public school law*. 2d ed. St. Paul, MN: West Publishing Company.

Board of Education of Aberdeen—Huntington Local School District v. State Board of Education, 116 Ohio App. 515, 189 N.E. 2d 81 1962.

Butterworth, J. E., and Dawson, H. A. 1952. *The modern rural school*. New York: McGraw-Hill Book Company, Inc.

Campbell, R. F.; Cunningham, L. L.; and McPhee, R. F. 1965. *The organization and control of American schools*. Columbus, OH: Charles E. Merrill Books, Inc.

Campbell, R. F.; Cunningham, L. L.; Mystrand, R. O.; and Usdan, M. D. 1990. *The organization and control of American Schools*. 6 ed. Columbus, OH: Merrill Publishing Company.

Cubberley, E. P. 1934. *Public education in the United States*. New York: Houghton Mifflin Company.

Deffenbaugh, W. S. and Covert, T. 1933. *School Administration Units*. Washington, DC: Superintendent of Documents.

DeYoung, L. A. 1942. *Introduction to American public education*. New York: McGraw-Hill Book company, Inc.

Edwards, N. 1995. *The courts and the public schools*. Rev. ed. Chicago, IL: The University of Chicago Press.

Guthrie, J. R. 1980. Organization scale and school issues. Eds. C. S. Benson et al., *Education finance and organization research perspectives for the future*. Washington, DC: U. S. Department of Health, Education, and Welfare, National Institute of Education.

Guthrie, J. W. and Reed, R. J. 1991. *Educational administration and policy. Effective leadership for American education*. 2d ed. Boston, MA: Allyn and Bacon.

Hanson, K. H. and Morphet, E. L. 1970. State organization of education: Some emerging alternatives. Eds. E. L. Morphet, and D. L. Jesser, *Emerging state responsibilities for education*. Denver, CO: Improving State Leadership in Education.

Isenberg, R. ed. 1954. *The community school and the intermediate unit*. The Department of Rural Education, National Education Association.

Knezevich, S. J. 1984. *Administration of public education*. 4 ed. New York: Harper and Row, Publishers.

National Center for Education Statistics. *Digest of Education Statistics 2000*. Washington, DC: U. S. Department of Education, Office of Educational Research and Improvement.

Miller, V. 1965. *The public administration of American school systems*. New York: The Macmillan Company.

National Center for Education Statistics. *Instructions for completing the nonfiscal surveys, 1994-95*. Washington, DC: U. S. Department of Education, Office of Educational Research and Improvement.

National Education Association (NEA). 1950. *The county superintendent of schools in the United States* (yearbook). Washington, DC: Department of Rural Education.

National Education Association. 1955. *Rural education—A forward look* (yearbook). Washington, DC: Department of Rural Education.

National Education Association. 1960. *One teacher schools today*. Research Monograph 1960-MI. Washington, DC: Author. pp. 12 and 15.

No Child Left Behind Act of 2001, Pub. L. 107-110.

Sher, J. P., and Tompkins, R. B. 1976. *Economy, efficiency, and equality: The myths of rural school and district consolidation*. Washington, DC: U. S. Department of Health, Education, and Welfare, National Institute of Education.

Stephens, E. R. 1991. *A framework for evaluating state policy options for the reorganization of rural, small school districts*. Occasional Paper No. 32. Charleston, WV: Appalachia Educational Laboratory.

Thurston, L. M., and Roe, W. H. 1957. *State school administration*. New York: Harper and Brothers, Publishers.

Valente, W. D. 1994. *Law in the schools*. 3d ed. New York: Macmillan Publishing Company.

Wagner, P. ed. 1950. *County government across the nation*. Chapel Hill, NC: The University of North Carolina Press.

Chapter 2

Stage Three: The "Golden Age" in the Development

It is to be recalled that the third stage in the development of the concept of an educational service agency covers the approximate time period of the early 1960s to the early part of the decade of the 1980s. It was during these years when action was taken in a fairly significant number of states to redefine the roles and responsibilities of the county office of education-intermediate unit, or when state interests moved to authorize early new service agency organizations. The volume of activity promoted a number of supporters of the concept to label the period the "golden age" of the movement, an apt title as will be shown.

EARLY STRUCTURAL MODIFICATIONS

The redesign of the county-intermediate unit had its first early beginnings in the mid-1940s. Writing in 1968, Fritzwater, Chief of the Administrative Services Division of the then U. S. Office of Education, pointed to the late 1940s as a time when "at least 32 of the 50 states have had organizational changes that can reasonably be regarded as having major significance in the operation and functioning of the state system" (p. 5). Moreover, he stated that from the late 1940s to the mid-1960s, 18 states made major changes in more than one level or type of administrative agency in the state system of elementary-secondary education (p. 6).

Fritzwater's classification of the structure of state systems of education in the mid-1960s is shown in Figure 2.1. He, like most other observers, reported that three basic types of intermediate units of school government existed in the 32 states with a three-tier structure: (1) supervisory units composed of two or more town school districts "for the purpose of sharing a superintendent;" (2) the county intermediate district, or, in some states, county superintendency; and, (3) multi-county or regional intermediate districts (p. 32). The state distribution of the three types is shown in Figure 2.2.

An overview of the restructuring of county-intermediate districts in a representative group of states is provided below. First, though, a listing of what are judged to be major precipitating factors that gave rise to the relatively widespread perceived need to revitalize these organizations is provided.

PRECIPITATING FACTORS CAUSING MIDDLE LEVEL REORGANIZATION

A number of significant developments, beginning in the mid-1960s, gave

Figure 2.1
Current Types of Intermediate District Structure

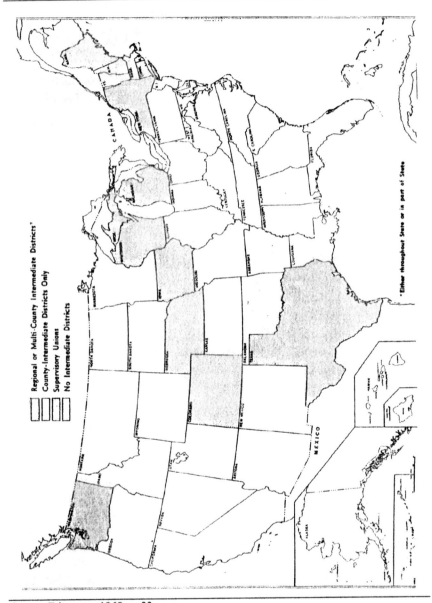

Source: Fritzwater 1968, p. 33.

Figure 2.2
Patterns of Structure in State Systems of Education, 1965

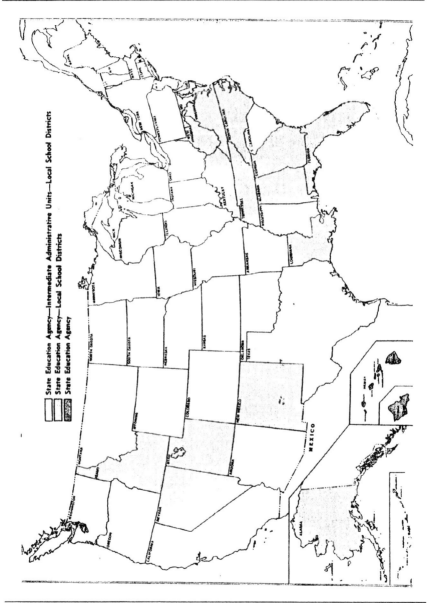

Source: Fritzwater 1968, p. 4.

rise to the strengthening of many county-intermediate districts as the policy choice of numerous state and local policymakers. Three are particularly significant:

1. The growing opposition to the mandated reorganization of rural, small school districts.

2. Title III of the federally enacted Elementary and Secondary Education Act of 1965, which provided bonus point incentives for local school districts to collaborate in the procurement of federal funds designed to promote innovative practices. States also occasionally added bonus point incentives for joint applications for Title III funds.

3. Mounting pressures on the states and on local school districts to address the need to enhance both the quality and equity of elementary-secondary education. These pressures were promoted in large part by a series of court cases challenging the constitutionally of state finance plans for the support of a system of elementary and secondary education as well as equal educational opportunities for disabled students.

Fritzwater (1968) also provides a useful classification of how states implemented major changes in the middle unit in their three-echelon structure (those outside of New England) since the mid-1940s. It is important to note that he attributes most state action to the huge reductions in the number of local school districts that occurred over much of the late 1940s, 1950s, and into the mid-1960s, a frequently defined era of the "Big Push" in the school reorganization movement. Fritzwater's classification of state activity consists of five categories and is presented in Table 2.1.

It is the fifth of Fritzwater's five types of changes made by the states concerning their county intermediate district structure that is of most interest. This fifth approach, what Fritzwater calls the intermediate unit restructuring option, continued well beyond the mid-1960s, the ending period for his analysis.

What follows are descriptions of structural developments in selected states that illustrate several of Fritzwater's fifth option, and importantly, an extension of his analysis from the mid-1960s to the mid-1980s, the approximate time period designated here as Stage 3: The "Golden Age" of the development of this concept, with the addition of still another, or sixth strategy.

STATE DEVELOPMENTS

The review of structural developments during the highly active period covered by Stage 3 is organized around the major strategies used by state and local interests to respond to the need to transform the existing middle echelon unit of school government in response to the growing needs of both local districts and the state or create a new one. The six transformation strategies are shown in Table 2.2 along with the identification of the states making use of each in the period. Note that some states (e.g., Massachusetts, New Jersey) made use of several strategies simultaneously.

In four of the six strategies, the existing county intermediate districts were maintained although characterized by vastly different approaches. In two of the

Table 2.1
Fritzwater's Classification of Five Major Types of State Changes in Their Three-Echelon Structure, 1945-1967

1. Abolishment of all county intermediate units (e.g., Idaho).
2. Elimination of part of the county intermediate districts without provision for replacement by another types (e.g., Mississippi, South Carolina, Indiana) and permissive legislation enacted in still other states (e.g., Minnesota, Missouri, Wyoming, Kansas, South Dakota).
3. Continuation of existing pattern without any basic strengthening of it—with few exceptions, these are states with county intermediate districts where there is no board and superintendent is elected (e.g., Arizona, Montana, North Dakota).
4. Strengthening of existing structure without enlarging its component school districts or service area (e.g., California, Michigan, Iowa, Oregon, Pennsylvania).
5. Establishment of enlarged intermediate districts, or restructured, intermediate service agencies by (a) abolishment of county intermediate districts and mandatory replacement with regional education service agency; (b) establishment of regional education service agencies without abolishment of county intermediate districts; (c) county option on abolishing the county intermediate superintendency and local district option on forming new type intermediate service agencies; (d) consolidation of small intermediate districts; and, (e) statewide plan for intermediate district enlargement, with provision for adoption by county boards of education.

Source: Fritzwater 1968. pp. 34-42.

Table 2.2
Major State Transformation Strategies—Stage 3

#1. Maintain county intermediate districts with no significant change in role.
- Montana—county offices of education
- New Jersey—21 county offices of education
- North Dakota—county offices of education
- Supervisory unions in New England states

#2. Maintain county intermediate districts, but strengthen role in provision of services to, especially, local school districts.
- California—58 county offices of education
- To a lesser degree—the 14 county offices of education in Arizona

#3. Maintain county intermediate districts but establish a new state network of regional educational service agencies having a major role in assisting local school districts, and to a lesser extent, the state.
- Massachusetts—creation of 44 Educational Collaboratives in 1974

Continued on next page

Table 2.2—*continued*

- Nebraska—the formation of 19 Educational Service Units in 1965
- New Jersey—the establishment of 4 Educational Improvement Centers in 1977
- Texas—the establishment of 20 Regional Educational Service Agencies in 1967

#4. Maintain county intermediate districts, but establish a new state network of regional branch offices of the state education agency to provide largely state determined technical assistance to local school districts.
- Michigan—the creation of 58 Intermediate School Districts in 1963
- Massachusetts—the organization of 6 Regional Educational Centers in 1966
- North Carolina—the establishment of 8 Regional Education Centers in 1971
- Ohio—the creation of 13 Field Service Area Coordinators in 1966
- Ohio—the establishment of 16 Special Education Regional Resource Centers in 1969
- Ohio—the creation of 25 Area Media Centers in 1972
- Ohio—the development of 27 Data Acquisition Sites in 1979
- Oklahoma—the formation of 20 Regional Education Service Centers in 1974

#5. Abolish county intermediate districts and replace with new state networks of regional educational service centers having an expanded service role for local school districts, and to a lesser extent, the state[1].
- Arkansas—the creation of 15 Educational Service Cooperatives in 1985
- Colorado—the establishment of 17 Boards of Cooperative Services in 1965
- Illinois—the formation of 58 Educational Service Regions in 1975
- Iowa—the establishment of 15 Area Education Agencies in 1975
- Indiana—creation of 9 Education Service Centers in 1973
- Minnesota—the establishment of 9 Educational Cooperative Service Units in 1973
- Oregon—the formation of 29 Education Service Districts in 1963
- Pennsylvania—the formation of 29 Intermediate Units in 1971
- Washington—the establishment of 9 Educational Service Districts in 1965
- Wisconsin—the creation of 19 Cooperative Educational Service Agencies in 1965

#6. Establish a new state network of regional educational service agencies where no county intermediate district currently exists, but may have in the early history of the state.
- Connecticut—the establishment of 6 Regional Educational Service Centers in 1972
- Georgia—the formation of 16 Cooperative Education Service Agencies in 1966
- West Virginia—the creation of 8 Regional Education Service Agencies in 1972

[1] The establishment of the New York Boards of Cooperative Educational Services in 1948 would be classified as an example of strategy #5.

four, a new system of regional educational service agencies was established. In strategy #3, the primary orientation of the new units was the provision of locally determined services to local school districts. In another, strategy #4, the primary orientation of the new units was the provision of largely state-determined services to local districts.

Strategy #5 was clearly the most popular state response. Here, the decision was made to abolish the county-intermediate districts and replace these with a new, frequently multi-county, state network of regional educational service agencies. This action was taken with the expectation that these entities were to be created to assist local school districts, as well as, in many cases, continue to perform certain administrative and supervisory functions previously assigned to the predecessor county-intermediate districts. Another somewhat popular state action was the use of strategy #6, the creation of a new state network of frequently multi-county regional educational service agencies where no middle echelon existed in the early 1960s, but, in several cases, many have functioned in the past.

Strategies #3 through #6 together clearly represent significant state and local efforts to strengthen the infrastructure of a significant number of state systems of elementary-secondary education. It is in these four categories of state policy choices where the most meaningful development of the concept of an educational service agency begin to take hold and be subsequently implemented in various forms all across the country, a story that continues to evolve to the present time.

AN EARLY TYPOLOGY

The relatively rapid developments in service agency formation and reorganization during the 1960s and 1970s resulted in the creation of state networks having a number of commonalities, yet significant differences as well, reflecting as this does the political traditions of the various states. One of the first attempts to unravel the major similarities and differences present in the educational service agency movement was undertaken by Stephens (1979), who argued that while few pure paradigms were in existence in the late 1970s, these organizations appeared to be developing along the following lines:

Type A: The special district pattern, a legally constituted unit of school government sitting between the state education agency and a collection of local education agencies. This pattern was built on the concept that ESAs should be established by the state, or the state and local education agencies acting in concert, to provide services to both the state and constituent local districts.

Type B: The decentralized SEA pattern, consisting of regional branches of the state education agency. This pattern appears to be supported by the view that ESAs should be established as arms of the state to deliver services for the state education agency.

Type C: The cooperative pattern, organized through sponsorship by two or more local education agencies of single- or multi-purpose entity de-

signed to promote shared services. This pattern is supported by the
view that ESAs should be established by consortia of local school
districts to provide services exclusively to members of the consortia.
(p. 3)

These broad distinguishing characteristics of the three dominant types of
ESAs appear to be a reflection of the differing schools of thought regarding the
role and function of ESAs. In general, the governance, staffing, programming
and financial features vary according to the locus of control; that is, whether the
primary orientation is toward the LEA as in Type C, the SEA as in Type B, or
shared between the SEA/LEA as in Type A.

The typology gave prominence to four central organizational characteristics, shown in Table 2.3, along with a description of the dominant patterns of
each of the three major forms of service agencies. The typology of ESAs was
developed and then tested against over 100 governance, organizational, staffing,
programmatic, financial, and other characteristics of what was judged to be all
state networks of ESA-type agencies in operation at the close of the 1970s. It is
to be stressed that the typology was constructed using a deductive, or an a priori
approach, as opposed to an empirical derivation that possesses greater predictive
capability. This choice was consistent with the immediate task in late 1979 that
called for the development of an initial classification system that would be of
value to the policy and professional communities in characterizing patterns and
trends in ESA state networks.

The use of only three basic types of ESAs in the typology also reflects a
commitment to what was, on a later occasion, referred to as the "Rule of Numerical Relevance" (Stephens 1992) that ought to be followed in classification
exercises that attempt to establish the primary orientation of organizations, especially those intended to inform the policy communities. This rule holds that the
number of classes in a typology should be limited to no more than a range of
five to seven in order that the dominant, most distinguishing, features of the
classes can be readily recognizable and understood, especially by those in the
policy-making communities (p. 88).

STAGE 4: THE RESTRUCTURING PERIOD

As noted earlier, the fourth stage in the development of the concept of an
educational service agency covers the approximate time period from the mid-
1980s to the present, the first years of the 21st century. Unlike Stage 3, which
witnessed the transformation of many state networks of older county intermediate districts into bona fide service agencies, as well as the creation of entirely
new state systems, Stage 4 can best be characterized as a period of reassessment
and redirection of that which was created in the preceding stage. The themes of
a number of the most significant restructuring efforts are introduced below. A
more in-depth discussion of each of these is provided in subsequent chapters.

It is true that many factors account for the new, widespread emphasis on
restructuring the state networks of educational service agencies. While the

Table 2.3

Stephens' Typology of Educational Service Agencies Based on Dominant Patterns of Four Central Characteristics

Type of ESA	Four Central Characteristics			
	Legal Framework	Governance	Program and Services	Fiscal Support
Type A: Special District ESA	Tends to be highly structured in legislation and/or SEA regulations	Tends to be lay control	Tends to be determined by member LEAs and the SEA or by statute	Tends to be a mix of local, regional, state and state/federal
Type B: Regionalized SEA/ESA	Tends to be structured in SEA regulations only	Tends to be professional advisory only	Tends to be almost exclusively determined by SEA	Tends to be almost exclusively state and state/federal
Type C: Cooperative ESA	Tends to be general (i.e., intergovernmental regulations and statutes) and/or permissive legislation	Tends to be composed of representatives of member LEAs	Tends to be almost exclusively determined by member LEAs	Tends to be almost exclusively local and state/federal

Source: Stephens, E. R. 1979, p. 3.

rationale behind these developments may have differed in some respects from one state to the next, it is possible to establish several dominant considerations that likely hold true in most cases.

FURTHER CHANGES IN THE CALCULUS

As stressed elsewhere in this chapter, the appropriate design for educational service agencies is not fixed. It is predicated on the world view held by state and/or local district policy makers for these types of organizations, and ultimately reflects and must be extraordinarily sensitive to the real and perceived needs of either the state or local interests, or a combination of the requirements of both. Since the publication of *A Nation At Risk* in 1983, the pressures on both local and state policy communities to improve public education have been the most intense in the post-World War II period, if not in the past century, and show no signs of abating. The most pervasive of the rising expectations for public education are in the time period covered by Stage 4 and include the following:

(1) The development of a state content standards system and the related push to align a student performance measurement system, a professional development system, and a finance system with the content standards;

(2) The development of an accountability system that includes sanctions for

less than satisfactory process against some prescribed benchmark, and the requirement that an individual school/school district make public the status of its efforts to achieve some prescribed benchmark;

(3) The emphasis on the use of technology in the instructional program;

(4) The continuing interest in the construct of "equal educational opportunity," mitigated in part by the introduction in some court cases of the construct "adequacy" in assessing state financial support for education;

(5) The continuation of problems facing critical components of the state system of education—the effect of out-migration on rural school districts and central city districts and, increasingly, the inner-ring districts in metropolitan areas. Together these population shifts weakened the infrastructure of the state system of education at a time when it was asked to do more.

These developments, and other pressures that local school districts meet additional legislatively mandated requirements, challenged many local school districts. At the state level, a frequently downsized state education agency was placed in a position to exercise a significant role in the planning and implementation of a state's comprehensive school improvement strategy. It is in this context that pressure mounted to make greater use of the existing educational service agencies. Also, service agencies themselves, independent of an external advocacy, begin to voluntarily assume greater leadership and service roles.

OTHER MAJOR FORCES PROMOTING RESTRUCTURING ACTIVITIES

An overview of eight further significant developments in the evolution of the concept of an educational service agency that have thus far occurred in Stage 4 is provided in Table 2.4. A brief introduction of the eight trends is provided below. As established previously, a more in-depth discussion of a number of the eight is provided in subsequent chapters.

Further solidification of the legitimacy of ESAs. The position that the state networks of educational service agencies were to be regarded as an integral part of the state system of elementary-secondary education was clearly reinforced in many states. Expressions of this movement were in some cases very explicit, as was the case in Iowa where, in 1989, the state board of education, in a mandated major report to the state legislature, stressed that the state's network of Area Education Agencies must play a major role if the board was to be successful in reaching its goal of building "a world-class education system in Iowa" (Iowa State Board of Education 1989, p. 5). Moreover, and importantly, there are ample examples of other proxy measures utilized by the states to clearly reinforce acceptance of the notion, especially in the state component in the state's educational delivery system (e.g., the assignment of a major role in the state's school improvement strategies, particularly, most recently, their central role in providing technical assistance to low-performing schools; and, the relatively significant increases in state funding for a number of state networks over the course of the time period covered by Stage 4).

As will be subsequently discussed, major steps have also occurred at the federal level to recognize the legitimacy and growing importance of educational

Table 2.4
Overview of Major Trends–Stage 4

1. Further solidification of the position that the existing state networks are to
    be viewed as an integral part of the state system of elementary-secondary
    education in state and local policy circles, and at the federal level as well
2. Reduction in the number of agencies in a number of states with Type A:
    Special District ESA state networks
3. Both the elimination of some state networks of Type C: Cooperative ESAs,
    and the creation of new networks of service agencies of this type in still
    other states
4. Changes in the governance structure of some networks by the inclusion of
    representatives of other educational organizations or other human services
    providers
5. Broadening of the mission of a number of networks beyond the traditional
    emphasis on equity, efficiency, and quality in the provision of services
6. Adoption in more states of a set of core required programs and services that
    must be offered by state networks
7. Adoption in a number of states of more rigorous performance accountability
    measures, including the use of a state accreditation system
8. Further strengthening of cooperation between service agencies serving met-
    ropolitan areas and the central city school district

---

service agencies in federal policy circles. It was during the last decade that service agencies were identified by Congress in several major federal programs as
one of the eligible recipients of funds. Indeed, the latest reauthorization of the
Elementary-Secondary Education Act of 1965—the No Child Left Behind Act
of 2001, requires states to make use of educational service agencies where they
now exist, or, where they do not, to promote the formation of new collaboratives
in order to carry out certain requirements of the legislation. Moreover, as cited
previously, it is only recently that the National Center for Education Statistics
began to require state education agencies to report on the number of operating
regional education service agencies and supervisory union administrative centers
as part of their periodic counts of the universe of education agencies in their respective states.

Reduction in number of agencies in state networks. In the last 25 years
questions have been raised in several of the states operating Type A: Special
District ESAs about the appropriate number of agencies for the state to operate.
In most cases, mandatory legislation was used to affect reductions. Curtailments
most typically occurred in those state networks formed in the 1960s and early
1970s, and involved networks that were formed as replacements for an original
state system of county intermediate units formed in the early history of a state.
Examples of the reductions in Type A: Special District state networks include:

Illinois—from 57 Regional Service Centers in 1979 to 45 in 2001-02

New York—from 44 Boards of Cooperative Educational Services in 1979 to

38 in 2001-02

Ohio—from 87 County Offices of Education in 1979 to 61 Education Service
    Centers in 2001-02

Oregon—from 29 Education Service Districts in 1979 to 21 in 2001-02

Wisconsin—from 19 Cooperative Education Service Agencies in 1979 to 12
    in 2001-02

The number of agencies in several states, including Iowa and Oregon, have
been under repeated legislative scrutiny, though no reductions were mandated.
Rather, permissive legislation was enacted in both states in 2001 that allowed
for the voluntary merger of service agencies. In Iowa, this resulted in a reduction
of agencies from 15 formed in 1975 to 12 in 2003.

   *Both the elimination as well as creation of Type C: Cooperative ESA State
Networks.* Several state networks of this type of service agency were eliminated,
including the 18 Educational Service Centers created in Illinois in 1985. The
functions of these units were transferred to the state network of Type A: Special
District ESAs, the Educational Service Regions. Three Intermediate Service Centers
were also formed in the Chicago metropolitan area. Also dissolved were the
four Educational Improvement Centers in New Jersey, formed in 1977.

   On the other hand, the cooperative version of a regional service agency enjoyed
significant growth in a number of states in the period covered by Stage 4.
These include new agencies in the states of Kansas, Kentucky, Montana, North
Dakota, New Mexico, and South Dakota.

   Changes in governance structures. Recent legislation enacted in several
states (e.g., Georgia, Texas) mandates or strongly encourages that the composition
of the governing boards of service agencies include representatives of other
educational organizations or other human services providers serving the same
region as the service agency. This development adds to the number of states that
have had a long-standing requirement of this type (e.g., Oregon), or a long-standing
permissive legislative authority to do so (e.g., West Virginia). Moreover,
many service agencies across the country now voluntarily make provision
for the involvement of representatives of nonpublic schools, as well as postsecondary
institutions and human services providers in the decision-making processing
of their agencies.

   A broadening of the mission of the agencies. What is perhaps the most
significant development that is also still unfolding in the time period covered by
Stage 4 has to do with state expectations for their system of service agencies,
especially those classified here as Type A: Special District ESAs. The common
state aspirations for the initial creation and continued support of the concept of
an educational service agency was that these units would address equity issues
of educational opportunity, especially for children in the state's small and often
rural school districts. Though this focus is still prominent, there appears to be a
growing awareness in state policy circles that the service agencies should be
viewed as a critical state asset for addressing equity issues including the opportunity
to offer high-quality and efficient programs throughout state system of
elementary-secondary education. This is perhaps most dramatically illustrated in
the relatively new, and deeper, involvement of numerous state networks in vari-

ous aspects of their respective state school improvement strategies. Now a state network of educational service agencies is generally regarded as a highly prized, accessible primary technical assistance provider for one or more of state initiatives.

Adoption of core programs and services. The recent increased involvement of numerous state networks of educational service agencies in state school improvement efforts has frequently been institutionalized through passage of legislation or enactment of administrative rules that establish a set of core programs and services that all agencies in a state system must provide. These core services most often center on the continuation, but now more targeted, programs and services such as staff development, curriculum development, technology support as well as instruction and a range of instructional support services for the disabled student. Other frequent recent core requirements are the engagement in some aspect of a state's technology initiative (e.g., Iowa, Nebraska, Oregon, Pennsylvania), and a prominent role in the provision of technical assistance to low-performing schools (e.g., Georgia, New York, Texas, and West Virginia).

Adoption of more rigorous performance accountability. Though late in coming, the performance accountability movement being implemented at the local school district level, and at all levels of general government, is beginning to touch the educational service agency movement. Most typically, the accountability strategy used by the states has been the development of a state accreditation system for its network of service agencies. In 1989-90, the six states of Georgia, Nebraska, Ohio, Oregon, Texas, and Wisconsin established a system for accrediting their service agencies. Most of these, however, were generally limited to a listing of standards only, with no performance measures cited (Stephens 1990). However, the current accreditation system in Texas clearly includes the requirement that the state network meet a range of specified standards and establishes performance measures on which to establish whether or not the standards have been met, exceeded, or failed to be met. The new accreditation system for the Iowa Area Education Agencies, adopted in 1997, also established both standards and performance measures on which the accountability of the agencies can be assessed.

Most recently, several states have begun to publish an annual report card on the condition of its system of service agencies. The vast majority of individual service agencies have for some time voluntarily issued annual report cards to their constituent school districts. The content and format of both state-sponsored and voluntary annual reports vary significantly, as will be established in a subsequent chapter.

Further cooperation with central city school districts. Another significant trend warranting mention is the increasing cooperative relations between service agencies located in metropolitan areas and the central city school district. Since their inception, the New York BOCES have had little interaction with the "Big Five," the states' five largest districts when BOCES were established in 1948. The two largest districts in both Nebraska (Lincoln and Omaha), and the two largest in Pennsylvania (Philadelphia and Pittsburgh) were all designated to function as a service agency as well as a local school district at the time the state network in each state was formed in the 1960s and early 1970s. The exclusion of the "Big Five" in New York reflected the prevailing view in the 1940s that the service agencies were to be a way to address the needs of rural, small districts. The exclusion of the two large districts in Nebraska and Pennsylvania may in part reflect this same position, though other considerations likely played a part as well.

However, in the vast majority of situations the state identified the geographic boundaries of its state network of service agencies to include all local districts, including large central city districts within the catchment area of a service agency. Large urban districts, with few exceptions, avail themselves of some but usually not all of the potential programs and services of their service agency.

This traditional situation has been undergoing change in recent years. There appears to be a realization on the part of urban school interests that substantial benefits can be realized in addressing their own special needs by collaborating with other metropolitan area districts, especially because of the demonstrable high quality of programs and services typically offered by their metropolitan area service agencies. On this latter point, it is generally acknowledged that some of the nation's exemplary service agencies serve regions in some of the largest metropolitan areas (e.g., Seattle, Portland, Los Angeles, San Diego, Houston, Detroit, Milwaukee).

FEDERAL AND STATE INFLUENCES ON SERVICE AGENCY DEVELOPMENT

In many respects, the evolution of the concept of the educational service agency parallels the course of major developments in the history of public education. This holds true from the early beginnings of the concept in the 19th century to the present day, the first years of the 21st century. This is so for at its very core, the continuously changing nature of the concept reflects the struggles of local school districts and those of the states to devise and implement strategies, sometimes acting in concert and sometimes unilaterally, to take action to meet ever increasing challenges that have unfolded over the past century. The evolutional track is also a story of the successful implementation of both the theory and practice of interorganizational collaboration. It is a story of how specific federal legislation as well as advocacy positions of federal executive branch agencies, particularly during the last half-century, put in motion incentives that greatly spurred development of the contemporary consensus view of the concept. Furthermore, it is a story of how key individuals have, over time, helped shape the policy agendas at both the state and federal levels that also set in motion events that resulted in the transformation of the concept. Finally, because of these reasons and more, it is to be recognized that the concept of an educational service agency is not a static idea but rather a continuously evolving one.

An overview of our position of the major factors contributing to the development of the concept during the last half-century is provided in Figure 2.3. Emphasis is given to this period because it is here where the present day forms of the concept clearly unfolded and where the implementation of the concept became most widespread across the nation.

For the most part, the discussion that follows focuses on the five categories of events cited in Figure 2.3 that caused state and local school districts to explore, either unilaterally or in concert, the concept of regionalizing the provision and/or production of some programs and services in response to the increasing pressures on both over the course of the last half-century:

♦ the increasing formal recognition of the concept in federal education legislation
♦ formal endorsement in federal legislation designed to improve local general government
♦ the increasing support of the concept in positions advanced by federal executive branch agencies, particularly during the critical early decades of the last half-century
♦ the advocacy of the concept in both state and national professional communities
♦ the advancements made in the theory and practice of inter-organizational relations

Formal Recognition in Federal Legislation. There is a general consensus that until World War II, the federal role in education was largely negligible. Since that time, however, most students of school government are also in agreement that the federal government has assumed an activist role in the promotion of programs that are viewed to be in the national interest. Campbell and his colleagues (1990) argue that "while federal participation and influence in education have been with us since the founding of the nation, the 20-year period from 1950 to 1970 is particularly noteworthy as a time of rapid growth of federal involvement" (p. 50). They also remind us that decisions rendered by federal courts have been just as significant as action taken by the Congress in the creation "of a national policy for education" (p. 50). The passage of other influential legislation, as well as new federal court decisions in the ensuing 10 or more years, would likely cause these authors to add the 1990s and early years of the present decade as an equally significant period of federal engagement in education.

The role of the federal government in the promotion of the concept of an educational service agency is also of great significance. The influence of the federal government is reflected in two basic ways:

♦ through the passage of legislation that provides incentives to the local and state educational interest to engage in collaborative planning and programming efforts that result in the promotion of the concept
♦ through the largely unheralded but critically important, issuance of position papers and reports that were designed to inform local and state leaders about the merits of regional, multi-jurisdictional, approaches to the issues facing local and state governments in both metropolitan and nonmetropolitan areas alike.

Figure 2.3
Factors Contributing to the Development of the ESA Concept, with Particular Emphasis on the Last Half-Century

Major New Pressures

- growing body of research on school effectiveness
- acceleration of national and state policy initiatives designed to improve school district performance
- incremental expansion of judicial definitions of equal access
- growing resistance to rural district reorganization as the policy choice for solving the "rural" problem

that together created mounting challenges for both

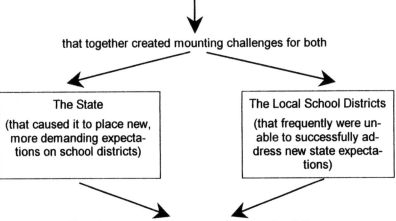

The State	The Local School Districts
(that caused it to place new, more demanding expectations on school districts)	(that frequently were unable to successfully address new state expectations)

That then caused the state and local school districts, either unilaterally or in combination, to explore the concept of the regionalizing of provision and/or production of some programs and services, a concept that was

- increasingly cited in federal education legislation
- formal endorsement of the regional concept in federal legislation designed to improve local general government
- increasingly supported in positions advanced by federal executive branch agencies
- advocated in state and national professional communities
- supported by advancements in the theory and practice of interorganizational relations

Identified in Table 2.5 are what we regard to be six milestones in Congressional action that has served to support the development of the concept of an educational service agency. However, two of the milestones stand out as most important. The first, passage of the Elementary and Secondary Education Act of 1965 (P.L. 85-864), is clearly the first of the two.

This is so because of two of the six provisions in the Act: (1) Title II, which offered grants to the states to provide instructional materials for both public and nonpublic schools; and (2) Title III, which provided grants to the states to promote innovative educational programs that include the use of supplementary educational centers and services.

Numerous states operating a long-standing system of county offices of education used one or a combination of both titles to undertake the planning and implementation of new multi-county regional educational service agencies to replace the older county offices. Other states with county offices used funds from these sources to create a new statewide system of educational service agencies, while still retaining, usually for political reasons, the county system.

Table 2.5
Major Milestones in Federal Legislation in Support of the Concept

Year	Legislative Action
1963	Passage of Vocational Education Act (P.L. 88-210)
	Eligibility of cooperatives of two or more districts established
1965	Passage of Elementary and Secondary Education Act (P.L. 85-864)
	Title II, support for school library resources, textbooks, and other instructional materials; and, Title III, support for supplemental educational centers and services
1967	Amendments to Elementary and Secondary Education Act of 1965
	Transferred Title III to state control
1975	Passage of Education for All Handicapped Children Act (P.L. 94-142)
	Eligibility of cooperatives of two or more districts established
1994	Passage of Goals 2000: Educate America Act (P.L. 1129)
	First statutory definition of an educational service agency—the term is to mean regional public multi-service agencies authorized by state statute to develop, manage, and provide services or programs to local education agencies
2001	Passage of No Child Left Behind Act (P.L. 107-110)
	Retained definition of an educational service agency but revised definition of a local education agency to include three additional entities that could qualify for local education status: educational service agencies, consortia of educational service agencies, and state educational agencies—other provisions (1) required states to consider providing professional development and technical assistance through education service agencies; and, (2) where education service agencies do not exist, the state is to consider providing these through other cooperative agreements such as a consortium of local educational agencies

Moreover, two of the primary programming initiatives of the reconstituted former county offices and the new service agencies were in the areas that were prioritized in both titles, the provision of media services, and special education, programming staples that continue to this day.

The second of the two critical milestones is the recent passage of No Child Left Behind Act of 2001, the latest reauthorization of the Elementary and Secondary Education Act of 1965. The act is significant for several reasons. On the one hand, it requires the states to consider utilizing their existing system of educational service agencies in the provision of two centerpieces of the legislation—professional development and technical assistance to schools as they implement the comprehensive provisions of the act. Singling out educational service agencies in this way, or for that matter, singling out any service provider in federal legislation has few precedents. Moreover, the legislation also asks those states without a system of educational service agencies to consider providing professional development and technical assistance through some form of cooperative arrangement between school districts, another unprecedented provision. Whether wittingly or not, the latter of the two options that the states are urged to consider might prove to be an example of the value of the incremental approach to changing state policy. That is, it may reflect an awareness that a number of existing, comprehensive statewide networks of educational service agencies had their origin in single-purpose consortia. Once the benefits of collaboration were more fully appreciated, support for a broader programming role was enhanced.

FORMAL ENDORSEMENT IN FEDERAL LEGISLATION DIRECTED AT LOCAL GENERAL GOVERNMENT

The concept of the regionalization of programs and services of local general government, particularly those located in metropolitan areas, was also introduced in a number of Congressional actions. Cited here are three major legislative acts passed in the mid-1960s and early 1970s, the approximate beginnings of Stage 3, "The Golden Age," of development of the educational service agencies concept. The significance of these three statutes should not be minimized for they clearly raised the visibility of the regional concept, and moreover, paved the way for the promotion of intergovernmental relations by removing legal constraints toward this end that may have been present in a state. The three acts are:

- ♦ the Housing and Urban Development Act of 1965
- ♦ the Public Works and Economic Development Act of 1965
- ♦ the Inter-government Personnel Act of 1970 (P.L. 91-648)

A 1982 report of the Advisory Commission on Inter-government Relations argues that the passage of the first two of these should be regarded as "the turning point for substate regionalism in the U.S." (p. 267). The first made it possible for area-wide organizations of locally elected officials, or councils of government, to be eligible for planning funds and grants from the federal government. The second provided federal funds for the creation of multi-county economic development districts.

The Commission asserted that largely because of these two acts, and others that followed, the governmental structure of the United States was literally changed "by inserting a nationwide system of substate regions between the local and state governments" (p. 6). The report also takes the position that the new substate regions should not be regarded as governmental units, but rather, and importantly, should be viewed as "intergovernmental mechanisms designed to fill the gap between existing levels" (p. 6).

The Inter-government Personnel Act is noteworthy in that it facilitated the ability of federal, state, and local governments and post-secondary institutions to provide for the temporary assignment (not to exceed two years, but could be re-newed for an additional period not to exceed two years) of personnel. This precedent-setting legislation also stands as clear evidence of the desire of the federal government to promote interorganizational collaboration and coopera-tion, the core underpinning of the concept of an educational service agency.

SUPPORT IN POSITIONS OF
FEDERAL EXECUTIVE BRANCH

Advocacy for the concept of regionalizing the production and provision of some functions heretofore viewed as within the domain of local governmental jurisdictions was also significant. Several reports in the decades of the 1960s and 1970s from, at that time, the highly visible and prestigious bipartisan com-mission, the Advisory Commission on Intergovernmental Relations (ACIR), are cited. The focus of the reports is on:

♦   the championing of inter-local agreements to facilitate intergovernmental cooperation
♦   early support for area vocational education programs
♦   a new emphasis on the need to develop more meaningful plans for the al-location of function between local and regional service providers
♦   the need to distinguish the provision and production of governmental functions

With the exception of the report that established the early support for area vocational education programs, all others were directed at general government jurisdictions at the local level, with education referred to only incidentally. However, may of the concepts and arguments advanced in the reports clearly could, and were, transferable to issues in education.

All of the reports were published under the auspices of ACIR. The first three were released by ACIR in the mid-1960s to mid-1970s, a key decade in the evolution of the concept of an educational service agency. Moreover, the four reports were not the only efforts of ACIR to promote ways to improve local government functions where there was a clear national interest, or of similar ef-forts by other executive branch departments and agencies during the last ap-proximate four decades.

We concentrate on the earlier work of the now disbanded ACIR because of the significance of its advocacy positions on issues that are central to the development of the service agency concept.

Facilitating Cooperation by Championing Inter-local Agreements. In a 1967 publication, the ACIR reiterated its strong endorsement of intergovernmental cooperation at the local level as "one basic method of broadening the geographic base for handling common governmental functions," particularly "when separate action by individual local units is uneconomical and when the consolidation or transfer of a function is not economically or politically feasible" (p. iii). The ACIR acknowledged that inter-local agreements and contracts have been in use for some time in local areas of the country and that a small number of state constitutions have provisions authorizing such agreements. However, the Commission also believed that the potential of this alternative strategy for improving the functions of local governments was greatly underutilized. To encourage the greater use of inter-local agreements, the Commission published a handbook that included: guidelines for the development of these agreements and contracts; and, a model statute to assist states in the adoption of legislation that would result in the greater use, and effectiveness of such agreements and contracts.

Early Support for Area Vocational Education Programs. In a 1966 report the ACIR noted that a number of states still had not created the legislative framework necessary to adopt area-wide vocational education programs despite the "considerable stimulus toward the adoption given by the Federal Government, particularly since the authorization of the grant-in-aid program under the Vocational Education Act of 1963" (p. 529). ACIR then proposed a draft statute for use by the states in the creation of ACIR's preferred alternative, the use of the county as the geographic catchment area for a hoped-for vocational education system. The draft statute was specifically targeted for use by those states having a significant number of small enrollment size districts.

A New Emphasis on Improvement in the Allocation of Functions. It is to be recalled that the decades of the 1960s and 1970s were previously referred to as a critical period in the evolution of the concept of an educational service agency. It was during this approximate time period when many of the existing state networks were formed as the policy choice for addressing, in particular, the issues of rural school district reorganization and strengthening what was widely criticized as the inept older county office of education. These same two decades are to be noted for another critical and timely debate in state and local general government circles on a topic that is central to the concept of an educational service agency and likely greatly influenced support for the concept in that it provided added rationale for advocates of the concept.

The focus of the debate centered on the complex question of which of the traditional functions of local government ought to be retained at the local level and which of these ought to be, for economic and other reasons, provided regionally. The positions advanced by ACIR on these questions appear to have been most influential in shaping the debate.

One of the first of ACIR's statements on this subject was published in 1963. In this initial report, 15 common governmental functions, one of them education, were ranked on a scale of "most local" through "most area-wide" in character. The 15 functions ordinarily represent 85% of the total expenditures of local government jurisdictions. The initial ranking made use of seven criteria, two economic and the remaining five centered on political, administrative, and social considerations that should be part of policy determination (pp. 5, 6).

The second ACIR report on this topic to be cited was published approximately a decade later, in 1974. Here the ACIR used what it called a "normative approach to functional assignment." According to the Commission, an ideal allocation system should reflect what was referred to as four basic characteristics: (1) economic efficiency, (2) fiscal equity, (3) political accountability, and (4) administrative effectiveness (p. 7). The report then stated:

> Taken together these characteristics suggested that functional assignments should be made to jurisdictions that can (1) supply a service at the lowest possible cost; (2) finance a function with the greatest possible fiscal equalization; (3) provide a service with adequate popular political control; and (4) administer a function in an authoritative, technically proficient, and cooperative fashion. (p. 7)

The Commission then restated seven criteria, first developed in 1963, that ought to be used in the development of what it referred to as the rational reassignment of functional responsibilities in a metropolitan area:

1. The governmental jurisdiction responsible for providing any service should be large enough to enable the benefits from that service to be consumed primarily within the jurisdiction. Neither the benefits from the service nor the social costs of failing to provide it should "spill over" into other jurisdictions.

2. The unit of government should be large enough to permit realization of economies of scale.

3. The unit of government administrating a function should have a geographic area of jurisdiction adequate for effective performance.

4. The unit of government should have the legal and administrative ability to perform services assigned to it.

5. Every unit of government should be responsible for a sufficient number of functions so that its governing processes involve a resolution of conflicting interests, with significant responsibility for balancing governmental needs and resources.

6. Performance of functions by the unit of government should remain controllable by and accessible to its residents.

7. Functions should be assigned to that level of government that maximizes the conditions and opportunities for active citizens' participation and still permits adequate performance (p. 7).

The third ACIR report on this topic to be cited, *A Handbook for Inter-local Agreements and Contracts* (1976), is of interest in that it included the results of a national survey of nearly 6,000 city governments with a population of at least 2,500 that had transferred one or more functions to another jurisdiction in the year 1975. Returns were received from nearly 60 percent of the government agencies. One line of inquiry asked the respondents to indicate the reasons why they transferred functions. The results in order of frequency mentioned were: economies of scale; avoidance of duplication; lack of facilities and equipment; fiscal constraints; lack of personnel; inadequate services; jurisdictional or geographic limitations; and, federal aid requirements/incentives (p. 38). We cite these results in that many of these same themes were frequently given prominence in the arguments put forth by advocates of the concept of a regional educational service agency.

Stephens (1970) also argued for the use of an allocation of functions approach for the production and provision of education programs and services. However, he asserted that in a field of public service like education that has a state constitutional requirement, the focus should be on an examination of the proper role of state, regional, and local jurisdictions, not just local-regional as was the point of interest of most statements on this subject in the 1960s.

The Need to Distinguish Provision and Production. The need to distinguish the provision and production of public goods and services is the theme of another report of the ACIR (1987). In the report, the ACIR took the position that the multiplicity of both general-purpose and special-purpose governments, including school districts, that are generally present in metropolitan areas, should not be a barrier to "good government or to metropolitan governance" (p. 1), a common concern raised in local and state policy circles and in academia.

Rather than being an impediment, the Commission argued that "the diversity of local governments can promote key values of democracy" and that "the multiplicity of differentiated governments does not necessarily imply fragmentation" but also so long as "such governments, interactively linked through a variety of arrangements can constitute a coherent local public economy" (p. 1).

What ACIR advanced as the solution is the necessity of distinguishing the provision and the production of public goods and services, where the former addresses the issues of what public goods and services will be made available to a community (or as increasingly the case in education, mandated by the state to be provided by all school districts), and the latter addresses how goods and services are to become available as stressed by ACIR. The criteria for organizing provision differ substantially from the criteria for organizing production. Provision criteria are concerned with how best to satisfy the preferences of citizens; production criteria have to do with the efficient management of human and material resources (p. 1).

We have no way of knowing the extent to which the line of argument advanced by ACIR informed local and state decision makers that it is important to consider the organizational capacity of school districts, in both metropolitan and nonmetropolitan areas, to provide programs and services mandated by the state and the federal governments, as well as to be sensitive to the need to think carefully about how best to produce a mandated requirement. We suspect, however, that the influence of this line of argument, given prominence by ACIR and others, was substantial, and resulted in the further support for the concept of an educational service agency and the subsequent assignment of an increasing role in the production of programs and services to agencies of this type.

ADVOCACY IN STATE AND NATIONAL
PROFESSIONAL COMMUNITIES

The development of the concept of an educational service agency has also benefited from the relatively extensive attention given to the significant problems and issues facing local governments in metropolitan areas in a number of professional fields other than education. This interest appeared to be especially high during the difficult decades of the 1960s and 1970s, as stressed earlier, a critical period in the evolution of the concept in the field of education.

Warren (1974), a political scientist, posits that the numerous proposals put forth during the 1960s and early 1970s to reform metropolitan governance reflect three different theories. Each of the three schools of thought can be distinguished by its placement on a centralization-decentralization scale: Policy Centrists, who promote the virtues of the existing fragmented system of local government; Consolidationists, who believe that the solution to metropolitan problems lies in the creation of a single, unified government for the metropolitan area; and Federationists, who attempt to strike a balance between the approaches favored by the other two (pp. 7, 8).

Warren then identifies what he believes are several existing alternative approaches used to capitalize on the virtues of both metropolitanism and localism available from the experiences of the United States and Canada. These are: (1) the urban county; (2) the multipurpose authority; (3) the metropolitan council; (4) the traditional federation; (5) consolidation-decentralization; and (6) the Council of Economic Development model (p. 6). He concludes with the observation that the six models are each similar in some respects, but they differ primarily in three ways: implementation (comprehensive to incremental); effect on existing units of local government (minimal to partial to substantial realignment); and, role of metropolitan government vis-à-vis local government (supreme, equal, subordinate) (p. 12).

The Warren piece is cited because it is instructive in establishing the nature of the debate that took place in many professional communities in the 1960s and 1970s and that continues to this day. This same debate carried over and subsequently influenced decisions reached in state and local policy circles concerning the relative costs and benefits of alternative designs of an educational service agency.

Other positions were certainly advanced in the 1960s and 1970s in support of the reform of local government through the use of some regional configurations for the delivery of some programs and services. Cowing and Hottmann's (1976) discussion of the optimal public services system in a metropolitan area tended to give prominence to economic factors, whereas Shulala and Merget (1974) tended to stress political consideration in their discussion of alternative models available to local governments engaged in reform efforts.

In the field of education at the national level, the Association of Educational Service Agencies (AESA) is the major professional association promoting and articulating the interests of its member organizations, that in 2003-04 numbered over 620 educational service agencies located in 42 states. The AESA has enjoyed rapid growth from its early beginnings in 1977 (Christiansen 2001). In the past eight years it is credited with successfully lobbying Congress for the first time to recognize educational service agencies in a major education statute (*Goals 2000: Educate America Act of 1994*), and more recently, influencing the Congressional decision to urge the state to utilize educational service agencies in the implementation of the numerous provisions of the *No Child Left Behind Act of 2001.*

At the state level, initial support for the concept largely originated in the professional education communities at the local level. It was frequently superintendents of rural small districts who took the lead in advocating for change in the role and function of the traditional county office of education, or where these were not in existence, took the lead in forming cooperative arrangements with other districts, as well as working for the removal of any legal inhibitions that hindered the creation of a cooperative.

In more recent years, the primary advocates at the state level in many cases clearly have been the well organized state professional associations to be found in a significant number of states, especially those with a statewide network of service agencies. In 2002-03, 10 state associations employed a full- or part-time executive director (AESA 2003 Membership Directory). Several of these 10 also employed a full- or part-time lobbyist, or contracted for this service.

Unfortunately, while there have been notable successes resulting from the advocacy of the concept at the state and national levels, particularly in recent years, supporters have been handicapped by the absence of a cumulative body of research on the impact of their work. Rather, over time they have generally had to rely on various forms of policy arguments to present their case that a state government or the federal government take certain action on their behalf that are less powerful than optimal. That is, most advocacy pieces originating in the educational service agency community across the country still are overly dependent on what Dunn (1994) would classify as modes of argument that are pragmatic (claims are based on argument from motivation, parallel case, or analogy), or the value-critical mode (claims are based on the basis of assumptions abut the rightness or wrongness of policies and their consequences) (p. 101).

Nonetheless, the national professional association in particular, and a number of the state level professional associations as well, clearly have in recent years experienced enough success that they would serve as interesting case studies of how and why these groups have formed, and equally of value, how they organize their work. Sipple and his colleagues (1997) might well add to, or reinforce, their position that certain interest group theories together help in understanding the reasons for interest group formation (e.g., order and disturbance theory, commitment theory, by-product theory, exchange theory, countervailing power theory) (pp. 442-445).

DISCUSSION

Substantial progress has been made over the course of the last three or four decades in adding to the cumulative body of knowledge on interorganizational relations, a central feature in the work of an educational service agency. Progress in this field of inquiry has most assuredly contributed significantly to the increasingly successful implementation of the concept in Stage 3 as well as influenced the restructuring of existing state networks in the latest stage, Stage 4.

Much of the progress in an understanding of what factors lead to the success of interorganizational arrangements, and what factors are to be avoided is the result of the commingling of systems theory (defined by Hoy and Miskel, 1978, as educational organizations that should be conceived as a unified whole, composed of interdependent, interrelated and integrated parts, and further, that the interdependence of the parts creates an order among them) and social exchange theory (generally defined, in this context, to mean that any activity, especially voluntary, between two or more organizations must result in the realization of their respective goals).

In an earlier piece, Stephens (1988) identified seven core propositions of what he argued represented a synthesis of what many students of interorganizational relations view as factors that cause an organization to seek out or be receptive to engaging in relations with another organization: (1) when the organization is faced with a situation of resource scarcity or other perceived need; (2) when the organizational leadership perceives the benefits to outweigh the costs; (3) when the organization has a common mission and perceives that attainment of its goals is more likely to be realized through interorganizational arrangements than by acting alone; (4) when there is a history of good relations, a positive view of the other, and both are in close geographic proximity; (5) when the organization can maintain its organizational identity; (6) when the organization members can maintain their prestige and authority; (7) and, when the organization has few or no other alternatives (p. 14). He then added what he regarded to be an important eighth proposition:

> However, there is more to be said regarding the promotion of interorganizational arrangements. One also needs to think about how best to implement this policy choice, once the decision is made to promote its use and design configurations are agreed upon. While implementation considerations are implied in a number of the seven previously cited core propositions, direct reference to this issue has received scant attention by specialists in the field. Therefore, what follows is one additional proposition that is directed to this important phase of public policy development. This proposition in particular flows from my own study and observation of state and local planning and implementation efforts to promote interorganizational arrangements that have extended over two decades: the successful implementation of widespread interorganizational arrangements is dependent upon a strategy of using state-induced external incentives to motivate local decision makers to seek out or be receptive to such efforts. (p. 14)

SUMMARY

Educational service agencies have undergone significant changes in the last 40 years. While originally established to serve needs of state departments of education and state legislatures, most state networks have largely evolved into becoming agencies that meet and balance the needs of the state and the local school districts that they serve. This has happened because states have come to realize their inability to meet all the needs of local districts at a time of reduced appropriations for state education agencies and because public demands for school accountability have required more proximate sources of assistance to local school districts, especially those that lack the resources and expertise to accomplish significant improvement. Recent federal legislation has recognized the value of service agencies and has encouraged their use in school improvement where they are available. This new phase of intergovernmental cooperation between federal, state and local authorities has somewhat been fostered by a growing body of theory about how to best allocate the development of programs and the delivery of services in general government as well as school administration.

REFERENCES

Advisory Commission on Intergovernmental Relations. 1963. *Performance of urban functions: Local and areawide* (September) Report M-21 revised. Washington, DC.

Advisory Commission on Intergovernmental Relations. 1966. *1967 state legislative program of the Advisory Commission on Intergovernmental Relations* (September) Report M-33. Washington, DC.

Advisory Commission on Intergovernmental Relations. 1967. *A handbook for inter-local agreements and contracts* (March) Report M-29. Washington, DC.

Advisory Commission on Intergovernmental Relations. 1974. *Governmental functions and processes: Local and areawide* (February) Report A-45. Washington, DC.

Advisory Commission on Intergovernmental Relations. 1976. *Pragmatic federalism: The reassignment of functional responsibility* (July) Report M-105. Washington, DC.

Advisory Commission on Intergovernmental Relations. 1987. *The organization of local public economies* (December) Report A-109. Washington, DC.

Association of Educational Service Agencies. *2003 membership directory*. Arlington, VA: Author.

Campbell, R. F., Cunningham, L. L., Mystrand, R. O. and Usdan, M. D. 1990. *The organization and control of American schools* 6th ed. Columbus, OH: Merrill Publishing Company.

Christiansen, L. 2001. *History: Association of Educational Service Agencies* (December). Arlington, VA: Association of Educational Service Agencies.

Dunn, W. N. 1994. *Public policy analysis: An introduction.* Englewood Cliffs, NJ: Prentice Hall.

Elementary and Secondary Education Act of 1965, Pub. L. 85-864.

Fritzwater, C. O. 1968. *State school system development: Patterns and trends.* Denver, CO: Education Commission of the States.

Hoy, W., and Miskel, C. 1978. *Educational administration: Theory, research, and practice.* New York: Random House Press.

Iowa State Board of Education. 1989. *Iowa's AEAs: Foundation for the future* (December). Des Moines, IA: Author.

Iowa State Board of Education. 1997. Chapter 72, Title XIII, Administrative Rule—

Accreditation of area education agency agencies. Des Moines, IA: Author.

National Commission on Excellence in Education. 1983. *A nation at risk*. Washington, DC: U. S. Department of Education.

No Child Left Behind Act of 2001, Pub. L. 107-110.

Shulala, D. E., and Marget, A. E. 1974. Transition problems and models. Ed. T. P. Murphy and C. R. Warren. *Organizing public services in metropolitan America* (pp. 179-187). Lexington, MA: Lexington Books.

Stephens, E. R. 1970. *The development of a model for the allocation of educational functions in a state school system: Some conceptual and methodological considerations*. Paper presented at the National Conference on Regional Educational Programs, October 10, Des Moines, IA.

Stephens, E. R. 1979. *Education service agencies: Status and trends*. ESA Study Series/Report No. I. Burtonsville, MD: Stephens Associates.

Stephens, E. R. 1990. An examination of state accreditation practices for education service agencies. *Research in Rural Education*, 6(3):1-9.

Stephens, E. R. 1992. Mapping the research task for the construction of a federal system for classifying the nation's rural school district. *Journal of Research in Rural Education*, 8, no. 3 (Fall):3-28.

United States Congress. *Goals 2000: Educate America Act of 1994*. Washington, DC: Author.

Warren, C. R. 1974. Developing alternative models for servicing metropolitan America. Eds. T. P. Murphy and C. R. Warren. *Organizing public services in metropolitan America* (pp. 3-14). Lexington, MA: Lexington Books.

Chapter 3

Educational Service Agencies in Contemporary America

INTRODUCTION

The concept of an educational service agency is clearly an evolving one, as the developments portrayed in the previous chapter attest. Moreover, the concept will most assuredly continue to evolve in the years ahead as educational service agencies, in most states, will likely always reflect and be responsive to changes that impact local and state educational interests. This has been true from the very earliest support and implementation of the first forms of a service agency, the traditional county office of education that performed largely supervisory and administrative roles, to the present day form of a service-oriented agency.

Presented in this chapter is a profile of the dominant discernable patterns of the major structural and organizational features of educational service agencies as these are evident at the time of this writing, the first years of the 21st century. As will be noted, both commonalities and diversity continue to characterize the service agency movement. This has been true from the earliest beginnings of the evolution of the concept. The objective of this status report is to establish what appear to be tendencies that are apparent in the workings of the major forms of networks of agencies, not a detailed treatment of each individual network. However, specific features of an individual state system are on occasion included to illustrate a pattern that is being described.

WORKING DEFINITIONS OF PRESENT DAY ESA

As cited in Chapter 1, the generic term, educational service agency, or ESA, has in recent years been used to define a category of organizations whose principal role is that of providing services for a collection of local school districts and/or for the state in a designated, bounded geographic region. A present day ESA can then be defined as follows:

> A regional public elementary-secondary education agency authorized by state statute or administrative code that exists primarily to provide instructional support and management and planning programs and services to local education agencies. It may also operate one or more specialized schools when so requested by local education agencies in its service region. This function, however, is secondary to its primary goal. Moreover, students in attendance at a specialized school administered by an ESA are ordinarily counted as holding membership in their home district.
>
> An ESA may also provide services of a technical assistance, consultative, or statistical nature for the state, but activities of this type are again

secondary to its primary mission. The technical assistance, consultation, or statistical functions performed by an ESA for the state, however, do not carry with them the responsibility for the ESA to levy sanctions against a non-complying local education agency to a state or federal directive. The voluntary roles performed for the state or those required by the state of an ESA, moreover, are also secondary to its primary role of providing programs and services to local education agencies. (Stephens 2001)

Though an admittedly lengthy definition of an ESA, it has substantial conceptual clarity and descriptive validity, two standards that ought to be uppermost in making choices concerning the best way to describe the essential features of an object. Several illustrations are offered that provide justification for the preferred working definition.

1. As will subsequently be established, virtually all ESAs created under state statute or administrative code or otherwise authorized were formed for the specific purpose of providing programs and services to local education agencies.

2. The definition notes that an ESA may operate a specialized school (e.g., a regional school for disabled students, a regional vocational-secondary school or center, a regional alternative school). This information also helps to clarify what appears to be confusion in a number of state education agencies' reporting practices to the National Center for Education Statistics on the type of elementary-secondary education agencies and elementary-secondary schools operating in their states. We return to the issue later in the chapter.

3. An attempt to more accurately reflect current practices also justifies the inclusion in the definition of an acknowledgment that a number of ESAs do, in fact, perform certain functions for the state of a technical assistance, consultative, or statistical nature (e.g., local education agency reorganization studies). Still others are engaged in implementing one or more state regulations governing some aspect of local education agency operations (e.g., processing teacher certification regulations, monitoring student truancy laws, validating student enrollment claims for state aid). The performance of these types of roles, however, is secondary to the primary mission of the ESAs. Indeed, many of the current state roles performed by those agencies are carryovers from functions earlier performed by county offices of education that were subsequently restructured as educational service agencies were designed to provide programs and services. The transfer to the new ESAs of any previous roles performed by a predecessor county office was most likely no more than the result of a decision that some substate regional agency in closer proximity to local education agencies than the state capital made good programming and economic sense.

The working definition also has several additional benefits that are likely to be viewed in some quarters as equally important as the three cited above. The nature of these further benefits address a crucial concern in definitional exercises—the utility of the working definition in the political and professional communities, especially in this case, the ESA community. Three additional advantages that speak to the utility issue are cited.

1. The definition is compatible with the language used in the 1994

amendments to the Elementary and Secondary Act of 1965 that for the first time in federal legislation included an explicit definition of the term. This legislation defined ESAs as: "regional public multiservice agencies authorized by state statute to develop, manage, and provide services or programs to local education agencies" (Goals 2000: Educate America Act of 1994, p. 1129). Importantly, this language has been carried over into the "No Child Left Behind" Act of 2001 (Pub. L. No. 107-110), the latest reauthorization of the Elementary and Secondary Education Act.

2. The definition is also comparable with the one used by the National Center for Education Statistics (NCES). In its seven category typology of all education agencies based on level of administrative and operational control, NCES defines regional education service agencies as "agencies created for the purposes of providing specialized educational services to other educational agencies" (National Center for Educational Statistics, p. 34).

3. Furthermore, and not surprisingly, the definition reaffirms the mission of the American Association of Educational Service Agencies (AAESA), which was renamed the Association of Educational Service Agencies (AESA) in 2000 in order to recognize its international membership. AESA is the single national professional association that devotes its energies to the improvement of practice in the nation's educational service agency-type organizations. It has a broad organizational membership eligibility guideline, possibly to enhance its impact to as wide a potential population as possible. AESA bylaws stipulate that a regular (voting) organizational membership is reserved for ESAs that are "created primarily for the purpose of providing educational services to multiple local education agencies" (American Association of Educational Service Agencies Bylaws 1996, p. 2).

SERVICE AGENCIES FEATURED IN THE PROFILE

The discussion of the principal dominant features of contemporary educational service agencies focuses on those that meet the working definition of an ESA and would be classified in the previously discussed Stephens typology as:

Type A: Special District ESAs, those that provide programs and services to both local districts and the state

Type C: Cooperative ESAs, those that provide programs and services primarily to member local districts

The third major type, the Type B: Regionalized SEA-ESA, is excluded for the principal reason that agencies of this type most typically are merely an extension of the state education agency, staffed by state agency personnel, and perform state-determined functions. Moreover, in many cases agencies of this type were created in response to a new federal or state initiative and funded from these sources. As a result, they typically come and go as such initiatives come and go. There are perhaps occasions where it is beneficial to include this variation in a discussion of service delivery in a state system of education. This is not so in the case of a discussion of the concept of an educational service agency, as this has been developed here.

A second selection criterion used to establish the principal focus of this chapter, and the remainder of the book as well, was the decision to concentrate on state networks or virtual state networks, defined here to mean those situations where all local school districts in a state are included in a region served by an ESA, or where three-fourths or more are included in a region served by an ESA. (There are a few states, New York for example, in which the largest cities in the state were deliberately excluded from inclusion in the catchment area of any service agency when the system was formed in 1948, probably because it was assumed by policy makers that such large entities had no need of assistance from a service agency.) The principal rationale for the use of this criterion is that a state network, or virtual state network of whatever of the two types, Type A or Type C, is chartered by the state. The likelihood, then, is greater that at least some primary reference sources are available. Even here, however, the availability of reliable information descriptive of each state system is minimal.

It should be noted that only an overview of the high-interest topic of the programming features is provided herein. This is consistent with the overriding objective of this chapter to provide a status report of discernable patterns in the major structural and organizational features of service agencies. Several of the major programming activities of service agencies are each the subject of more in-depth treatment in subsequent chapters, as is another emerging high visibility structural feature, the accountability systems under which the networks function.

NUMBER AND TYPE OF EDUCATIONAL SERVICE AGENCIES

A total of 25 statewide or virtual statewide networks of educational service agencies were in operation in the 2003-04 school year. Of this number, 13 most resemble what is classified here as a Type A: Special District ESA network, and 12 are classified as a Type C: Cooperative ESA network.

Presented in Table 3.1 is a listing of the 25 systems, the title of the units, the number of agencies in each state system, and their designation as either a Type A or Type C. Type A: Special District agencies are by far the most dominant of the total of 529 in that the 392 agencies of this type represent approximately three-fourths of the total. The state systems are depicted in Figure 3.1, which illustrates three heavy concentrations in the west coast, and much of the Midwest and upper Mid-east regions of the country.

A Conservative Count

It is to be stressed that the total of 529 agencies represent those that are part of what is being focused on here, statewide or virtual statewide networks. Excluded are a significant number of educational service agency-type organizations currently operating in many states, particularly in states outside the southeastern section of the country where the boundaries of many local school districts tend to be coterminous with county governments. Such countywide local districts tend to be larger and thus are seemingly presumed to have the capacity to serve their own needs. For example, a recent National Center for Education

Table 3.1
*Statewide and Virtual Statewide Networks of Type A and
Type C Service Agencies, 2003-2004*

State	Title of Agencies	Number of Units in Network	Type A	Type C
AZ	County Office of Education	15	15	
AR	Education Service Cooperatives	15		15
CA	County Office of Education	58	58	
CO	Boards of Cooperative Services	22		22
CT	Regional Educational Service Centers	6		6
GA	Cooperative Education Service Agencies	16	16	
IL	Educational Service Regions	45	45	
IN	Education Service Centers	9		9
IA	Area Education Agencies	15	15	
KS	(various titles used) [1]	11		11
KY	Educational Cooperatives	9		9
MI	Intermediate School Districts [2]	57	57	
MN	Educational Cooperative Service Units	10		10
NE	Educational Service Units	18		18
NM	Regional Education Cooperative	10		10
MS	(various titles used)	8		8
NY	Boards of Cooperative Educational Services	38	38	
OH	Educational Service Centers	61	61	
OR	Education Service Districts	21	21	
PA	Intermediate Units	29	29	
SD	(various titles used)	7		7
TX	Regional Education Service Centers	20	20	
WA	Educational Service Districts	9	9	
WV	Regional Education Service Agencies	8	8	
WI	Cooperative Education Service Agencies	12		12
	Total	529	392	137

Notes:
[1] Various titles are used; many have the terms "education service center" in addition to a geographic designation (e.g., southwest, south central, northwest, northeast).
[2] Original title is Intermediate School District; some have exercised a later adopted option to be called either a Regional Education Service Agency, Education Service Agency, Education Service District, or Regional Education Service District. Ten of the agencies have selected one of the four options, usually preceded by the title of the county(ies) served.

Figure 3.1
Statewide or Virtual Statewide Networks[1] 2000-2001

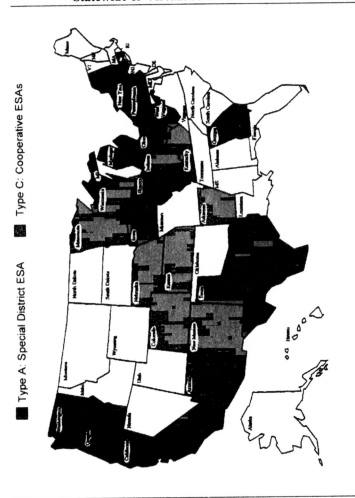

Statistics (NCES) publication (*Digest of Education Statistics 2002*) reports that in 2001-02:

♦ Massachusetts had 33 regional education service agencies
♦ Montana with 21 regional education service agencies
♦ South Carolina had 14 regional education service agencies
♦ Virginia with 34 regional education service agencies (p. 96)

Though these states have a significant number of agencies, they do not appear to provide service to enough local districts to enable the state to claim a "virtual" state system.

Moreover, AESA counts among its members still other service agencies (e.g., Alaska–1, Missouri–1, New Jersey–10, North Carolina–3, Utah–4, Wyoming–3), agencies that are not counted in the NCES tabulation. Yet, all meet the requirement that to hold voting membership they must be an agency established primarily to provide services to a collection of local districts.

However, in both of these two categories, the NCES count and the membership definition of AESA, the examples cited do not represent developments in states that meet the definition of a statewide or virtually statewide network. It is for this reason only that they are excluded.

Nor does the count of 529 include what must be an even more significant, but largely uncounted, number of collaborative activities between two or more local districts that are authorized by some form of generic statutory permissive legislation for local governments to enter into intergovernmental contracts, or inter-local agreements. No systematic tracking of these types of arrangements on a national level is known to exist, in part because of the short-term life cycle of many of them.

ESTABLISHMENT, ALTERATION, AND DISSOLUTION PRACTICES

A limited number of strategies were used to establish the 25 state networks that are the focus of this status report. So, too, is the limited extent of the use of various types of criteria to establish the geographic regions of a network, the related issue of the membership status of local schools and local school districts, and provision for the alteration and dissolution of a network once formed. However, clear and differing patterns on these issues can be noted with regard to the 13 Type A: Special District ESA state networks when compared to the 12 Type C: Cooperative ESA networks.

Establishment Patterns

Two principal strategies were used to create the existing state networks, each largely peculiar to the type of network. Eleven of the 13 Type A: Special District ESA networks are the result of the enactment of mandatory legislation. The two exceptions, the Arizona and California systems, were both created with the adoption of their respective state constitutions in the early years of statehood; and, as expected, all 12 of the Type C: Cooperative ESA networks were the result of passage of permissive state legislation authorizing the formation of either a specific number of agencies or making possible the establishment of a service agency wherever there was interest, a movement that ultimately resulted in the creation of a statewide or virtual statewide network of agencies.

Criteria Used to Establish Geographic Boundaries

For the most part, permissive legislation authorizing the establishment of the Cooperative ESA networks is silent on the geographic configuration that a service agency of this type might ultimately serve. However, this is not true of Special District networks that were formed most often through passage of mandatory legislation, or in the case of the Arizona and California systems that were created as constitutional offices. Their number was fixed at the outset.

The geographic boundaries of the 58 California and original 14, now 15, Arizona county offices of education were, as expected, straightforward. They were to be coterminous with those of the county government. Beyond these two cases, a variety of criteria have been utilized in establishing service areas for ESAs. In several instances, a minimum enrollment figure was used; for example, a minimum of 5,000 students or 8,000 students for the Michigan and Ohio systems, respectively. The criteria used to restructure the boundaries of the Illinois system also call for a minimum enrollment figure of 43,000, but also state that the boundaries are to be coterminous with all county governments included in the geographic region of a service agency.

Another common practice is to align the geographic boundaries of a Special District network so that they are coterminous with some other existing state sponsored substate region. For example, the boundaries of the original 15 Iowa service agencies, formed in 1975, closely followed the boundaries of the state's 15 area community colleges. The 20 Texas agencies, created in the mid-1960s, closely follow regional economic planning regions identified by the state earlier in the decade.

The criteria used in 1970 to establish the boundaries of 27 of the 29 Intermediate Units in Pennsylvania (excluding Philadelphia and Pittsburgh, both designated as service agencies as well as local school districts), represent early legislative efforts to be explicit in the design of the state network. The enabling statute (School Laws of Pennsylvania, 1971) stipulated that: "the arrangement of the IUs shall reflect consideration of the number of public school students; ease of travel within each IU; and, the opportunity to provide adequate basic services" (pp. 84-85).

As will be discussed below, several state networks have experienced major alterations in the number of units over the years. In a number of the efforts accomplished through legislative action, legislatures have tended to be more expansive in establishing criteria that are to be honored in the realignment activities.

Membership Status of School Districts

Differences are clearly to be noted concerning the membership status of school districts and the type of service agency network. For the most part, all school districts in Special District networks are by legislation technically a member of one service agency and may participate in its programs and services; however, they are not required to do so. The automatic membership status of school districts was usually established in legislatively predetermined geographic boundaries or in any subsequent modification in the number of agencies in the state network.

A relatively recent pattern in several states is the inclusion of specific statutory language that makes it possible for a local school district to receive services from any service agency in the state, not just their home agency (e.g., Georgia, Iowa, Texas). However, school districts in many states have for some time regularly participated in programming activities of agencies other than the one where their district is located. This has been made possible in part by inter-local agreements between two or more service agencies. Also in recent years, several state education agencies have awarded federal program funds (e.g., Ei-senhower staff development) to a single service agency with the requirement that it provide services to school districts located in two or more adjacent service agencies.

There are two notable exceptions to the general pattern of the automatic membership status of local school districts. In the case of the New York BO-CES, the so-called "Big Five" school districts of Buffalo, Rochester, Syracuse, Yonkers, and New York City, have by statute been excluded from membership in a BOCES and have been since the early formation period of the network. City school districts and exempted village school districts in Ohio continue to be excluded from official membership in a service agency. However, recent legisla-tive action in both states has removed legal barriers that have in the past pre-cluded nonmembers from participation in the programming activities of the ser-vice agency whose prescribed geographic boundary embraces the districts.

What clearly is the most comprehensive membership requirements estab-lished by legislative action for a Special District network concerns the 16 Geor-gia RESAs. Not only are all school districts required to be a member of the ser-vice agency in their region, but the legislature has also stipulated that the Department of Technical and Adult Education facilities and institutions, the University System of Georgia facilities and institutions located in designated geographic areas, and every state supported postsecondary institution not only are to be members, but "shall be an active member of an RESC" (HB 1187—A Plus Education Reform Act of 2000, p. 89).

School district membership in a Cooperative ESA network is, without ex-ception, voluntary, and most typically is achieved by the payment of a member-ship fee. In some state networks of this type, the geographic boundaries of the network were established in the adoption of a state plan for the development of the network, as in the case of the Connecticut RESCs. A local school district in the geographic area served by a service agency in Connecticut can voluntarily hold membership in its service agency. In other situations, the typical pattern is for contiguous school districts to form a service agency and hold membership in that which it helped create. The Indiana network would be an illustration of this practice. In other cases, membership is program-specific, and a service agency in the state may have different combinations of local school districts for a par-ticular program or service. A local school district may simultaneously be a par-ticipant in programs supported by several service agencies.

The state statutes are generally silent on the membership status of nonpub-lic, charter, and private schools, though in several cases, as will be established, legislation has been enacted that requires a state network to provide certain pro-grams and services to, especially, nonpublic schools. This is particularly true where a program is funded in whole or in part by federal funds. Schools of these types are thus not represented in the formal governance structures of a service agency, though a common practice is for representatives of these schools to serve as advisory groups of an agency.

Alteration and Dissolution Practices

The efficacy of the number of agencies in a state network, particularly the Special District types, has seemingly been an issue in many states since their early formation period. A state legislature of course has plenary authority to dissolve an entire state system of service agencies should it so choose. The typical legislative response to concerns regarding the number of agencies in its state network is to take action that:

♦ Delegates responsibility for the determination of the efficiency in the number of agencies to the chief state school officer or state board of education.
♦ Mandates a reduction in the number of agencies.
♦ Allows for the voluntary merger of two or more agencies.

A discussion of each of these three major state strategies follows. First, though, it is to be noted that the only way to alter or dissolve two Special District state networks, those in Arizona and California, is through an amendment to the state constitution. As noted previously, the county offices of education in both states are constitutional offices.

Delegation of responsibility. The legislatures in two states, New York and Texas, have granted the state commissioner of education authority to affect a modification in the number of agencies. Over the years, the state commissioners in New York have from time to time reduced the number of BOCES from the 90 operating in 1948, the year the network was established, to the present day 38. Reductions have typically occurred to coincide with the vacancy in the office of the district superintendent, a state employee and the chief executive officer of a BOCES. The state commissioner in Texas has the authority to provide for no more than 20 RESCs (the original and current number), but has the discretion to reduce this number and determine the location and geographic boundaries of the units so long as all local districts in the state have an opportunity to receive the programs and services of an RESC.

Mandated reductions. Several state legislatures have in the past taken action to mandate changes in number of agencies in their respective networks. These actions have in all cases resulted in a decline in the number of agencies. For example:

♦ The Illinois ESRs were reduced from 78 in 1974 to the present number of 45.
♦ The 21 currently operating ESDs in Oregon represent a decline of 9 below the number operating in 1963.
♦ Washington reduced the 14 ESDs operating in 1965 to the present 9.
♦ Ohio currently has 61 operating ESCs, down from 87 in 1995.

Voluntary mergers. Most states also have provisions for the voluntary merger of agencies as an option to the use of a mandate to affect a reduction in the number of units. These provisions vary across the states, but typically include these time-honored democratic precepts that must be honored before a merger can take effect:

- ♦ A proposed merger must be approved by the governing boards of each affected service agency. Should the agency have taxing authority (as in Michigan and Oregon), the merger must be approved by the electors of the affected local districts as well.
- ♦ Public hearing(s) are to be provided to allow representatives of affected local districts and the public to provide comment on the proposed merger.
- ♦ The proposed merger must meet certain minimal criteria established by (usually) the state board of education.
- ♦ The proposed merger must be approved by the state board.

Other state practices. Another relatively recent state strategy is now available in four states that could result in the mandated reduction in the number of agencies in a state network. The accreditation systems in Iowa, Ohio, Oregon, and Texas require that a nonaccredited agency is to be dissolved, and the programs and services of the discontinued agency transferred to one or more contiguous agencies. This mandated responsibility rests with the state board of education in Iowa, Ohio, and Oregon, and with the state commissioner of education in Texas.

Action by the Ohio legislature in 1995 is the only known recent example of the use of a financial incentive to affect an alteration in the number of agencies in a state system. In dissolving the 87 existing county offices of education and replacing these with what in 2000-01 were 61 Education Service Centers, the legislature provided a one-time $60,000 grant for each newly merged ESC to ease the financial cost associated with the merger.

MISSION

Certain patterns are also evident in state expectations of the networks, as these are ordinarily expressed in an explicit statutory declarative mission statement, or in the more common form, a statement of purpose. This is especially true for the Special District ESA network. However, there are also a number of noteworthy differences among states in their goals for service agencies that warrant mention.

Themes of Statutory Provisions

Certain themes regularly appear in the statutory language that establishes a state's expectations for its system of service agencies. Though the language varies, the most common hoped-for outcomes center on the anticipation that the network will promote efficiency, quality, and access to programs and services, as shown in Table 3.2, which also portrays the themes of other less frequently cited state expectations.

It is also a common practice for the states to combine several of the themes cited in Table 3.2 into a single declarative statement. An example of this would be the Oregon statute (Oregon Legislative Assembly, Chapter 334 1999) that defines the mission of the states 21 Education Service Districts to be that of "assuring the opportunity for each child to an equitable and excellent education . . .

Table 3.2

State Expectations of Networks Cited in Mission Statements

MOST COMMON THEMES

- Promote efficiency in delivery of programs and services.

- Provide programs and services that are effective.

- Promote equity in state system of elementary-secondary education by providing students and schools access to programs and services.

OTHER FREQUENTLY CITED THEMES

- Promote cooperation and coordination among school districts.

- Promote cooperation and coordination between school districts and other human service providers.

- Assist state-level bodies and/or state officials in the discharge of their statutory responsibilities.

- Provide services to special populations of students and/or school districts with limited enrollments.

assist the state board . . . deliver essential programs and services . . . help achieve coordination and cooperation . . . and, allow private agencies to participate" (334.005). The anticipation that a state network should provide for the development of leadership personnel for local school districts is specifically cited in only one state proclamation, that for the Iowa AEA system (Accreditation of Area Education Agencies 2001).

Individual Service Agency Mission Statements

Like most organizations, education service agencies all across the country have formally adopted mission statements to serve as a guide to the work of their enterprise. Of interest here is a content analysis of the mission statements of the 15 Iowa AEAs as these were stated in the mandated comprehensive plans or annual reports that were submitted to the state education agency in 1997-98. Five lead questions were posed for the review of the 15 mission statements: (1) What is it the AEAs do?; (2) In what ways do they do it?; (3) For whom do they do it?; (4) How do they do it?; (5) Toward what end? The results of this exercise are reported in Table 3.3.

GOVERNANCE FEATURES

A pronounced difference exists in the method of selection of the governing boards of Cooperative ESA networks and those of Special District networks. As shown in Figure 3.2, the chief executive officers of member school districts tend to play the most prominent role in the governance of Cooperative ESAs, either as active members of the governing body or through their involvement in the election of one of their peers to serve in this capacity. In contrast, the selection

Table 3.3

Content Analysis of Mission Statements of Iowa AEAs, 1997-98

1. What is it that AEAs do?
    Provide <u>Services</u> (n=12) and <u>Leadership</u> (n=11)
2. In what ways do they do it?
    With <u>Quality</u> (n=6), <u>Excellently</u> (n=3), <u>Effectively</u> (n=3), <u>Efficiently</u> (n=2), <u>Economically</u> (n=2), <u>Equality</u> (n=1)
3. For whom do they do it?
    <u>Children/student learners</u> (n=10), <u>Schools/districts</u> (n=10), <u>Families</u> (n=6), <u>Communities</u> (n=5), <u>Educators</u> (n=2)
4. How do they do it?
    <u>Support</u> (n=6), <u>Partnerships</u> (n=5), <u>Cooperation</u> (n=3), <u>Assistance</u> (n=3), <u>Facilitation</u> (n=3), <u>Catalysts</u> (n=2), <u>Collaboration</u> (n=1)
5. Toward what end?
    <u>Maximizing Potential</u> (n=2), <u>Enhancing Learning</u> (n=2), <u>Fostering Success</u> (n=1), <u>Providing Opportunities</u> (n=1), <u>Achieving Systemic Change</u> (n=1)

<u>Source</u>: Stephens and Good 1998.

Figure 3.2

Variations in the Method of Selection of Governing Boards

COOPERATIVE ESA NETWORKS
▼

- Automatic appointment of all superintendents of member school districts to serve on the board.

- Superintendents of all member school districts elect, from their members, members to serve on board.

SPECIAL DISTRICT ESA NETWORKS

ALTERNATIVE ELECTION PROCESSES

- By eligible voters within service area of agency

- By members of member school district boards sitting in convention—equal vote

- By members of local school district boards sitting in convention—weighted vote based on enrollment of school district

- By members of member school district boards sitting in convention—weighted vote based on population of school district

ALTERNATIVE APPOINTMENT PROCESSES

- Automatic appointment of both president of member school district boards and superintendent of member school districts

- Automatic appointment of one representative from each member organization

- By members of service agency board from non-education community members

processes used to establish the make-up of the governing boards of Special District service agencies, which are prescribed in statute, make use of alternative election methods and tend to limit the membership of professional staff. However, members of the governing boards of member school districts are the most prominent participants in three of the five alternative election procedures.

Election by the general population is a requirement in approximately one-third of the 13 Special District networks, those in the states of California, Illinois, Oregon, and Washington. Four of the 57 Intermediate School Districts in Michigan are elected by the general population; the remaining 53 are elected by members of the boards of component school districts, each district having one vote.

Some state networks are allowed to have a variable number of members, so long as a prescribed minimum or maximum is honored. Additionally, the statutes governing two networks either require or allow non-voting members to serve on a service agency board. The Oregon ESD boards are required to appoint two non-voting members, one each from the employment sector and the social services sector in the region served on an agency. The West Virginia RESA boards are also authorized by statute to appoint non-voting membership to members representing other educational and human services providers. The 15 Arizona County Offices of Education have no formal governing board.

Powers and Duties of Governing Board

Governing boards of service agencies tend to have a number of common powers similar to those enjoyed by the governing bodies of other public educational organizations. These typically include: the appointment of a chief executive officer, other employees upon the recommendation of the chief executive office; adoption of a budget; and general oversight of the operation of the service agency. However, the powers and duties of governing boards tend to be more extensively enumerated for boards of Special District networks that: (1) Perform state prescribed core programs and services to school districts; (2) Perform certain administrative and supervisory functions for the state; (3) Are selected by popular election or by election of board members of constituent districts; and, (4) Have a degree of taxing authority.

The statutory powers and duties of a number of governing boards are quite unique. Examples of some of the most noteworthy of these uncommon state requirements granted or placed on a governing board include the following: (1) The California county boards are not the employer of record for the employment of certified staff; the county superintendent is. However, they may contract with or employ individuals to provide special services to the board (e.g., legal, financial, engineering, administrative). (2) The Iowa AEA boards must meet at least annually with the boards of the regional area community college to discuss coordination of programs and services and other common interests, as well as meet annually with the board of any component school district if requested by the latter to do so. (3) A Michigan ISD board, in fulfilling the numerous duties required of it by law or administrative rule, may not "supercede or replace the governing board of a component school district, nor can it control or otherwise interfere in the rights of either component school districts, or public academies," with the disclaimer "except as provided for in statute." (4) Oregon ESD boards have been granted the most sweeping oversight of local school district operations, including: the authority to examine and audit all component school district budgets; approve or reject, increase or reduce any item in the budget; give final approval of the district budget; levy school district taxes; or appropriate school district funds. They may also collaborate in joint planning for the delivery of health care, employment training, and social services with other service providers. (5) County offices in California also have the responsibility of reviewing the budget of a local school district and then make recommendations to the state.

Advisory Groups
The extensive use of advisory groups to help shape the planning, delivery, and evaluation of programs is a central feature of most educational service agencies. Moreover, it would appear that the deep engagement of representatives of school districts cannot be solely attributable to a state statutory requirement, as in the case in several states (e.g., Illinois, Iowa, Oregon, Pennsylvania, Ohio), nor fully explained by virtue of the involvement of many service agencies in federally funded programs that require the establishment of an advisory group (e.g., special education programs, vocational-technical education). Rather, the need to involve stakeholder groups in the decision-making processes appears to be an accepted feature of the organizational culture of service agencies across the country.

PROGRAMMING PATTERNS
Educational service agencies of both types, Special District and Cooperative, engage in a long and varied list of programming activities in an effort to be responsive to the needs of constituent school districts and, particularly in the case of state networks of Special District ESAs, to the needs of the state as well. Presented below are several of the most discernable patterns in the programming practices of service agencies, including those that are enumerated in state mandates and those identified by the state as discretionary programs. Also reviewed are patterns in the roles played by state networks of Special District ESAs in the state's regulatory system covering school district operations.

Also described below are other relatively new practices that appear at this time to be the beginnings of several major and potentially significant patterns in the programming efforts of state networks of service agencies:

- the more prominent role played by several state networks in their respective state school improvement strategies
- the requirement that the agencies devote extraordinary attention to the provision of support services to low-performing schools and school districts
- the mandated as well as voluntary creation of what can be referred to as "super-ESAs," the combining, but not merging, of several service

agencies in order to concentrate the human and fiscal resources of each for the development, production and delivery of highly specialized programs and services.

It is to be stressed that the description of the programming patterns of service agencies is intended to provide an overview of what these are. As established earlier, a number of the topics introduced here are each the subject of more detailed treatment in other chapters.

Major Programming Patterns

The most comprehensive national survey in recent years of the programming activities of service agencies was conducted by the Association of Educational Service Agencies (AESA). Participants in the survey, completed during the 1999-2000 school year, were the approximately 500 member organizations of the association, including agencies in all 25 state networks that are the focus of the review presented in this chapter.

The AESA survey classified potential programs and services into three conventional categories that have long characterized the work of service agencies across the country:
♦   Educational programs offered to students of school districts
♦   Curricular and instructional support services to staff of school districts
♦   Administrative/management services for school districts

Selected results of the survey are reported in Table 3.4. Highlighted in the table are those programs and services reportedly offered by at least one-half of the respondents that numbered 438, or 88 percent of the membership of AESA in 2000-2001. The list of reported programs and services offered by the 438 participants in the survey that did not achieve the one-half or more threshold is a very long one.

In the category of curricular and instructional support services were: teacher centers (29.9%); instructional printing (34.5%); and program evaluation (36.5%). In the category of administrative/management services for school districts were: teacher/administrator credentialing services (33.6%); management planning services (25.1%); insurance services (34.7%); special needs transportation services (34.9%); personnel recruitment services (42.5%); energy management services (23.7%); school maintenance management (23.5%); safety-risk management (30.8%); and program audits (23.1%).

The AESA survey also requested respondents to establish whether or not the agency provided programs and services to three categories of participants other than regularly enrolled K-12 students. The results of these probes indicated that: 2.8% offered adult education programs and services; 74.8% offered early childhood programs and services; and, 47.9% offered programming for incarcerated children and youth.

Statutory Requirements

Statutory pronouncements concerning what programs and services agencies are to engage in for the most part focused on Special District networks. And

Table 3.4
Major Programming Activities of ESAs, 1999-2000

Category/Major Programming (offered by at
least 50 percent of member organizations)

Category: Educational Programs Offered Students Enrolled in School Districts
- Special education instruction and support services
- Itinerant therapy and instructional services
- Vocational education instruction
- Gifted and talented instruction
- Hospital/homebound instruction
- Alternative school instruction

Category: Curricular and Instructional Support Services to Staff of School Districts
- General staff development services
- Leadership training services
- Learning resources library services
- Curriculum development services
- Telecommunication services
- Technology services
- Student testing/evaluation services

Category: Administrative/Management Services for School Districts
- Cooperative purchasing services
- Computer services
- Financial management services

Source: Association of Educational Service Agencies 2000.

here also there are differences in how the states approach this issue. Three different approaches concerning the specificity of enumerated programming requirements are in use:

1. In some statutes, a relatively long list of required programs and services are cited as requirements that must be met by all agencies in the state network.

2. In other cases, the statutes cite specific programs and services that the agencies may provide should certain conditions be met.

3. In still other cases, a combination of both specifically required programs and services is cited, along with a largely open-ended *carte blanche* approach that makes possible the offering of any number of different discretionary programs and services, again so long as certain conditions are met.

This third approach, a combination of both specific and optional requirements, is the most dominant strategy used to structure the programming efforts of Special District ESA networks. Illustrative examples of the combined approach used in the two states of Georgia and Iowa are presented in Table 3.5.

Table 3.5

Illustrative Examples of Both Specific and Discretionary
Statutory Programming Specifications

State Network	
Georgia Regional Education Service Agencies[1]	Required Programs ● school improvement planning ● staff development with emphasis on improving student achievement and accountability ● curricular and instructional services, including implementation of state core curriculum academic assessment and evaluation ● instructional and management uses of technology ● statewide mentoring program ● alcohol and drug abuse ● assist instructional care teachers ● support alternative teacher certification program Discretionary Programming and Conditions ● Governing board may provide any additional service and assistance to its member schools ● offer any service and assistance for purchase by any school system in the state
Iowa Area Education Agencies[2]	Required Programs ● school community planning ● professional development services ● curriculum, instruction, and assessment services ● services that support multicultural, gender-fair approaches ● media services ● school technology services ● leadership development services Discretionary Programming and Conditions ● management services ● services requested by 60 percent of school districts or districts representing 60 percent of enrollment, if funds available ● auxiliary services for nonpublic schools for fee ● other educational programs if approved by state board of education

Sources:
[1] Georgia – H.B. 447. A Plus Education Reform Act of 2000.
[2] Iowa – Chapter 72, Accreditation of Area Education Agencies. (1997).

Most enabling legislation creating Special District networks also addresses the issue of discretionary programs and services. A common statutory requirement for the offering of a discretionary program is that it must be requested by school districts. Another common condition is that discretionary programs must be self-supporting.

One notable exception of the general self-supporting requirement for the offering of discretionary programs is the practice used in New York State. Here, a BOCES can offer, and receive a state subsidy for, a discretionary program that is requested by two or more school districts. This is a relatively generous state policy, when compared to other states. However, it is consistent with long-term state goals to address the issues of efficiency and equity in the state school system. Moreover, before an "aidable" discretionary program can be offered, it must first be approved by the chief state school officer. As required by statute, the commissioner is to apply the following criteria to each request. The program: must provide additional opportunities for pupils, particularly those with handicapping conditions; is expected to result in cost savings to the school district; will provide greater opportunity for students to earn credit in academic subjects; and, will insure greater and more appropriate use of a BOCES's facilities (Article 40, 7d (1)).

Joint Service Agreements

Most state networks of both Special District and Cooperative types have clear legislative authority to enter into joint service agreements with other agencies and organizations. This authorization is frequently specifically cited in the enabling legislation covering Special District networks, and in the case of Cooperative systems, through the ability to enter into joint service agreements as a result of the passage in the early 1970s in all states of a general intergovernmental relations statute authorizing public sector agencies to enter joint service agreements.

In several state statutes, specific types of other eligible organizations are identified. In a majority of cases where this is done, collaboration with another educational service agency(ies) is referenced most often. Also, in a majority of cases, the legislative language used is permissive in nature ("may" or "can"), rather than mandatory. One statutory provision that is more direct in conveying legislative intent is a provision of the Iowa statute (Chapter 323.2(5), 1997) that states that the AEA network "shall contract, whenever possible, with other school corporations for use of personnel, buildings, facilities, supplies, equipment, and programs and services."

Data on the number of joint service agreements entered into by service agencies is seldom traced in any systematic way. However, this practice is probably very significant, especially in some of the more proactive state networks. Moreover, the deep engagement of most service agencies across the country in the provision of instruction and/or instructional support services for students with exceptional learning needs would likely result in the development of close relationships with other human services providers.

The results of one statewide survey that does provide data on the extent of joint collaborative action with other agencies are included in a 1994-95 report by the Michigan Association of Intermediate School District Administrators (Collaborative Services Survey of Michigan Intermediate School Districts, 1994-95). The 1994 survey of the collaboratives engaged in by the Michigan ISDs revealed a significant number, 2,080, of them. This figure included 248 reported collaboratives in the category of "business, industry, and/or chambers of commerce." Another 551 collaboratives were reported in the category "other agencies." This latter figure did not include collaboratives established with other ISDs or colleges and universities. The results of a similar, but unpublished, survey completed in Iowa in the early 2000s suggest that there are also large numbers of voluntary efforts between the AEAs and other governmental entities in that state as well.

Role in State Regulatory System

Few state networks of Type A: Special District ESAs, and not any of the Type C: Cooperative ESA systems play a significant role in their respective state regulatory systems governing the operation of school districts. What roles that are performed by some of the Special District networks are largely administrative in nature (e.g., monitor teacher certification requirements, monitor compulsory attendance requirements, process school district reorganization proposals, distribute school district state aid). There are no known examples of service agencies being granted the ultimate power of a state's regulatory system, the levying of a sanction for noncompliance with a state or federal regulatory requirement. However, there seemingly continue to be substantial concerns in many states surrounding the issues of whether or not Type A: Special District ESAs now engage in regulatory functions, or the opposite position, should have a role in a state's regulatory system.

Enhanced Role in State School Improvement Strategies

One of the more recent patterns in the programming efforts of state networks of service agencies has been the more visible role they have been asked to play in support of state school improvement strategies. In a number of cases, the state has mandated a supportive role in a new state school initiative. In other equally significant cases, the state professional association of service agencies has voluntarily put the energies of the association behind a new state school improvement strategy. Selected examples of both recent state-required and voluntary roles being played by state networks are briefly described in Table 3.6. The examples cited are not an exhaustive list. Additional details of the role played by service agencies in a state school improvement strategy are provided in subsequent chapters.

STAFFING PRACTICES

A number of patterns in the staffing practices of the state networks are also discernable. Highlighted here are the methods of selection and statutory roles assigned to the chief executive officers of the agencies, staffing levels of selected networks, prevailing practices concerning state certification requirements, and collective bargaining practices.

Chief Executive Officer

Method of selection. Appointment by the service agency governing board,

Table 3.6
Selected Illustrations of Recent State Network Roles in Support of a State School Improvement Strategy

California County Office of Education

- State has organized 58 offices into 11 "super regions" for the planning and administration of state-initiated school improvement initiatives.

Connecticut Regional Educational Service Centers

- In mid-1990s, the six RESCs were asked by the state to engage the public in planning to address regional disparities in educational opportunities in their respective service areas.

- Most recently, the state has provided RESCs with capital funds and operating monies to build and administer regional elementary, middle, and senior high magnet schools open to urban, suburban, and rural students.

Georgia Regional Education Service Agencies

- New statutorily-prescribed core services clearly focus on the need for 16 RESAs to provide support services to schools in their school improvement efforts (e.g., planning, staff development in support of state core curriculum, academic assessment and evaluation).

- Agencies are designated in statute as lead agency in their service region to organize and support "instructional care teams to assist low-performing schools."

Illinois Educational Service Regions

- The 45 ESRs have been designated by the state to serve as the lead agencies in the state-supported Standards Driven Professional Development Project.

Iowa Area Education Agencies

- New statutorily-prescribed core services and accompanying administrative rules clearly focus on the need for the 15 AEAs to provide support services and technical assistance to schools in their school improvement efforts (e.g., planning, staff development in support of core content areas, and in implementation of instructional technologies, assessment and evaluation).

- AEAs have been designated by the state to administer the Iowa Collaborative Instructional Improvement Centers to assist schools in the development of standards-referenced assessment models and staff development specifically targeted on student assessment.

Michigan Intermediate School Districts

- The 57 ISDs are designated by the state to provide support services for the Michigan Curriculum Framework project; ISDs are divided into a small number of "super ISDs."

- The 57 ISDs also are designated by the state to provide support services for the Michigan Literacy Progress Project; agencies are divided into a smaller number of "super ISDs."

Continued on next page

Table 3.6—*continued*

New York Boards of Cooperative Educational Services

- The state has organized 38 BOCES into nine "super regions" for the planning and administration of state-initiated school improvement initiatives.

- State uses nine "super BOCES regions" to create nine Regional School Support Centers to provide assistance to low-performing schools.

- State also uses these same "super regions" to support nine Regional Leadership Academies.

Oregon Education Service Districts

- State designated 21 ESDs as the lead agencies in the Oregon Public Education Network, a partnership between U.S. West and ESDs, to provide for a clearinghouse for the development of electronically-based products and staff development on instructional uses of technology.

- The 21 ESDs voluntarily contracted with McGraw-Hill to develop assessment tests in math and reading in grades not covered by state assessment program.

Pennsylvania Intermediate Units

- State designated 29 IUs as the lead agencies for implementation of Partnership for Educational Excellence Network, a program that provides technical assistance to schools to address requirements of new state standards.

- State professional association of IUs voluntarily participate in a statewide cooperative purchasing program that includes a special focus on the development of specifications, bidding, and purchase of technology software.

Texas Regional Education Service Centers

- New statutorily-prescribed core services clearly focus on the need for the 20 RESCs to assist schools in their school improvement efforts (e.g., assist schools in improving student performance, assist legislature and state commissioner in the implementation of their initiatives).

- Statute also prescribes that RESCs are to pay particular attention to low-performing schools; state commissioners annual evaluation of each RESC reinforces this requirement.

Washington Education Service Districts

- State designated nine ESDs to provide technical support to Commission on Student Learning, a recent major school improvement agenda launched by the state.

- ESDs voluntarily support the Washington State Information Processing Cooperative that, among other services to schools, develops specifications, bidding, and purchase of technology equipment for all schools in the state.

---

rather than by popular election, is the most common state-prescribed method used to select a chief executive officer. The three exceptions to this pattern are for the networks in Arizona, Illinois, and California where county voters are authorized to choose between election or appointment. Six of the 58 California county superintendents are elected.

The appointment power of a governing board in three states, however, is qualified. In New York and Texas, the appointment is subject to the approval of the chief state officer. Statutory requirements in the state of Washington require that the governing board involve a review committee in the selection process. The three-person review committee is to be composed of two superintendents of component school districts appointed by the service agency governing board and one representative appointed by the state superintendent of schools. The committee's role is to screen all candidates and then recommend three individuals to the governing board that makes the final selection. Governing boards of many individual service agencies in other states also voluntarily engage school district personnel in various phases of the selection processes used to appoint, not just the chief executive officer, but for other key leadership positions as well.

Role and function of the position. The role and function of chief executive officers of Type A: Special District ESA networks tend to be far more specific than those of cooperative networks, as expected. Statutory requirements typically specify that the executive officer is required to: (1) serve as the executive officer of the governing board; (2) prepare the agency budget; (3) recommend the appointment of staff to the governing board for its approval; and, (4) assure that the service agency is in compliance with all state and federal requirements.

Several variations of this general pattern are noteworthy. The California county superintendents are empowered to appoint certified staff, once the board has approved a program where the certified staff is to be assigned. Moreover, the county superintendent, not the board, is the employer in all employer-employee negotiations. Additionally, the district superintendents of the New York BOCES technically serve as the representative of the state commissioner in her/his supervisory district, and, as such, can potentially exercise significant review and oversight authority over school districts.

Staffing Levels

Extant data on the total staff employed by the agencies in an individual state network is limited. Selected data (including all staff: administrators/supervisors, professional and support staff) reported by agencies participating in the previously cited 1998-99 survey completed by members of the Association of Educational Service Agencies indicate that for that school year:

♦ The total number of staff members of a majority of responding service agencies in the Arizona, Illinois, Oregon, and West Virginia systems was less than 50 full-time equated (FTE).
♦ The total number of staff members of a majority of responding service agencies in the Michigan, Texas, Washington, and Ohio systems was from between 50 and 100 FTEs.
♦ The total number of staff members of a majority of responding service agencies in three state networks—California, New York, and Pennsylvania—exceeded 300 FTEs.
♦ Five of the 16 responding Georgia service agencies reported a staff

level of from 100 to 149 FTEs.

♦   Fourteen of the 15 responding Iowa AEAs reported a staff level of
    from 150 to 199 FTEs. (Association of Educational Service Agencies
    2000)

The Texas Education Agency is one state education agency that regularly
tracks staffing patterns of its state network of service agencies. In the fall of the
2000-01 school year, the 20 RESCs employed slightly less than 4,000 full- and
part-time staff (3,943) that were reportedly assigned in this way: over one-half
(56 percent) assigned to programs and services designed to provide instructional
and instructional support services to schools; 35 percent assigned agency functions that support administrative support services to school districts/schools; and
nine percent assigned to the operations of the center (Regional and District
Level Report 2000).

Other Patterns

Two other patterns in the staffing practices of state networks of educational service agencies are apparent. Of most importance is the state requirement
that all professional staff meet appropriate state certification requirements where
these are in place. This pattern holds irrespective of type of network, Type A:
Special District or Type C: Cooperative. State certification and licensure requirements of course differ in the comprehensiveness of their coverage, especially those involving specialists that might be added to the staff of a service
agency in response to a new, emerging need. Most states include the minimal
requirement that an individual must at least hold a teaching certificate. Secondly, collective bargaining agreements are typically the norm in those states
where there is a strong tradition of these practices in both the public as well as
the private sector.

FINANCIAL FEATURES

Significant variation is present in the financial features of state networks of
ESAs, perhaps more so than of any other aspect of their structural and organizational characteristics.

Major Types of Funding Sources

A number of patterns are evident in the funding sources used to support the
work of the two major types of state networks of ESAs. A majority of both the
13 Type A: Special District and 12 Type C: Cooperative networks tend to draw
on a combination of state, local/regional, federal, and other sources to underwrite their activities. Beyond this common feature, however, significant differences are present between the Special District and Cooperative systems. That is:

♦   As a group, the Special District networks are the recipient of greater
    state aid in both dollar amounts and as a percent of total revenue;
    moreover, and importantly, networks of this type are more likely to re-
    ceive multiple forms of state support from the list of six major types of
    state funding sources cited in Figure 3.3.

Figure 3.3
Major Types of Funding Sources

State sources	• Appropriation—administration of state-mandated administrative functions • Appropriation—general ESA administration • Appropriation—general ESA programs/services • Appropriation—ESA capital improvements • Categorical—specific ESA programs/services to LEAs • Service contracts/grants—specific ESA programs/services to LEAs
Local/regional sources	• Local tax—general ESA administration • Local tax—general ESA programs/services to LEAs • Local tax—specific ESA programs/services to LEAs • Membership dues • Service contracts—specific ESA programs/services to LEAs
Federal sources	• Categorical grants/contracts—specific ESA programs/services to public and nonpublic schools
Other sources	• Service contracts—specific ESA programs/ services to other public and nonpublic entities • Gifts and grants—specific ESA use • "entrepreneurial" —product sale; broker role; partnerships with other public and nonpublic entities

Source: Stephens, E. R. 2000.

♦   As a group, the Cooperative networks are heavily dependent on one of the four types of local funding sources cited in Figure 3.3, service contracts with school groups.

The previously cited 1998-99 survey conducted by the Association of Educational Service Agencies (AESA) provides some insight on the sources of funding of the membership of the Association. A total of 438 member organizations, representing both Special District and Cooperative service agencies, participated in the survey. The 438 figure includes some states not classified here as a statewide or virtual statewide network. The results of the AESA survey are shown in Table 3.7.

Table 3.7
Revenue Sources, 1999-2000

Percent Interval		Source			
		Federal	State	Local	Other
0-19					
	number	223	112	113	232
	percent	58.5	29.2	30.4	82.3
20-39					
	number	109	109	93	26
	percent	28.6	28.4	25.0	9.2
40-59					
	number	33	94	78	14
	percent	8.7	24.5	21.0	5.0
60-79					
	number	10	38	33	5
	percent	2.6	9.9	8.9	1.8
80-100					
	number	6	31	55	5
	percent	1.6	8.1	14.8	1.8
Total ESAs Reporting		381	384	372	282

Source: Association of Educational Service Agencies 2000.
Note: A total of 438 ESAs in 31 states, that included eight states not classified here as a statewide or virtual statewide network, responded to the survey. The 438 include both Special District and Cooperative ESAs.

Independent Taxing Authority

Only two complete networks, the Michigan and Oregon systems, and the fiscally independent California county offices of education (that represent 50 of the 58 county systems) enjoy taxing authority.

Both the Michigan and Oregon networks have clear statutory limitations on the exercise of their taxing authority. In Michigan, annual property taxes for operating purposes are not to exceed 1.75 mills, an upper limit established and approved by electors in 1993. Property tax levies to support area vocational-technical and area special education programs are not to exceed levels established in 1993, but may be increased if approved by electors. The agencies, subject to approval of the electorate, may also levy a regional enrichment tax that is not to exceed three mills, revenues of which must be redistributed to school districts based on general population of the districts. An Oregon service agency can levy a tax in the amount necessary to cover its own operating expenses, and for the implementation of all resolution programs and services approved by two-thirds of the component school districts that also represent a majority of the student population.

TOTAL EXPENDITURES

Individual ESAs. The AESA national survey also requested that respondents indicate the approximate amount of their annual budget for the year 1999-2000. The results of this probe are presented in Table 3.8. Nearly two-thirds, or 64.2%, of respondents reported that their annual budgets were less than 10 million dollars. Three agencies indicated their annual budget for that year was in excess of 100 million dollars.

State network expenditures. Data on the recent total expenditures of several state networks of Special District ESAs are also instructive. The data illustrate the great diversity that exists between state networks that are similarly classified as Type A: Special District ESA networks. These data represent one proxy measure of the fiscal capacity of different state systems.

- 15 Iowa Area Education Agencies—252.1 million in 1999-2000
- 58 Michigan Intermediate School Districts—989.4 million in 1999-2000
- 29 Pennsylvania Intermediate Units—102.2 million in 1999-2000
- 20 Texas Regional Education Service Centers—399.9 million in 2000-2001
- 9 Washington Education Service Districts—102.2 million in 1999-2000 (general fund expenditures only)
- 8 West Virginia Regional Education Service Agencies—29.9 million in 1999-2000
- 61 Ohio Education Service Centers—171.8 million in 1998-1999 (Stephens 2000, May)

State Funding Formulas

A number of states made use of a formula in the appropriation of state funds to support the work of the network. This is especially true for state networks of Type A: Special District ESAs. The design of the formulas differed

Table 3.8
Individual Agency Annual Budgets, 1999-2000

Interval In Millions	Number Reporting	Percent of Total Reporting
1-9	273	64.2
10-19	73	17.2
20-39	49	11.5
40-59	13	3.1
60-79	5	1.2
80-99	9	2.1
100>	3	0.7

Source: Association of Educational Service Agencies 2000.
Note: Only 438 ESAs in 31 states, that included eight states not classified here as a statewide or virtual statewide network, responded to the survey. The 438 include both Special District and Cooperative ESAs.

substantially in these two principal ways:

- ◆ the type of state appropriation that is to be formula-based
- ◆ the variables used in the construction of a state formula

The prevailing pattern is for a state to make use of a formula-based system for the appropriation of whatever type of recurring state aid is provided. For example, if a state has established a set of renewable core services that are to be provided by its network of service agencies, then this is likely to be a formula-based appropriation. Short-term service contracts or grants may or may not be formula-based.

A number of variables are used in the design of the state aid formulas. These include: (1) the number of public school students in a service region, which is the most frequently used variable; (2) fixed amount for each service center; (3) core service costs; (4) number and enrollment size of school districts; (5) number of schools; (6) number of nonpublic school students; (7) number of square miles and/or other geographic features; and, (8) a specific set-aside for rental of facilities.

It is a common practice for most states to include multiple variables in their base state appropriations. For example, as will be described below, the Iowa formula is based on: core services, total public school enrollment, and the total nonpublic school enrollment. The Georgia formula incorporates most of the preceding list of eight variables, all except the number of nonpublic school students, and a set-aside for rental of facilities. An overview of the formula used in eight Type A: Special District networks in the year 2000-01 is provided below.

Georgia RESCs. The state allocates a base amount for each of the 16 RESAs, an amount that is to cover: the salary and benefits for one director, one secretary, one bookkeeper, and five consultants, plus an allowance for operations of the agency (e.g., supplies, travel, equipment, and for miscellaneous operational costs). This base amount is supplemented by what is referred to as "local needs variables" that consist of: number of school districts greater than six; the number of school districts having less than 3,300 enrollment; the number of schools greater than 30, the total number of school district/school FTE staff; and the total square miles of the RESA in excess of 2,500. The state share of the combined base amount and "local needs variables" is computed at 80 percent; a local school district assessment pays the other 20 percent.

Iowa AEAs. In contrast to the Georgia state aid formula, the formula used in Iowa is relatively straightforward; three funding streams are used: special education aid (state cost per pupil times enrollment in the AEA plus a weighting factor); media services aid (state cost per pupil times enrollment); and educational services aid (also cost per pupil times enrollment).

New York BOCES. BOCES's state aid is calculated in three categories: service aid, administrative aid, and facilities aid. Service aid and administrative aid are calculated using the base year approved service costs and BOCES administrative expenditures; that is, approved expenses for the base year times the highest of three aid ratios—millage, tax rate, full value-resident weighted average daily attendance, or the .360 minimum with a maximum of .90. Approved service costs are distributed among component school districts based service costs are distributed among component school districts based on participation. Administrative service costs are distributed among component school districts by either of three methods: (1) by dividing the total administrative expenses by the resident weighted average daily attendance of pupils residing in all component districts within the BOCES, and multiplying the result by the resident weighted average daily attendance of pupils in each component district; (2) the ratio of the component school district's total full value to the total full value of all component school districts within the BOCES; or (3) resident enrollment of component districts.

The state places limitations on allowable BOCES service aid and BOCES administrative aid. Subject to approval of the state commissioner, aidable shared services include: school nurses, attendance supervisors, supervisors of teachers, dental hygienists, psychologists, teachers of art, music, physical education and career education subjects, guidance counselors, and the operation of special classes for students with disabilities. Limitations on shared services include the following:

- Employees' salaries are aidable up to $30,000 annually (2000-01).
- Charges for pupils with disabilities are not aidable. (The aid goes directly to school districts)
- Aid to reimburse expenditures for transporting students to and from BOCES classes and expenditures for approval for LEP programs conducted through a BOCES are sent directly to school districts.
- BOCES administrative aid is available to support expenditures of the agency's central office. As established elsewhere, the New York BOCES are one of three state networks where a limitation is placed on administrative costs (in this case, they are not to exceed 10 percent of total expenditures). The administrative budget must also be approved by the majority of governing boards of component districts.

The BOCES facility and formula calculates current year approved expenditures times current year full value (property) per weighted resident average daily attendance aid ratio—with no minimum aid ratio and a maximum of .90.

Ohio ESCs. An ESC's budget request to the state board is comprised of two parts. Part A is a direct reimbursement from the state's general fund and is computed in this way: (1) salaries, retirement, and travel allowance for each approved supervisory teacher; (2) an additional salary for approved supervisory teachers for extended service not to exceed three months; (3) an allowance equal to 15 percent of salaries; and (4) an allowance for travel, limited to either a monthly or yearly amount for each approved employee. Part B reimbursement is received in two ways: (1) for costs in excess of $6.50 times average daily membership (ADM) of the center, and (2) if the ESC provides services to city or exempted village school districts, state reimbursement is also received for costs in excess of $6.50 times the sum of the center's ADM and the city or exempted village district served. Cost not in excess of $6.50 times ADM served shall be apportioned by the state board among local school districts or on the basis of total enrollment in each district. If the budget is in excess of $6.50, excess costs shall be apportioned by the state board among local school districts on basis of total enrollment, provided a majority of local school district boards approve. If approved, the amount is deducted from state funds to the local school districts.

Other major state apportionment practices include:

♦ ESCs are eligible for state funding for special education, including the purchase of school buses.

♦ If an ESC provides contracted supervisory services to an exempted village or city district, these cost are also deducted from state funds after being apportioned among all parties to the contract, but not to exceed one supervisor for the first 50 classroom teachers, and one supervisor for each 100 additional classroom teachers.

♦ In addition to the apportionment under Part A above, each single county ESC receives $37 times (minus large cities and unfunded city-county contracts) the sum of the ADM of city and exempted village districts having a service contract in effect in 1997.

♦ In addition, each multi-county (three or more counties) ESC receives $40.52 times the sum of the local school district ADM and the sum of the ADM of city and exempted village districts having a service contract in effect in 1997.

Pennsylvania IUs. The state aid formula consists of three parts: each IU receives a minimal constant amount related to the state's previous appropriation to its predecessor county office of education; one-half of the remaining legislative appropriation for the IU times an IU's share of the total statewide student enrollment count (both public and nonpublic enrolment); and the other half of the remaining total state appropriation divided by 29, the total number that includes the Philadelphia and Pittsburgh IUs.

Texas RESCs. The state commissioner is required by statute to distribute the state appropriations annually to the 20 RESCs for the funding of core services for a center's basic cost of providing core services. The schedule used by the state commissioner must be based on three factors: the minimum amount of money necessary for the operation of a center; an additional amount that reflects the size and number of campuses served; and an additional amount that reflects the number of students in a service center's region, as well as the impact of the geographic size of a service center region on the cost of providing core services.

Washington ESDs. The legislature has directed the state superintendent to prepare a biennial budget request for the operation of the nine ESDs based on a formula that reflects: the core service cost, which is to receive primary weighting; a weighted factor constituting a geographic factor which shall be used to weight the larger sized ESDs; and, a weighting factor based on the number and size of local school districts. In operationalizing the statutory requirements, the formula used by the state superintendent to distribute state aid consists of an appropriation to each ESD of monies for: salaries for the ESD superintendent, differing FTEs, or fractions thereof, for curriculum specialists, fiscal officers, and support staff; some maintenance and operational expenses for both staff and board members, and for facility costs.

West Virginia RESAs. The state appropriation for the eight RESAs is 0.63 percent of the total state school aid; 60 percent is divided equally among all agencies; 40 percent is based on student enrollment in an agency's service region.

Other Required Financial Practices

State networks of both types, Type A: Special District and Type C: Cooperative, also function under a number of other statutory requirements concerning the fiscal dimensions of their work. Most common are the requirements that: (1) they use a state-prescribed process for the development of their annual budget; (2) they use a state-prescribed, uniform accounting system to record both revenues and expenditures; and, (3) they conduct an annual audit.

Approval of the budget by parties other than the governing board of an individual service agency is also a common statutory requirement for Special District ESA networks. States vary, however, in designating the third-party having this responsibility. For example, the state board of education or chief state school officer must approve the service agencies' budgets in Georgia, Iowa, Ohio, Texas, and Washington. State education officials also share this authority in two other states.

♦ In California, the consolidated budget of fiscally independent county offices of education must be approved by both the county supervisors and the state superintendent of schools; the budgets of fiscally dependent county offices of education must be approved by the county board of education and county supervisors, and the school service budget approved by the chief state school officer.

♦ In New York, the governing boards of component school districts must approve the administrative budget of a BOCES, with the chief state school officer having the approval authority over the entire budget.

Local school officials also play a prominent role in the approval of still another state network, the Pennsylvania IU system. Here, the statute requires that an IU budget must not only be approved by a majority of component school districts, but also by a majority of the weighted votes of members of the governing boards of component school districts. Additionally, voter approval is required for the budgets of area vocational technical and area special education programs administered by the Michigan service agencies.

Three states also impose limitations on the percent of expenditures that can be devoted to administrative costs. The statutory limitation in Iowa is 5 percent of an agency's total expenditures, and 6 and 10 percent in Pennsylvania and New York, respectively.

ACQUISITION OF FACILITIES

Consistent with variations that are to be found in many of the structural and organizational features of ESAs, diversity is also true in how these organizations may acquire physical facilities to house their programs and service activities. Three major practices in use are:

1. The majority of state networks are authorized by the state to hold ownership of one or more facilities, but have limitations on how this can be accomplished. Most rely on the use of lease-purchase agreements, a permissible option

in most states. Authority to receive gifts and grants is also a common feature of the legal framework under which service agencies function.

2. A minority of agencies are provided facilities by county governments. This practice is generally limited to those two state networks that are constitutional offices, the Arizona County Office of Education, and the fiscally dependent California County Boards of Education (the fiscally-independent County Boards of Education may lease, lease-purchase, hold and convey real property). Three other networks that are provided facilities by a county government are the Arizona, Illinois and Ohio systems.

3. Two state networks can levy a tax to build or purchase facilities. The Michigan ISDs and Oregon ESDs can levy a tax to build or purchase facilities to house their special education and vocational/technical programs. Voter approval is required in both states. The New York BOCES are authorized to borrow funds from a state agency to acquire facilities.

In recent years, the Connecticut centers were designated by the state as one of the eligible parties to receive state funds to construct and operate regional magnet schools as part of a state initiative to address equity issues in elementary-secondary education. Many of the centers have been successful in competing for these funds.

REFERENCES

Accreditation of Area Education Agencies. 2001. October. Des Moines, IA: Iowa State Department of Education. (72.4(8)).

Association of Educational Service Agencies. 2000. January. Arlington, VA: unpublished report.

Association of Educational Service Agencies. 1996. By-Laws. Arlington, VA: Author.

Georgia General Assembly. 2000. H.B. 1187—A Plus Education Reform Act of 2000.

Goals 2000: Educate America Act of 1994. Pub. L.

Iowa General Assembly. 1997. Chapter 273.5. Area Education Agencies.

Michigan Association of Intermediate School Districts. 1994. *MAISA collaborative services survey of Michigan intermediate school districts, 1994-95*. November 28. Lansing, MI: Author.

National Center for Education Statistics. 2001. *Digest of education statistics*. Washington, DC: U. S. Department of Education.

National Center for Education Statistics. 1997-98. *Instruction for completing non-fiscal surveys of the common core of data*. Washington, DC: U. S. Department of Education.

New York General Assembly. 1959. Article 40 7d(1). Boards of Cooperative Educational Services.

Regional and District Level Report. 2000. *A report to the 77th Texas legislature from the Texas Education Agency*. December 1. Austin, TX: Author.

School Laws of Pennsylvania. 1971. January. Harrisburg, PA: Department of Education. Author.

Stephens, E. R. 2000. *A report to the joint Iowa Department of Education—Area design team*, Section I. 10-11. May. Edmond, OK: Author.

Stephens, E. R. 2000. *Financial characteristics of selected state networks of educational service agencies*. Report prepared for the Oregon State Board of Education ESD Task Force and the Oregon Coordinating Council on School Finance. April. Edmond, OK: Author.

Stephens, E. R. and Good, K. 1998. *AEA system evaluation.* December. Oak Brook, IL: North Central Regional Educational Laboratory.

Chapter 4

Structure and Organization of ESAs:
A Commentary

We have attempted so far to provide a description of the major tendencies and patterns of two types of statewide or virtual statewide networks, those classified here as Type A: Special District ESAs and Type C: Cooperative ESAs. Emphasis in the profile has been given to seven major categories of the structural and organizational features of the state systems, not characteristics of individual service agencies within one of the state networks, as these are discernable in the early years of the 21st century.

What follows is a commentary designed to give additional perspective to the material so far presented. This is followed by several general observations on the education service agency movement as it is evolving at the turn of the century. For both topic-specific and general observations, use will be made on occasion of data provided in earlier attempts to profile the dominant structural and organizational features of state networks in existence in the late 1960s, the late 1970s and the late 1980s. These earlier state profiles include many, but not all, of the 23 state systems focused on in the preceding chapter.

TYPE AND NUMBER OF STATE NETWORKS

There has been relatively little change over the past few decades in the total number of Type A: Special District ESA state networks discussed in this book. Rather, changes that have occurred in this type of network have resulted in a reduction of the number of agencies in several states; there has been only one increase in the number of agencies in the 13 state systems of Type A: Special District ESAs, that is Arizona as a result of the creation of one new county government.

The most rapid growth in the past year has been experienced by Type C: Cooperative ESAs, where in several states the number of units is approaching the threshold number used here to be labeled a virtual statewide network, the inclusion of at least three-fourths of the school districts in a state.

The resiliency of the Type A: Special District ESA networks is quite remarkable in that many networks of this type have been the subject of periodic legislative inquiries, not just about the efficiency of the number of units in the system, but even questioning whether they deserve continued support. The success of state systems in surviving regular close legislative scrutiny can be attributed to the commingling of a number of factors. One of these is clearly the growing professionalism of the service agency community in the state, not just in lobbying efforts, but as well in recognition of the need to become a truly systemic state network of service agencies, not just a collection of largely autonomous agencies. Certainly the downsizing of a number of state education agencies over the past decade has brought to the forefront limitations in the infrastructure of the state system of elementary-secondary education. This has been accompanied by a growing recognition in state policy circles that the state network of service agencies is well positioned to provide needed support services.

There continues to be great difficulty in establishing with greater precision the number of service agencies in each of the two major state networks featured in this text, Type A: Special District ESAs and Type C: Cooperative ESAs. We are confident that the number in each of the two types in operation in 2001-02 cited in Table 3.1 are accurate (392 units in the 13 Type A, and 137 in the 12 Type C state networks). However, at present, there is no governmental agency that maintains a comprehensive data system of educational service agencies, despite their growing significance.

In recent years, the National Center for Education Statistics has attempted to address this issue in its Education Agency Type Code used in surveys of state education agencies for the compilation of the highly valuable annual publication of the *Digest of Education Statistics*. This code classifies education agencies within the geographic boundaries of a state according to the level of administrative and operational control. The code has seven categories. Two of the code categories in particular are the source of much of the difficulty in arriving at a more accurate count, a problem compounded by the apparent indifference of some state agencies in completing the survey:

   ♦   Code 3: Supervisory union administrative center, or county superintendent's office serving the same purposes.
   ♦   Code 4: Regional education services agency, agencies created for the purposes of providing specialized educational services to other educational agencies.

The inclusion of "county superintendent's office" in Code 3 likely accounts for errors in how some states classify county offices that in fact provide both administrative and educational programs to school districts, the definition, as in Code 4, of a regional educational service agency. Moreover, in some states (e.g., Montana and North Dakota), some of the county superintendent's offices limit their role to the provision of administrative functions only, and should be classified in still another code, Code 2, while other county offices do in fact engage in both administrative and educational programming.

The anticipated entry of still other service providers resulting from the provisions of the No Child Left Behind Act of 2001 is likely to further complicate the goal of establishing a more accurate count of the number and type of operating service agencies in the country.

Definitional issues are, of course, central to the development of a useful typology of education service agencies. Along these lines, we would maintain that that the basic features of the typology used in this book continue to have utility in understanding the primary orientation of service units.

It is to be recalled that the Stephens typology, developed in 1979, argued that it is useful to classify different forms of service agencies operating at that time into three major types based on tendencies that center on the four central characteristics of legal framework, governance, programs and services, and fiscal support. We take the position that these four characteristics continue to be of value but would add a fifth major category—the primary orientation of the accountability practices engaged in by a type of service unit.

The revised typology is shown in Table 4.1, a revision which adds a focus on tendencies that prevail in the accountability practices of the state and whether these are either mandated or voluntary. Where mandated accountability practices are in place for Type A: Special District ESA state networks, such as an accreditation system having both standards and performance measures, submission of an annual progress report and a periodic third-party client satisfaction survey are invariably required. Such requirements were not established in the late 1970s.

Table 4.1
Revised Typology of Educational Service Agencies Based on Dominant Patterns of Five Central Characteristics

Type of ESA	Five Central Characteristics				
	Legal Framework	Governance	Program and Services	Fiscal Support	Accountability Practices
Type A: Special District ESA	Tends to be highly structured in legislation and/or SEA regulations	Tends to be lay control	Tends to be determined by member LEAs and the SEA or by statute	Tends to be a mix of local, regional, state and state/federal	Tends to be both state mandated and voluntary directed at state and member districts
Type B: Regionalized SEA/ESA	Tends to be structured in SEA regulations only	Tends to be professional advisory only	Tends to be almost exclusively determined by SEA	Tends to be almost exclusively state and state/federal	Tends to be structured in SEA regulations only
Type C: Cooperative ESA	Tends to be general (i.e., intergovernmental regulations and statutes) and/or permissive legislation	Tends to be composed of representative of member LEAs	Tends to be almost exclusively determined by member LEAs	Tends to be almost exclusively local and state/federal	Tends to be based exclusively on voluntary practices evaluated by member districts

ESTABLISHMENT, ALTERATION, AND DISSOLUTION OF ESAS

The formation of many of the statewide networks in the 1960s and 1970s whereby all local school districts were assigned to be a member of a service agency and eligible to participate in its programs and services suggest that, in the establishment of the network, state and local leaders were sensitive to the potential benefits of creating a truly statewide network of support services for local districts. However, the optimal number of units in many of the Type A: Special District ESA networks continues to be a regular source of controversy in many states. This suggests that political compromises were required to create the new systems and that state policy makers, from the very beginning, may have intended to reduce the initial number of units, though incrementally.

The numbers of units in several states have, in fact, been reduced, especially in recent years. However, our review of these developments suggest that the prime motive for the reductions has been to reduce administrative costs, not necessarily to improve the effectiveness of the service agencies.

Whether this is actually the case or not in all instances, the context for addressing the issue of the efficacy in the number of units in a state network has also changed dramatically in recent years. For example, the new emphasis on individual school campuses rather than school districts is now the focus for sustained school improvement efforts. There is also widespread support for site-based management movement and a renewed celebration of the concept of small school size. So, too, has been the development in many states of a statewide technology infrastructure.

Some of these developments raise the question in several states of whether or not more, not fewer, service agencies are needed and whether the current configuration limits the effectiveness of a service agency providing accessible support services to all campuses and districts in its catchment area. On the other hand, the development of a statewide technology infrastructure for use in delivering some, but certainly not all, services may support the views of those who advocate a reduction in the number of agencies.

Legislation that facilitates the voluntary merger of service agencies appears to be gaining momentum. This is especially true where fiscal incentives have been a part of the legislation package, as is true in Ohio, or where a rigorous accreditation system for the service agencies is in place, as in Iowa.

It appears highly unlikely that the use of mandatory legislation to create a state network of Type A: Special Districts will ever approach its almost exclusive use as the state policy option of choice that it enjoyed in the formation of a majority of systems of this type. This observation is based in large part on the now widespread opposition to state mandates of whatever type, and, perhaps more critical, to the growing support for choice in the delivery of support services to school districts.

The practice in a few states of supporting more than one statewide service delivery network, consisting of agencies that overlap or are in direct competition with the existing network of educational service agencies, is likely to receive greater scrutiny.

MISSION STATEMENTS

What Is the Network to Do?
Though the language varies, as established in the preceding chapter, the one dominant expectation held by all states in creating a network of service agencies and continuing its support is the expectation that it will contribute to solving the pervasive and challenging issues of assuring *equity, efficiency, and quality* throughout the state system of elementary-secondary education. All three of these issues have been at the forefront of policy debates for much of the post-World War II era, and are likely to be at the center of attention well into the future, as is the additional expectation that the state network address the adequacy of programs and services provided to especially low-performing districts.

GOVERNANCE PRACTICES
There are two major issues relating to the governance of educational service agencies that demonstrate the variety of practices by which educational service agencies are governed: the multiple methods used for the selection of school board members and the concomitant powers and duties of these different kinds of boards.

Selection of Board Members
The democratic ethos of representative government is well-entrenched in the selection processes used to establish the governing boards of the Type A: Special District ESA state networks, though a variety of implementation strategies are used. A desire to make the service agencies as responsive as possible to their component school districts appears to be one of the prime rationales for the practice of having representatives of local school boards be involved in the election of the service agency board. Further, the various voting arrangements discussed in the previous chapter are seemingly viewed by state interests as a way to achieve two major objectives—strengthening the responsiveness of the service agencies to their member school systems while also seeking to adhere to the "one man, one vote" principle. The diverse methods used to select or elect the governing boards of Type A: Special District ESA state networks probably illustrates as no other feature that the structural and organizational diversity among state networks of this type generally reflects the political norms and traditions of the state where they operate.

Powers and Duties of Governing Boards
There are significant differences among the states in identifying specific powers and duties for the agencies. The expressed powers and duties of governing boards of state networks which are expected to perform administrative, supervisory, and ministerial functions are, as expected, far more comprehensive

than those networks that do not.

Of special interest with regard to the administrative and supervisory roles required of a state network are the two cases—the Illinois ESRs and the Oregon ESDs—where these roles involve significant oversight of the activities of member local school districts. The Illinois ESRs and their chief executive officer, a popularly elected official, perform what probably is the longest list of administrative and supervisory functions over local school districts, many of which are carryovers from roles performed by the replaced county office of education. The Oregon ESDs, on the other hand, though having fewer oversight responsibilities, exercise what likely would be viewed as the most sweeping of any state authority granted a state network. They are authorized to examine and audit all constituent school district budgets, and approve or reject an increase or decrease of any item in the budget. How this statutory authority is exercised across the 21 ESDs is not known. Nonetheless, it is embedded in statute and is not an exact carryover function from the replaced county office of education. Rather, it appears to represent a deliberate policy choice to strengthen the accountability of local school districts to the ESDs. This is one of the strongest examples of a seldom-addressed issue in discussions of the accountability of service agencies, the equally important question of the accountability of member school districts to contribute to the success of the service agency.

Also noteworthy is the Oregon requirement that the ESDs must appoint two nonvoting members to their governing boards, one from the employment sector and one from the social services sector in their catchment area. State interests were careful to align the mission statement (help achieve intergovernmental coordination) (Chapter 334.005) with how the agencies were to be governed. State leaders in Oregon appear to be sensitive to the wisdom that "form should follow function."

Many service agencies of both Type A: Special District ESAs and Type C: Cooperative ESAs represent a form of regional governance, not another form of the less politically unpopular regional government. This is particularly true of those agencies where the policy-making authority is assigned to representatives of local school districts, the principal governing body of the vast majority of Type C: Cooperative ESAs. It is also arguably true of the numerous governing boards of Type A: Special District ESA state networks who are elected by and from local school district boards, and where the service agency board cannot substitute its judgment for that of a local district board.

The need to make a distinction between whether or not an ESA represents a form of regional governance, not regional government, is critical. For example, it should dispel one of the major myths put forth by proponents of the concept of local control by raising the specter of a new layer of government imposed over a local district.

PROGRAMMING FEATURES

Both constancy and change characterize the major programming efforts of the networks over the past approximate two decades since the completion of the last national profile in 1978-79 (Stephens 1979). Special education support services continue to be a major function of all service agencies, though many ESAs no longer offer classes for exceptional children. So, too, is the continued prominence of professional development services, curriculum development, and learning resources library services (what used to be called media services). However, more ESAs of whatever type, more so than in the past, are now engaged in serving individuals outside the mainstream K-12 student population, and now market and provide many more administrative/management support services. Moreover, many ESAs are engaged in numerous curricular and instructional support services that were not priorities in the late 1970s (e.g., telecommunications and technology services, student testing and evaluation, leadership training). Since curricular and instructional support services are believed to be significantly related to improving student achievement, state networks have seemingly made the most significant changes in the breath and depth in their programming in these areas.

What has not changed is the underlying rationale that seems to explain the dominant programming features of the ESA state networks. It has seemingly always been a priority of state and local interests to assign functions to service agencies that (1) require a concentration of students with special learning needs, (2) require a highly specialized staff and/or facilities, or, (3) permit significant economies of scale to be realized.

Three of the most recent state legislative pronouncements of required core services provide a relatively comprehensive enumeration of specific mandated programs and services (the Georgia RESAs, the Ohio ESCs, the Iowa AEAs). In recent years, state interests seem more determined than in the past to assure that the required activities of the state networks are closely aligned with the state school improvement strategy, or with what the research literature has identified as important ways to support school improvement.

A strong majority of the statutes grant specific authority to a Type A: Special District ESAs state network to offer discretionary programs and services, typically accompanied by the qualifier that these must be requested by component school districts. Moreover, another common practice is for the statute to specifically caution that all such discretionary programs are to be provided for a service fee. The inclusion of authority to offer discretionary programs outside required core programs and services clearly reflects an awareness on the part of state interests that the needs of local school districts and schools differ not only across a state, but frequently among districts within a single service agency as well.

Though at this time it is only a "mini" pattern, two of the most recent rewrites of the basic statutes governing the Type A: Special District ESA state networks, the Georgia RESAs, the Texas RESCs, both adopted in the past six years, make clear that a local school district may purchase a service from any service agency in the state. As established earlier, this move likely represents in part a growing interest in state policy circles to inject competition into the network, as well as honor the seemingly widespread commitment to promote choice in the delivery of public services.

A small number of states have statutory provisions that provide a disincentive to a school district that chooses not to participate in a program or service that is approved by a majority of component districts in a service agency, and that is to be funded in whole or in part by the component districts. Both the Pennsylvania and West Virginia statutes speak to the issue of how to protect the programming decisions of a majority of school districts, once made.

The inclusion of specific language in the statutes granting Type A: Special District ESA state networks legislative authority to enter joint service agreements with others is a fairly common practice (cited in eight of the 13 states). Most of these references grant permissive authority to enter such agreements, and then cite specific types of organizations as potential partners. Only one, the Iowa statute, is both prescriptive ("AEAs shall contract, whenever possible, with other school corporations for use of personnel, buildings, supplies, programs and services") as well as permissive. The inclusion of specific reference in the statute to joint service agencies, whether prescriptive or permissive, would in part suggest that state interests are desirous of promoting interorganizational relations, in this case involving the state network and others. Nor can the absence of such provisions necessarily be viewed as a lack of state interest. This is so because, beginning in the early 1970s, most states enacted legislation adopted from model intergovernmental relations legislation enacted by the federal government.

As suggested earlier, the provision of needed support services for a state's large number of rural school districts likely was the raison d'être in the minds of many members of state policy circles in the initial support for a state network of service agencies. It is also likely that the needs of rural systems continue to be of primary interest for the continued support of a state network in many cases. However, there now appears to be significant recognition in more than a few states that educational service agencies can make important contributions to addressing the needs of large central city and other poor metropolitan area districts. While in most states, large metropolitan area districts have always been eligible to participate in the programming of a service agency, this participation has historically been limited. There is some evidence that the involvement of large metropolitan districts in the work of service agencies has expanded in recent years.

Moreover, at the present time, some of the nation's most comprehensive educational service agencies are located in and serve all districts in their respective metropolitan regions. There is face validity to the frequent claim advanced by supporters of a more prominent role of service agencies in metropolitan areas nationally can indeed help in addressing many of the pervasive problems facing education in a metropolitan setting.

STAFFING PRACTICES

A number of prevailing norms in the staffing practices generally found in elementary-secondary education hold true for a majority of the state networks, whether Type A: Special District ESAs or Type C: Cooperative ESAs. One area where this is apparent is in the appointment of the chief executive officer, a responsibility of the governing board of the agencies in a strong majority of cases. However, in a small, but growing number of states, all operating Type A Special District networks, a governing board's authority to appoint a chief executive is no longer unilateral. A short-list of potential candidates for the position must first be approved by the chief state school officer (e.g., New York, Iowa, Texas) or by some other third party (e.g., Oregon, Washington). The involvement of a third-party in the selection process is a relatively new development. It likely is a reflection of recent efforts to expand the role of a state network in a state school improvement agenda.

Small but significant changes are also occurring in the heretofore unchallenged role of the governing board of a Type A: Special District ESA in the evaluation of the chief executive officer of its agency. A requirement calling for a state evaluation of the chief executive officer of a service agency is cited in statute in only one case, the Texas RESCs. However, the results of the required accreditation reviews of all or selected parts of the operations of three additional state networks (New York BOCES, Oregon ESDs, and the Iowa AEAs) presumably can be used to reflect on the effectiveness of these individuals. Perhaps of even greater significance, the required submission of an annual progress report, one of the requirements of the accreditation systems in place in Oregon, Texas, and Iowa can, and likely is, also used to reflect on the work of the chief executive officers. Statutory requirements calling for some form of evidence regarding the work of a state network no doubt was in part promoted by the expectation that doing so would provide important insights on the performance of agency leaders.

With one possible exception, there do not appear to be any discernable patterns concerning statutorily required roles and responsibilities of chief executive officers of Type A: Special Districts. In a majority of cases where specific duties are enumerated, these tend to be administrative or supervisory in nature. Surprisingly, in only three cases do the statutes specifically single out a chief executive officer to work directly with component school districts in their school improvement efforts, the Iowa AEAs, the New York BOCES, and the Washington ESDs. The requirements of the chief executive officers of the Iowa AEAs and the New York BOCES are the strongest in making the connection between the expected role of these officials and the school improvement efforts of component school districts. Of note, both the Iowa and New York statements are relatively new, adopted in both cases in the mid-1990s. This suggests that in two of the most recent rewrites of the basic statutory pronouncements on the roles and responsibilities of a state network, explicit, not implied, expectations are being made on chief executives to give priority to assisting component school districts in their school improvement efforts.

Two other prevailing norms in the staffing practices generally found in elementary-secondary education that also hold true for a majority of state networks of whatever type over time relate to the need that both professional and specialized support staff meet all existing state certification requirements. To a lesser extent, but still in the majority, staff members are covered by collective bargaining agreements.

FINANCIAL PRACTICES

There has been little change over the past decades in the primary sources of revenues for different types of state networks. That is, Type A: Special District ESA systems are still largely dependent on combination of state aid, local revenues, especially service contracts with local districts, and federal grants and contracts. Type C: Cooperative ESA state networks continue to rely on service contracts and federal grants and contracts, though a small but increasing number receive state categorized funds in support of their role in a state school improvement initiative.

It is highly unlikely that any new state network of whatever type will join the now limited number of Type A: Special District ESA state networks that possess the ability to impose a limited regional tax.

The most universal design feature of state aid formulas used to support the work of a state network is the inclusion of a strong weighing for the total enrollment base of an individual agency. This is clearly a supportable position from one perspective of the equity of the formula: equal state funds for each child who will benefit from the efforts of the service agency. However, the absence in most state aid formulas of consideration of the wealth of a service unit, or recognition of other contextual differences in which an agency functions raises legitimate concerns concerning the adequacy of the formula. Service agencies serving largely sparsely or densely populated regions incur differing costs in delivering support services to school districts.

Unfortunately, at this time most states that provide funds for the state network do not align these funds with a state's school improvement agenda, one of the widely accepted requisites of comprehensive school improvement. There are, of course, several notable exceptions to this observation, particularly in those few states that have adopted an accreditation system that identifies a set of core programs and services to be offered by the agencies.

Also, only a small number of states base part of their formula aid or other categorical aid to service agencies on the expectation that the agencies are to devote extra resources in assisting low-performing schools and school districts, a new priority of many state school improvement agencies given even greater visibility as a result of the passage of the No Child Left Behind Act of 2001.

One of the notable recent changes in a growing number of state aid formulas is in the computation of the *total* enrollment of a service agency. Both public and nonpublic enrollment data is now included in more state programs than in the past, reflecting the institutionalization of the child-benefit theory in state appropriations to service agencies. This development in part reflects a movement by the states to align state aid with long-standing federal requirements in program areas where service agencies are deeply involved, such as special education, vocational/technical education, and technology.

The principle of imposing rigorous checks and balances on the financial practices of public sector organizations has been carried over to many state networks of service agencies, especially Type A: Special District ESAs. These include the use of such traditional checks as a prescribed annual budget preparation calendar, a prescribed budget format, a prescribed uniform accounting system, and a prescribed financial audit process. In addition, many Type A: Special District ESAs networks must now have their annual budget approved by the state.

The close monitoring of the capital improvement plans of many Type A: Special District ESA state networks and the limited ability of many to acquire space, usually restricted to rental, lease, or short-term lease-purchase agreements, suggests that state interests in these cases are anxious to maintain a degree of fluidity in their networks. That is, there seemingly is a desire in many states, wherever possible, to have some control over those factors that might complicate a need in the future to restructure the networks. Placing restrictions on long-term capital debt is certainly one effective strategy to follow in achieving this goal.

GENERAL OBSERVATIONS

We conclude this commentary by offering several general observations concerning the educational service agency movement as this is unfolding across the country.

1. Many of the state networks formed in the 1960s and 1970s continue to exist, and in many instances, thrive. This suggests an admirable degree of resiliency in meeting changing requirements of member school districts in the case of Type C: Cooperative ESAs, and in meeting the changing expectations of both member districts and the state in the case of Type A: Special District ESAs systems. State networks are now in what should be regarded as the maturity stage of the life cycle of organizations, yet they have so far successfully avoided some of the common problems that contribute to organizational obsolescence.

However, the great variations in the organizational capacity of individual service agencies in most state networks of the Type A: Special District ESAs remains a huge handicap for the further development of many of the networks. It is likely that achievement of complete parity in the human and fiscal resources available to all units in a state system is a remote, likely unattainable, goal even with the greatest commitment by the state to do so.

The variation in the organizational capacity of members of a Type A: Special District ESA state network has been the case since the early formation period of the systems. While this situation has been a source of much of the conflict surrounding a number of state networks over the years, it apparently has not been raised as an issue of such profound import that it caused the dissolution of the system. While this may be true of the past, it will not likely continue to be the case as new demands are increasingly placed on state networks, and parallel demands for greater accountability are also forthcoming. Weaker units will become increasingly unable to meet the demands placed upon them.

2. Despite the unequal organizational capacity of individual units in a state network, it would seem that the collective expertise of the staff of all the agencies in a state network represent a significant state resource in that they possess the necessary intellectual capital needed by a state to affect sustained school improvement. A strong majority of agencies across the country have historically been engaged in many of the prerequisites of meaningful school improvement efforts (e.g., curriculum development, staff development, instructional enrichment support). Moreover, a strong majority are located within easy reach of their constituent schools and school districts, thus facilitating accessibility, another near absolute requirement of an external service provider.

3. One of the developments in recent years that is particularly noteworthy is the seemingly growing awareness in some state policy circles that the state network of service agencies should be viewed as a systemic state network, not a collection of unorganized, separate entities. This observation especially applies to Type A: Special District ESA state networks, though there are examples of where this apparently new mindset is present in some states sponsoring a Type C: Cooperative state network. Moreover, it could be argued that, after all, state interests had in mind a state network when the service agencies were initially formed. It is of course true that while a state network may indeed have been created, it was frequently not perceived as a systemic state network, nor, it follows, did the individual agencies comprising the network necessarily function as a system.

A number of factors have come together in recent years that help explain what we perceive as a major shift in how state interests now view their state networks. Not the least of these is the seemingly more widespread understanding of the concept of a systemic state network of educational service agencies, a concept that we would define as:

> a collection of separate, nonhierarchical organizational entities established and supported by the state to serve as a statewide system for the development, production, and/or delivery of programs and services deemed essential for promoting a common set of needs for school districts/schools and those of the state, as well as to promote cooperation and coordination among and between school districts/schools and others; as such they constitute a systemic statewide support network within the state system of elementary-secondary education.

Moreover, though the individual organizations function under a degree of state oversight concerning the need in part to honor a common mission, governance, programming, and fiscal requirements, and thus are in important ways, mutually interdependent, they also enjoy a degree of discretionary authority to set policy governing their own affairs.

4. One of the long-standing contentions in discussions of the role of service agencies, particularly state networks of Type A: Special District ESAs, relates to whether or not the networks should be directly involved in mandatory functions imposed by the state or local districts and schools. We believe the frequently arbitrary position taken by stakeholders at all levels, the state, the service agencies, and local districts and schools, that the service agencies should

not have any role is erroneous, and given recent developments in a majority of state networks of this type, a myth. Moreover, and important, holding on to a rigid position against any role in the state regulatory process not only has potential negative consequences for the implementation of effective state regulatory practices, but is detrimental to the interests of local districts and schools, and to the state network as well.

One useful way to establish our position of this point is to breakdown the sequential steps typically followed in the implementation of a state regulation on local districts and schools. These steps in the process are ordinarily eleven in number, as shown in Figure 4.1.

Service agencies have a unique perspective and vantage point in substate regions of the state. Most ordinarily have in their catchment area a diverse collection of local districts and schools—wealthy and poor, large, medium and small, urban, suburban, and rural. Clearly this unique perspective on the potential impact of a regulation would be of value, for example, in establishing the nature of the need for the regulation (step 1), the exploration of alternative requirements of a sound regulation (step 2), and, the selection of the most effective regulatory language (step 3). Moreover, many state networks are already deeply engaged in a number of the steps as a result of their increasing involvement in the implementation of state school improvement strategies such as: the dissemination of regulation (step 6); the provision of technical assistance (step 7); and, the implementation of state regulation (step 8). All of these roles serve to enrich the regulatory cycle for both the state and local districts and schools.

As established in Figure 4.1, we strongly argue against a role of the state network in the levying of a sanction against a district or school that is in non-compliance, a role that would be severely detrimental to its service role. Moreover, such a role is arguably not legal unless there is a clear state mandate embedded in statute to do so.

5. Finally, a frequent interest of those studying profiles of state networks is to raise the question—can the dots included in the profiles be connected in any meaningful way? That is, if feature A is true for a state network, what is the likelihood that features B, C, D will also be present? Equally important is the reverse question—if feature A is not true for a state network, then how likely is it that features B, C, D will also be absent?

With regard to the state networks in question, and based on the data provided, the answer to whether or not the dots can be connected unfortunately has to be one of those frequently necessary, but in many respects, distasteful mixtures of both "yes" and "no" answers. Examples of where the response is a "yes" include these very broad general associations: a (relatively) close link between the specificity of required core services and the allocation of state funds to support the work of a network; and, the (relatively) strong measures of state oversight on the workings of a network and the increasingly recognized role of a network in support of local school improvement efforts.

Examples abound of where a "no" response to the issue of connecting the

Chapter 4

Figure 4.1
Typical Sequential Steps in the Implementation of State Regulatory Functions

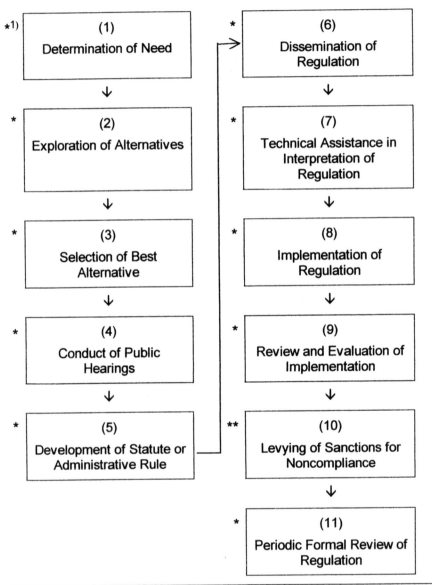

*Steps in the process that are enriched as a result of service agency involvement
**The single step in the process where the service agency involvement would be detrimental to the service agency.

dots must be given, reflecting as this does a long-standing observation concerning state networks of ESAs—the great diversity in the particulars in the design features of state networks. Some of the more obvious illustrations include:

- Inclusion in the mission statement of two of the networks, the Texas RESCs and the Washington ESDs, is the expectation that the networks are to assist the chief state school officials in the furtherance of her/his responsibilities, yet the two seemingly play significantly different roles in the promotion of state priorities, with the larger role clearly assigned to the 20 Texas RESCs.
- Perhaps an even more critical difference is evident in the important issue of the locus of authority for policy development. State oversight of the Texas RESCs is now relatively comprehensive, yet the service agencies are reminded in statute that they are not to be engaged in any regulatory responsibility concerning local school districts. This situation can be contrasted to the New York BOCES, where the chief executive officers, in part a state employee, are relatively limited in initiating offering programs and services that, in many cases, must first be requested by multiple school districts.

Therefore, caution should be exercised in attempting to link, couple, combine, join, or (especially) correlate the structural and organizational features given prominence in the state profiles and the patterns described here. However, there clearly are design features that appear to account for the successful functioning of many state networks of whatever type, Type A: Special District or Type C: Cooperative ESAs. Some of these center on commonly recognized needs of all organizations cited by Selznick (1949) over a half-century ago: (1) security of the organization as a whole in relation to the social forces in the environment; (2) stability of the lines of authority and communication; (3) stability of informal relations within the organization; (4) continuity of policy and the sources of its determination; and, (5) homogeneity of outlook with respect to the meaning and the role of the organization.

We also hold the position that organizations such as education service agencies also have additional, unique basic needs if they are to be effective. Some of these are related to Selznick's list of five, while others are not. We believe that the critical issue of the discernable, and frequently elusive goal of providing stability for a service agency, especially for Type A: Special District ESA networks, is best achieved under the following conditions: (1) they operate under a relatively clear mission statement and role responsibilities that are codified; (2) there is a relatively definite source of funding that is aligned with the mission and expected role, and, is also codified; (3) to the extent possible, the relationships with the state education agency are based on formal policy statements of the state board of education, and thus are not subject to the whims of a single individual; and, (4) the individual units in a state function as a systemic state network, not a collection of loosely–coupled organizations.

An example of the efforts of state policy makers in Iowa, in a series of strategic, not random, decisions to connect some of the important data, in this case, important structural features of a state network is described in a recent evaluation report by Stephens and Good (1998) of the Iowa AEAs. According to the authors of the report, the current AEA structure is one of the soundest of any of the statewide or virtual statewide state networks of educational service agency-type organizations presently operating in the nation at that time. This is not to say that there are not certain features of the structure that have been put in place to support the network that cannot be improved upon. When considered as a whole, however, the existing structural features account for much of the past success of the network.

The structural features of the Iowa AEAs account for the health and much of the performance of the state network. These consist of what were referred to as five "old pillars," and two "new supports," all of which, importantly, have been either wholly or partially codified. Together, the five pillars and two supports are viewed as the strengths of the network in both a relative sense and in absolute terms. The five pillars, shown in Figure 4.2, have been in place in their

Figure 4.2
One View of the Essential Structural
Features of the Iowa AEA Network: One More Time

The Five "Old" Pillars and the Two "New" Supports

The AEA State Network				
1	2	3	4	5
a relatively clear mission statement and role responsibilities	a complete statewide network that includes all LEAs	a relatively definite source of funding that is aligned with mission and role	a relatively close working relationship with LEAs, non-public schools, and the SEA	a relatively substantial degree of discretionary authority to set policy governing both external and internal workings
that are codified	that is codified	that is codified	that is in part codified	that is in part codified
6				
an <u>accountability system</u> that, in addition to fiscal and legal measures, has been broadened to include the expectations that the state will also provide oversight of the processes, procedures, and outcomes of an AEA's efforts				
7				
an <u>accreditation system</u> that is intended to demonstrate that an AEA is honoring some value practice concerning the processes and procedures it uses, as well as meets, exceeds or fails to satisfy desired outcomes				

Source: Stephens, E. R. 1998.

essential form since the inception of the network in the mid 1970s. Pillar One changed the most, and generally in the direction of greater, not lesser, expectations. While many AEA accountability measures have been in existence for many years, only recently have outcome expectations and the way these are to be measured been made explicit. Both features are part of the new accreditation system put in place in 1997. The recent expansions of the accountability and accreditation systems are the two new supports that serve to reinforce the systemic nature of the structural features.

The systemic nature of the AEA structure, as outlined in the report, argues that there is an interrelationship among the five pillars and two support systems. This means, for example, that a negative change in one of the pillars would likely have an impact on the other four and, subsequently, on the health and performance of the network. The complete removal of one of the five would likely have near-fatal consequences for the state system.

The network, moreover, may have survived and even flourished in the past, absent the inclusion in its accountability system of the measurement of its outcomes or an accreditation system that is built around standards, indicators of quality, and sanctions for poor performance. This clearly would not be the case today with an emphasis at all levels of government on performance measurement. Therefore, the new accreditation standards must be successfully implemented. They are not only the glue that holds together all other structural features and give added substance to the accountability system, but also give substance and meaning to the five pillars as well (pp. 181-183).

REFERENCES

No Child Left Behind Act of 2001. Pub. L. No. 107-110.
Oregon Legislative Assembly. 1999. S.B. 259 § 5(4).
Stephens, E. R.. 1979. *Education service agencies: Status and trends.* ESA Study Series/Report No. 1. Burtonsville, MD: Stephens Associates.
Stephens, E. R. 1998. Presentation, Staff Retreat, Western Hills AEA 12. August 17. Sioux City, Iowa (unpublished).

Chapter 5

The Impact of ESAs on Teaching and Learning

Looked at from a traditional lens, the core role of public schools is to help students grow intellectually; that is, to acquire knowledge. In a correlative way schools are also expected to help children grow toward emotional maturity as well as to care for and strengthen their bodies.

More recent articulations of the core role of education have defined more complex functions for the schools. Sarason (1998) has argued that the role of schools is not simply to communicate knowledge but also to create what he called "contexts for productive learning," situations that enable students to encounter ideas and concepts that "take on meaning for and application to personal experiences" (p. 8). It is, therefore, not enough for schools to serve up knowledge for student mastery, a process that is assessed all over the country largely through standardized test scores, an effort given even greater prominence by the No Child Left Behind Act of 2001. Knowledge must be gained in such a manner as to empower the individual to use knowledge for his/her own purposes, an outcome that is virtually never evaluated.

Another recent commentator about public education, Carl Glickman (1998), argues that schools generally misapprehend their main purpose, which is to "provide an education that is consistent with the dream of a fully functioning democratic society" (p. 5).

It is no wonder that local school district leaders struggle to bring coherence to school improvement efforts. They must keep teachers abreast of the exponential growth in content knowledge, train them to use productively new technologies for learning, help students from disadvantaged homes to succeed at defined high levels of performance defined by state curriculum standards, and force feed a new language, English, to a new generation of immigrant children, who must also be successful on high stakes tests. If this were not enough, they must constantly assess the public's expectations of public schools and deal with social critics such as Glickman and Sarason, who argue that the school leaders don't even understand the essential function of public education. However, it must be concluded that if schools don't understand their basic purpose, neither do members of the public who, through their elected and appointed representatives, have been instrumental in shaping the contours and contexts of contemporary education.

It is clear that contemporary thinking argues that school buildings are thought of as the locus of fundamental change (Fullan 1998; Goodlad 1992) rather than school districts. School buildings cannot, by themselves, bring about significant educational improvement. Most local school districts also lack the human and financial resources to assure adequate levels of training for staff at each building. Educational service agencies have been playing an increasing role in assuring quality instruction for students wherever they may go to school, whether traditional public or charter school.

THE ROLE OF ESAs IN SCHOOL IMPROVEMENT

There are many variables in the process of helping a school improve the performance of its students: pupil-teacher ratios, organizational structure, the appropriateness of equipment and facilities, the level and kind of parent and community support, to name just a few. However, two elements stand out as especially critical—*time* and *money*. Both of these resources must be adequate to the task and, since they are always in short supply everywhere, whether relatively or absolutely, they must be carefully targeted toward key goals. Educational service agencies have been instrumental in helping local districts maximize the power of both the time and money available to them.

Time

One consultant who came fresh to the area of school improvement quickly learned a harsh lesson: "We could buy time for the school staffs, but they had no space to install it. Organizational activities were crammed into every available corner of the day" (Donahoe 1993, p. 299). Even districts with a comfortable bank balance are hard pressed to keep training levels of staff at a high level, including building and district leaders, because of the press of daily duties. New research findings, improvements in technology, creative teaching strategies, and ad hoc problem areas (e.g., school violence and responding to the threats of terrorist violence) are numerous and require large blocks of time to master. It would be virtually impossible for a single district staff member to learn the material sufficiently to teach it to others (even if this person had the time to teach it). Building principals and classroom teachers would have even less time to try to master all of these areas. Listed below are just some of the more contemporary issues that need to be included in the repertoire of the contemporary teacher:

Understanding new research findings about brain functioning and their application to classroom practice:

- Using newer computer software to increase higher level thinking skills of students
- Discovering web-based resources for classroom teaching
- Understanding the revised National Teachers of Mathematics teaching recommendations
- Merging the insights of phonics-based and whole language-based reading instruction
- Developing higher order thinking skills in the classroom
- Using classroom diversity to improve instruction
- Incorporating HIV/AIDS information in the health curriculum

This is, of course, not a comprehensive list of issues for today's classroom teachers and administrators to master. It is merely representative of the incredibly varied body of knowledge that is necessary to assure a successful and safe school.

In this complex environment educational service agencies have taken on the responsibility of hiring and continuously training high-quality personnel to search the horizon for new developments in education and to deliver training in these areas at convenient times and places locally. Sometimes service agency staff go to other states to take training and return home to offer instruction locally; at other times ESA staff scan the environment for individuals who have created new knowledge and bring them into the area to provide training themselves.

In addition, accessibility of training close to the school makes it feasible for staff to be able to acquire training without serious degradation of time available to carry out regular tasks; namely, teach classes or manage a building.

Money

"Time" and "money" can be thought of as two sides of one coin. Buildings and districts don't have the time to train local staff to master all these emerging trends because they lack the money to expand the length of the teachers' contracts in order for staff to have adequate time to learn all these, and other, topics.

FINANCING SCHOOL IMPROVEMENT EFFORTS AT ESAs

As was noted earlier, service agencies in different states use different funding sources to acquire the necessary money to staff the agency with adequate expertise to provide training to local district personnel. There are potentially four major sources of funding for the operations of service agencies: state aid, local taxing authority, state and federal grants, and sale of services.

In some states, such as Connecticut and Wisconsin, less than 5 percent of revenues come directly from the state as aid. Service agencies in these environments generate the bulk of their revenues through the sale of services, of which training programs are a major component. Such service agencies are creative and highly responsive to their local districts because they must be if they wish to survive. They listen closely to their customers to learn of their needs and desires for staff training. They also communicate carefully with their local districts (that is, their customers) to, in effect, help them recognize a need. Often district personnel, overworked and understaffed, are unaware of cutting edge concepts in education and opportunities for training teachers and administrators that can make a significant improvement in classroom instruction. The service agencies work at making district personnel aware of these opportunities.

As a result programs are frequently offered that will satisfy a number of districts. Very popular programs can generate significant funds for the service agency. Programs that might be of interest to a limited audience (teachers of autistic children, for example), though not money makers, become financially feasible because an audience for the program can be aggregated from a number of districts. Pricing of programs is usually on a cost-plus basis; that is, the cost of a program to participants is usually defined at a rate that it will cover the actual costs of presenting the program plus an additional amount that will contribute to covering the general operating costs of the service agency. Some service agencies also include an amount that will provide the agency with funds to cover capital replacement and building improvement costs.

NEW DIRECTIONS IN ESA CURRICULUM AND INSTRUCTION SERVICES

For many years the standard practice for the delivery of curriculum and instruction services at educational service agencies was to bring the audience to the service center to hear a speaker or to work as a group on curriculum issues. In the area of general education the service centers saw their primary focus as adult (teacher and administrator) education. They would train the staff members who would return home to render an improved instructional program directly to the students. Many changes have occurred over the last 25 years that are forcing changes in the operating mode of service agencies. Listed below are just some of the forces requiring a change in delivery systems.

Cost

When teachers and/or administrators have to travel to a central location, a whole series of costs must be paid by someone, be it the district sending staff for training, the person doing the travel, or, less likely, the ESA offering the training. The most basic of costs are mileage expenses, but in rural areas or in large states where ESAs serve a wide geography, those coming to a central location for training frequently must be housed overnight and provided meals. Poorer districts, which may be most dependent on the service agency to keep staff at advanced levels of training, are often the least able to bear these costs and therefore are reluctant to send their people.

Substitutes

Although the need to acquire substitutes for classroom teachers while they are away at training sessions represents a substantial cost factor for local districts, the bigger problem is the general lack of substitute teachers to cover even the normal absences of classroom teachers for illness or personal business (Smith 1999; Dorward, Hawkins, and Smith 2000). Classrooms cannot be left without a qualified teacher in charge. At a time of concern about the safety of children even when they are in school, most administrators are reluctant to leave their buildings for a day or even a half-day.

Technology

Ten or fifteen years ago the "sage on the stage" was perhaps the only viable methodology to make new information and techniques available to teachers and other staff members. Therefore, the common process of inviting an audience to the service center was the most logical and efficient method to make information widely available. This is obviously no longer the case. Information can be transmitted in many modes: through learning packages available on the Internet, on computer disks, and by means of interactive television programs that might be originated from almost any location. Audiences may interact with seminar leaders in synchronous and asynchronous modes via computers. Technology has become so powerful, so easy to use, and so universally accessible that a fully accredited high school education is now completely available on the Internet (Trotter 1999).

All of these factors, and others, have been altering the manner by which training to help teachers, administrators and other staff members is being delivered.

Higher Standards for All Students

For a good part of the 20th century, though the curriculum was considered a "local control" issue, with curriculum guides written at the school district level, the force that really drove the curriculum was the textbook industry. In states such as Texas and California, where texts in each subject area were adopted by the State Board of Education, teachers at the district level had few options but to make the locally adopted curriculum mirror the content that was available in textbooks produced for each grade level by national publishers.

In 1957, with the launching of the Russian "Sputnik" rocket, a national concern about the viability of the existing curriculum, especially in math and science, brought other players into the curriculum development arena, especially those universities funded to create more substantial and theoretically sound curricula in biology, chemistry and physics, and mathematics (Helgeson, Blosser, and Howe 1977).

The 1983 publication of *A Nation at Risk* created an even greater American concern with the quality of public education. Its call for higher standards for all students has continued to reverberate throughout the nation into the 21st century. The high school was changed most radically. The so-called general curriculum was largely eliminated. Requirements for all the core subjects were increased in virtually all school districts (Clune 1989; NCES 1997). Subjects previously taught in college (calculus) were moved to the high school, high school subjects (algebra) were moved to middle school, subjects taught at upper elementary grades (reading) appeared in the new kindergarten curriculum because reading skills were included in state-developed standards.

There have been several consequences of these forces acting singularly or together on the way service agencies deliver training programs and curriculum services.

Site-based Training and Curriculum Development

Local school districts have been asking that service agencies reconsider the location of training programs and curriculum development activities. Ideally districts would like to have all training programs delivered after school and on-site in the local district. Such a delivery system would obviate the need for travel expenses and, more importantly, eliminate the often-fruitless effort to find substitute teachers. Teachers and administrators would be able to remain at their work stations during the day. But such a radical change is virtually prohibitive for service agencies. Instead of aggregating a lot of teachers in one place and raising the knowledge base of teachers from many districts in one training program, it would be necessary for ESA staff to replicate programs again and again in each district. In those ESAs with large numbers of constituent districts (some larger ESAs serve 30, 40, and 50 or more local districts) such a training methodology is impossible. Bringing in high-priced speakers from other places to appear at multiple sites would be cost prohibitive.

Therefore, a trainer-of-trainers model has become a popular delivery system. Rather than offer a training program to all the teachers in all districts of the ESA constituency who might be interested in a particular program, or perhaps a series of programs in those cases where a topic is very popular, the service agency solicits one or more local district personnel who will be trained in the new topic, either by ESA staff or a guest presenter from outside the area, and then return to the home district to train other staff members—on-site and, if preferred by local officials, after school.

This methodology is finding expression in curriculum development services as well. In past years local district personnel, from teachers to curriculum personnel, would be invited to the ESA building to hear presenters in subject areas such as reading, math, science, health, and other subjects describing new knowledge in the field or new techniques and materials for teaching the subject. Audience members would then return to the local district to work on curriculum documents to guide instruction in the local district or, at least, guide in selection of textbooks to position the instructional program to use the latest knowledge and materials.

This methodology suffers from the same drawbacks as offering all training at one location: cost, inconvenience, and the problems in finding substitute teachers when needed. Now more and more ESAs are using their in-house talent, who are current in these new ideas because of the high levels of training to which they are exposed in the normal course of their work, and are developing "core curricula" for the various grades and subjects. Such curricula flesh out benchmarks often provided by the state education officials. They provide the framework defining the scope of topics to be covered from the beginning of a course to the end and a sequence of topics that will be the content from grade to grade. Such curricula can identify the most recent instructional materials for use in teaching the program including new computer software, useful Internet sites, videos, and other ancillary materials. Such documents can then be provided to local districts to be used as written or they can be modified by local staff slightly or significantly. Of course, local district staff leaders are still free to continue to develop their own curricula, rely on textbooks, or use curriculum "frameworks" produced by state departments of education. A major benefit of a curriculum document developed at the regional level is the ease of adding information about new videotapes, CDs, computer programs, web-based resources and other supporting materials as soon as they become available.

Distance Learning

The origin of many ESAs was rooted in the need to provide direct instruction to special populations. Two populations in particular proved appropriate for regional solutions, special education and vocational education. (Chapter 6 will develop these topics in depth.) Disabled students, especially those who were severely disabled, became legally entitled to local district programming as the result of state and federal legislation passed in the early and mid-1970s. It was not cost efficient for each district, especially small ones, to create special classrooms for low-incidence handicap categories. Another need leading to the creation of regional programs was vocational education, which usually had small numbers of students interested in a particular career area and almost all areas required the acquisition of expensive training equipment.

However, it is a newer responsibility for service agencies to provide direct instruction to general education students. This is no longer an unusual phenomenon. This growing trend has resulted because of advances in technology and in the growing realization of the capacity of ESAs to provide instruction to all students, especially those with special requirements.

The higher standards and expectations that developed in response to the *Nation at Risk* report made clear to many local districts that they were too small or too poor, often both, to provide a wide range of course work for more advanced high school students, especially in math, science, and foreign language. Therefore, ESAs developed a variety of methodologies to deliver such courses in a distance-learning mode.

Perhaps the first vehicles for doing this were Instructional Television Fixed Service (ITFS) television networks. By installing satellites to receive programming from across the country and offer this programming at the service agency and later by transmission to local districts, students were able to participate in advanced courses. Nationally famous speakers were also made available to teachers, administrators and other staff at the district level.

In recent years a few ESAs, at their own initiative and through their own bonding authority, have developed or used fiber optic networks to transmit course work and speakers to their constituency. Also, these networks permit local programming done within any district on the network to be made available to any or all other districts that are part of the network. It is the ESAs that have taken the leadership to create these networks though the cost of creating the network is usually shared by all participants.

Virtual Learning

For some time now there have been college courses, even degrees, training programs and other learning opportunities available through the Internet. Listed below are some of the more current programs offered over the Internet. Information about them is available on websites and promotional materials produced by the service agencies.

The University of Nebraska, in partnership with a private company, now offers a fully accredited *high school* experience through virtual learning (*Education Week* 1999). Indiana University does the same (Carr 1999). The Virginia Internet High School offers the entire core academic courses required for graduation from a Virginia-accredited high school (Rutkowski 1999).

Michigan and Pennsylvania have created "virtual high schools," which offer courses not available in small high schools or advanced courses not offered in most high schools, including advanced placement courses. The Kansas Virtual Learning Project is a cooperative effort among all the state's education service centers to design, develop and deliver web-based courses for students. In 2001 over 30 courses were available for students through their local districts. The Ohio Valley Educational Cooperative (Kentucky), in cooperation with the U.S. Department of Education and schools throughout the state, has developed a collection of 70 online courses for grades six through 12 in core subject areas. All course are offered in English and Spanish. The Wisconsin Virtual High School is offered under the auspices of CESA 9 in Tomahawk, Wisconsin.

A few ESAs have stepped into this environment and begun to offer virtual high school courses that they themselves have developed. Such courses are unlikely to become the standard method for receiving high school instruction but are almost certain to meet special needs; for example, the student heavily involved in music and/or athletic programs who cannot take a desired class which is offered only when the band practices or who, during football season, is too busy to take a course offered only in the fall. The availability of online classes can meet real learning needs of students and not engender the real or perceived fears of teachers that newer technologies threaten their careers.

Two of many examples of an ESA utilizing technology to improve instruction on a small scale are the DeQueen-Mena Educational Service Center (Gillham, Arizona), which serves a largely rural constituency. The agency utilizes a full-motion, two-way interactive video to deliver instruction to four schools simultaneously. The French River Education Center in North Oxford, Massachusetts distributes online professional development software created by WebEd, Inc. throughout the state. Course topics include offerings in general administrative development, assessment, classroom management, crisis management, differentiated instruction, special education topics and various approaches to teaching the basic subjects. The Darke County Educational Service Center (Greenville, OH) provides an intranet communications system linking every classroom in the county. This is a tool that permits access to a wide variety of resources for curriculum development, professional education, and communication.

In more metropolitan environments Partners to Access Virtual Education (PAVE), a collaborative effort between the Lancaster-Lebanon Intermediate Unit 13 in East Petersburg, Pennsylvania, its districts, and private online providers, partner to offer online courses for students. In a similar environment the Tri-

Valley Distance Education Consortium (ESU #10 in Kearney, Nebraska) provides two-way audio-visual educational programs to a more nonmetropolitan audience.

Newer entities now coming into being are partnerships for the use of technology that include varied partners. On a regional scale the Tuscola ISD (Caro, MI) Information Systems Department provides consulting and operations services to the county medical care facility, the county road commission and a library in addition to its natural local school district constituency.

The Illinois Century Network (ICN) is a much larger entity. It serves 22 counties in Illinois through a high-speed pathway that reaches K-12 schools, community colleges, and private colleges and universities. Regional Office of Education # 41 (Edwardsville, Illinois) is the fiscal agent for this comprehensive use of modern networking capacities. In Education Service Center 12 (Waco, TX) EDLINK 12 services 50 school districts, three charter schools, three private schools, four Educational Service Center locations and three higher education institutions (Baylor, Temple and Texas State Technical). The state of Iowa has completed a fiber optic network which allows the Heartland AEA (Johnson, IA) to use transmissions from the Quest Internet program from the Classroom Connect Company to interact live with scientists in Africa, others in the Caribbean following the route of Christopher Columbus to the New World as well as programs live from the Galapagos Islands, Australia, Central America and the Amazon.

Assisting Low-Performing School Districts

Though educational service agencies were developed by state policy makers primarily to provide assistance to poorer, often rural, school districts, assistance that they were free to solicit or ignore, in some states some functions of the ESA now come with a state mandate. State education department officials realized that the many due process provisions for parents that came attached to the Education of All Handicapped federal legislation in 1973 and similar state legislation passed in generally the same time frame would make it almost impossible for state officials to handle all the complaints that might arise. The ESA became a convenient locus for the adjudication and resolution of such complaints. Though this is not a universal responsibility of service agencies throughout America, carrying out monitoring and compliance responsibilities on behalf of the state is a requirement in several state networks of Special District ESAs. Though the most common manifestation of this role is found in special education, service agencies in some states monitor school district performance in other areas as well.

Most service agency leaders do not rejoice at having these monitoring responsibilities. They feel that they are best positioned to help their local districts when district staff perceive the service agency as a nonregulatory body. Districts fearful that the ESA may punish them in one sphere may well be disinclined to admit to service agency personnel the full scope and depth of problems they may be having even in areas not subject to monitoring, thus limiting the potential value of services to the district.

This problem, if it is accepted as a problem, is increasing. Many state legislatures and superintendents of public instruction take the view that if service agencies aren't fully committed to and involved in helping the worst performing districts in its area, their existence may not be justified. More and more states are now calling on regional agencies to assist districts with high concentrations of poorly performing students, whether the local districts want them involved or not.

For example, the leaders of the 20 service agencies in Texas each meet annually with the state superintendent and are required to show how their agency has been of assistance to low performing districts and what effects their work has been having in improving test scores on the state tests, the Texas Assessment of Academic Success (TAAS).

In 1998 Virginia set up three centers to work with failing school districts. Essentially field-based offices of the state education department, as of 2002 there were eight centers, dubbed Governor's Best Practice Centers, one located in each of the educational regions of the state. As described by Layman and Harmon (2001) these centers had several defined roles:

◆   to support the work of instructional leaders to improve student achievement
◆   to collect and disseminate research-based information about effective instructional practices
◆   to promote collaboration within school divisions and across regions to use resources effectively and efficiently
◆   to facilitate effective communication about Virginia's education reform initiatives to all who work with students.

While the initial purpose of these centers was to offer smaller, poorer, often more rural districts a "helping hand," they quickly transitioned into the role of conducting academic reviews of "warned" schools that were failing to meet student achievement benchmarks for 20% or more of their students. (In 2000 there were 211 of 1800 public schools on the warned list.) Though local schools were not "required" to accept the research and information provided by these centers, they were given a report that identifies areas of strength, areas that need improvement and recommendations for school improvement planning. (These entities have since been eliminated.)

Annual reports required of ESAs in Iowa must document the targeted assistance provided to each local district in improving student learning in core content areas and teaching skills in the basic curriculum areas (Stephens 2001).

Program Examples

Listed below are a very few of the many examples of targeted programs sponsored by individual educational service agencies designed to assist local districts in serving the wide range of needs and interests of students and parents in their pursuit of increased learning. Again, information about these programs is available on agency websites and in promotional materials produced by the agencies. Other examples of efforts of an entire state network of service agencies to enhance teaching and learning are described in several of the remaining chapters.

Math and Science Education. The Texas Rural Science Collaborative, sponsored by the Region VI Educational Service Center (Huntsville, TX), brings together teachers from six targeted school districts to help teachers present science instruction more effectively and thereby improve scores on the Texas Assessment of Knowledge and Skills (TAKS) tests. Content includes learning how to teach using a process-based instructional mode and provides basic equipment and materials.

In a similar strategy Education Service District (Vancouver, WA) 112, with four-year funding of 2.5 million dollars, is attempting to help elementary teachers use a "hands on/minds on" approach to science teaching. This effort is a collaboration that involves ESD 112, Washington State University, and the Hewlett-Packard Corporation and serves seven local districts.

The Southeast Kansas Education Service Center (Greenbush, KS) operates a Mobile Space Station (MSS) on behalf of 33 local school districts. It is designed to increase math, science, and technology skills by immersing students in aspects of living in the International Space Station. The program is to serve 24 fifth to eighth grade students at a time.

This same agency is one of a number of educational service centers around the country that sponsors and/or operates an outdoor learning center for use by students from constituent districts, the Greenbush Outdoor Wildlife Learning Site (OWLS). The Western Suffolk BOCES (Dix Hills, NY) offers a four-day teacher environmental education program in the summer. Participants receive a curriculum guide of discovery learning activities correlated to state math, science, and technology standards. Teachers may then make use of the equipment, resources and special instructional staff at one of the three outdoor "learning laboratories" operated by the service agency. Also, BOCES staff teach specialized courses for grades one through 12 on such topics as Marine Studies, Bay Investigations, Fisheries Resources, and Marine Mammals at identified sites on and off Long Island.

The Wayne-Finger Lakes BOCES (Newark, NY) has an Instructional Materials Center that provides, for a fee and for a defined number of weeks, instructional kits in science plus unlimited teacher training in use of the kits plus continuous materials revision.

The BUBL (Bathysphere Underwater Biological Laboratory Project) at Monroe BOCES #1 (Fairport, NY), run in conjunction with the Rochester (NY) Museum and Science Center, offers students from local districts a type of virtual reality underwater experience in a Deep Submergence Vehicle (DSM). It includes video animation scripted to bring an underwater environment to life. Also, this service center operates a "Challenger Learning Center," wherein middle school students can experience various aspects of a mission to Mars.

Curriculum, Assessment, and School Improvement. The Peoria County Office of Education (IL) serves as state coordinator for a program that focuses on aligning standards and developing effective assessments. School building teams come to the center to learn how to assure that the designed curriculum, the instruction program in the classroom and the tests used to assess learning are all aligned.

Education Service Center VI (Huntsville, TX) uses "School Effectiveness Audits," which make use of the correlates of effective schools and report what is happening on the day an audit team visits a school. The goal of such audits is to enable principals to be able to document changes made as a result of each audit and ultimately to show upward growth in school scores while maintaining a 90% satisfaction rate on the part of principals with the audit process.

The DeQueen-Mena Educational Service Cooperative (Gilham, AZ) scores standardized tests for local districts and reports back test data with interpretations. The scoring service says local districts save three dollars per student in comparison to a private vendor. Education Service Center 12 (Waco, TX), like many other service centers throughout the nation, also assists local districts in analyzing student data so that local officials can make data-driven decisions about how to improve instruction.

The Santa Cruz County Office of Education (CA) joined with the Santa Cruz County Business Council and a local business that had won the Malcolm Baldrige National Quality Award to work with local school districts to improve student achievement by using the Baldrige Education Criteria for Performance Excellence approved by Congress in 1998. The agency created the California Center for Baldrige Education, which now serves businesses as well as school districts (Santa Cruz County office of Education 2002).

The Northern Indiana Educational Services Center (Mishawaka, IN) has developed an online tool for constituent districts to survey their graduates. Local districts can customize the surveys, using their own questions, colors, and logos.

Arts Education. The Peoria County Office of Education (Illinois) organizes a six-week "Spring Celebration" which gives students in grades K-12 from 130 schools in five counties opportunities to perform, exhibit, and otherwise demonstrate their abilities in fine and applied arts. Funding for this activity is supplied by a large number of businesses in the area.

Parent Education. "Parents as Teachers," a program operated by ESD 112 (Vancouver, Washington), provides home visits to parents to offer ideas about how to encourage learning and manage children's challenging behaviors. Project staff also coordinate play groups for families, set up group meetings among parents, and sponsor vision and hearing testing.

The Dequeen-Mena ESC (Gilham, AZ) also offers a "Parents as Teachers" program to help parents feel competent and confident as teachers of their children. It is operated through a reciprocal referral process with the departments of Health and Human Services as well as local school districts and other programs designed to assist families at risk, including teen parents who have not yet finished school.

SUMMARY

Education service agencies have evolved in their range of services to school districts. Many were created out of a need to provide education to special populations, especially special education and vocational education students, forms of education that were too expensive to offer at the local district level. Because such programs served a narrow range of students and often required expensive equipment or very small class sizes to provide a quality program, they were often beyond the financial capacity of some districts while other districts were too small to aggregate enough students to provide these programs in a cost efficient manner. Providing such programming on a regional basis through service agencies became the solution of preference in many states.

In recent years educational service agencies, largely because of a favorable record of serving these special populations successfully, have taken on significant roles in general education, both by redefining their essential role and mission and by utilizing newer technologies to serve staff and students in the critical work of improving schools and raising student achievement. They have also become very active in helping local districts improve administrative services both in terms of quality and cost efficiency.

REFERENCES

Clune, W. 1989. *Graduating from high school: New standards in the states.* New Brunswick, NJ: Center for Policy Research in Education, State University of New Jersey.

Carr, S. 2000. Indiana U's virtual high school criticized over accreditation. *The Chronicle of Higher Education,* 46:A48.

Donohoe, T. 1993. Finding the way: Structure, time and culture in school improvement. *Phi Delta Kappan,* (December):298-305.

Dorward, J., Hawkins, A., and Smith, G. G. 2000. Substitute teacher availability, pay, and influence on teacher professional development: A national survey. *ERS Spectrum,* 18:40-46.

Fullan, M. P. 1992. Getting reform right: What works and what doesn't. *Phi Delta Kappan,* 74(10):745-752.

Glickman, C. D. 1998. *Revolutionizing America's Schools.* San Francisco: Jossey-Bass Publishers.

Goodlad, J. 1992. On taking school reform seriously. *Phi Delta Kappan,* 74, no. 3 (November):232-238.

Helgeson, S. L, Blosser, P. E., and Howe, R. W. 1977. *The status of pre-college science, mathematics and social science education: 1955-1975.* Volume 1. Columbus OH: Center on Science and Mathematics Education, Ohio State University.

Layman, R. W. and Harmon, H. L. 2001. Role of regional best practice centers in academic review of low performing schools. Paper presented at annual conference of the Association of Educational Service Agencies. December, Marco Island, FL.

National Center for Education Statistics. 1997. *High school course taking in the core subject areas: Indicator of the month* (NCES Report 97-925). Washington, DC: Author.

National Commission on Excellence in Education. 1983. *A nation at risk: The imperative for educational reform: A report to the nation and the Secretary of Education.* Washington, DC: US Government Printing Office.

Rutkowski, K. M. 1999. Virtual schools: Charting new frontiers. *Multimedia Schools,* 6:4-79.

Santa Cruz County Office of Education. 2002. *Report to the 2002 community: Working together to make a difference.* Santa Cruz, CA: Author.

Sarason, S. B. 1998. *Political leadership and educational failure.* San Francisco: Jossey Bass Publishers.

Smith, G.G. 1999. Dealing with the substitute teacher shortage. *School Administrator, 56*(April):31.

Stephens, E. R. 2001. State sponsored annual report cards on the work of state networks of ESAs. Report to the Iowa Department of Education—Area Education Agency Design Team.

Trotter, A. 1999. For-profit company to offer high school diploma over Internet. Class.com, Inc. is spin off from the University of Nebraska at Lincoln. *Education Week*, (April 21):12.

Chapter 6

Services to Students with Special Needs

It is a truism that every student is exceptional in some way. Virtually all students within what is considered the normal range of ability are intelligent in some way and perhaps most in several ways (Gardner 1983). However, some students have exceptionalities that suggest they may need special assistance and sometimes special facilities to reach their full potential. Though this statement includes children with handicapping conditions, one of the first and most prominent of the special populations served by educational service agencies, it includes many other children with special needs.

Since the range of human talent and ability is so wide and the circumstances that affect the lives of the 75 million American citizens under age 18 so disparate, it is almost impossible to identify by name the exceptionalities that might require special treatment if a child is to be prepared for a successful life as an adult. Children who are mentally and physically handicapped probably present the largest number of those considered exceptional, about 10 percent of the population between ages three to 21, the age range required for service under the federal Education of All Handicapped Children Act. Some states have a wider age range. Michigan has the largest range for required services under its state law, age birth to 26. Other more traditional areas of special services to students include vocational education, gifted and talented of all types (artistically, academically) those learning to speak English for the first time (bilingual and ESL students), and compensatory education students (Title I, Head Start).

In the last 25 years schools have added other special populations to those who needed special attention including the following: pregnant teens; and, non-traditional learners and non-school completers (alternative high schools and middle schools).

Another, relatively new, special population now coming into prominence is represented by children who are served through child care programs initiated by school districts in response to parent requests. These programs, mostly sustained through the payment of parent fees, may or may not be of acceptable quality. Though fees may cover direct costs, it is very possible that infrastructure costs (use of heating and lighting rooms, additional insurance, additional maintenance and repair expenses) are overlooked as school districts seek to respond to the desires of their constituency at affordable costs. Frequently, school districts may be charging minimal fees because of political pressures to initiate such programs at costs lower than those charged by private child care providers, yet may not be charging anywhere near the full cost to deliver these programs when costs of utilities, additional insurance, opportunity costs if building spaces were used for other purposes, etc. are factored in. Thus, this becomes another local constituency that may need the assistance of the educational service agency if quality programs are to be offered within school district financial resources.

The rest of this chapter will examine the role(s) that educational service agencies are continuing to play in responding to several significant special populations.

SPECIAL EDUCATION

There has long been considerable political debate about the number of tax dollars that should be expended in support of children who deviate, in one way or the other, from the normal range of intelligence or physical capacities. The area of special education offers the most conspicuous example of public debate about the magnitude of finite education resources that should be expended to serve a special population, especially those whose serious disabilities will prevent them from ever earning a living without special accommodations. The causes of this debate are well-known.

For much of the twentieth century parents of severely disabled students had three possible options, none of them ideal: (1) keep the child at home; (2) attempt to institutionalize the child; (3) send the child to a regular school and hope that the child could keep up with other children and not be the subject of taunting by peers. In the post-WW II years states slowly began to recognize the special needs of some children and created some funding for classrooms in regular schools designed for children with less severe disabling conditions such as mild retardation. As the number of handicapped children began to leave their homes and institutions to seek placement in regular school programs and as parents demands for regular classroom programs for more severe conditions began to crescendo, states began to realize the cost effectiveness of aggregating students from several districts into centralized classrooms. In addition, as the costs of providing for more and more disabled students began to increase, several states such as Michigan and New York created some of the first state-sponsored educational service agencies in the nation with the key goal of managing centralized services to handicapped students. In addition, Michigan authorized the new service agencies to hold special tax elections in their service area to generate funding for a more complete range of programs and services to all handicapped students if citizens were willing to bear the costs. The availability of local funds left the state with the obligation to pay only for residual costs after factoring in revenue from these local levies.

The Federal Government and Education of the Handicapped

In 1975, Congress passed the Education of All Handicapped Children Act, (PL 94-142), which imposed on local school districts the obligation to provide special educational programs for children who qualified for them. This legislation was the culmination of many years of increasingly successful efforts on the part of advocates of disabled children in state and federal legislatures and in the courts to assure the rights of these children (Levine and Wexler 1981).

The law was passed with the stated goal that the federal government would gradually move toward the goal of covering 40 percent of the excess cost of educating these children (Jeffords 2002) beginning at 5 percent for fiscal year (FY) 1978, 10 percent for FY 1979, 20 percent for FY 1980, 30 percent for FY year 1981 and 40 percent for each fiscal year after that (Levine and Wexler 1981). The other 60 percent of costs would continue to be covered by state and local tax revenues. Though the law, now called the Individuals with Disabilities Education Act, has been reauthorized or amended five times since it was originally enacted, the federal government has never come close to reaching the 40 percent target. Also, just before the initial federal legislation, some state governments had passed legislation requiring programs for these same children. Those states that moved before the federal legislation was passed were unable to collect federal funds for programs already operating with state funds. Federal dollars could be used only "to supplement and, to the extent practicable, increase the level of state and local funds expended for the education of handicapped children and in no case supplant such State and local funds" (PA 94-142 of 1975). Growth in special education populations was explosive as more children were identified under "Child Find" activities and as children, formerly institutionalized and supported by other government and private agencies, began to become clients of local school districts. Newer understandings of disabilities led to the identification of new and discrete populations such as children who were determined to be autistically impaired. Students with this very challenging disability can cost between $30,000-50,000 per year to educate in today's cost structure.

Laws and interpretations of laws were then expanded to include not only educational expenses for exceptional children but also programs and services that made education possible, including medical services such as catheterization. These costs escalated rapidly during the period of the 1970s-1990s. State aid to special education, to the extent that there was any categorical aid directed toward the education of these children, rapidly began to fall behind the demand for new staff, new classrooms and buildings, special equipment, individualized transportation programs and so forth. While services to handicapped children were guaranteed under provisions of federal and state laws, adequate financial support to respond to these escalating costs was not.

Not too long after the special education "revolution" came into law, it became clear that local school districts would drown in red ink if they attempted to serve every handicap classification with the district's own programs and within its own facilities. The creation of educational service agencies was accelerated either through state effort or by the initiation of voluntary cooperatives among local districts where service agencies did not exist. Such a strategy was justifiable in both economic and educational terms.

   ♦ Aggregating students from several districts within one center justified the hiring of a highly specialized teacher, who were scarce anyway.
   ♦ More students could use expensive specialized equipment, thereby justifying its cost.

♦ This additional tax base, when permitted by law and authorized by local voters, relieved the pressure on local districts to devote a disproportionate number of dollars to handicapped students and away from general education students.

Today's ESA is likely to service its constituent local school districts in helping to educate disabled students in one of two major program delivery systems, often both:

1. The ESA hires teachers who have special training in the various disability areas defined by state and federal statute and makes these staff members available to visit districts either to consult with local faculty who may lack significant education and experience in the areas they are teaching or to actually teach classes or assist in other ways, e.g., repair of specialized auditory equipment used with deaf students, recommend acquisition of newly designed equipment for helping physically impaired students, and so forth.

2. The service agency directly operates special programs for low incidence handicapped students (blind, deaf, autistic, severely emotionally impaired and others) whether at its own facility, in one or more local district classrooms which service children drawn from several districts in the area, or in a building specially designed and built for and operated by the service agency on behalf of some or all local districts at a location reasonably proximate to the geographical center of the area to be serviced.

Programs commonly offered by or through educational service agencies include the following:

♦ Physical and occupational therapy;
♦ Audiological and amplification services for deaf and hard of hearing students, psychological services (used primarily in identifying, evaluating and assisting schools with educational planning for special education students);
♦ Special classrooms and specially trained teachers (serving blind, deaf and hard of hearing, severely emotionally impaired, autistic, and cognitively disabled students);
♦ Mobility training for blind students (Learning how to move about the community, including the use of public transportation);
♦ Assistive Technology. (Providing special devices and equipment for children with severe impairments of bodily function. On a regional level the Wisconsin Assistive Technology Initiative is a statewide project supported by all 11 Cooperative Educational Service Agencies [CESAs] in the state. It provides information to local school districts about assistive technology available to disabled students, provides a lending library of such equipment so that local district staff can use such equipment before deciding to purchase, and offers a forum whereby instructors can share experiences, both successful and unsuccessful, in using this technology.)

Preschool Special Education

In addition to serving disabled students of normal school age in classroom programs, ESAs provide Early Intervention program support or program delivery for very young children (ages 0-5) provided in the "least restrictive environment" whether at home, child-care centers, or school or service agency sites.

For example, the preschool programs of the Genesee Valley Board of Cooperative Educational Services (LeRoy, NY) are open to children between birth and age five with a special need that may hinder their development (e.g., speech and language, behavior, fine or gross motor skills, medical, cognitive skills). Referrals are accepted from parents, school districts, and community agencies. Center-based programs are maintained at four sites.

Examples of Other Special Education Programs

ESAs often sponsor and operate special education programs beyond the normal school year. These offerings expand opportunities for children with disabilities to learn academics and grow as persons as well. Such programs can include the following.

1. Summer camping programs, whether in-school "camps" with field trips, swimming, picnics, and other outdoor activities or residential-type camps. For example, Education Service Center 12 (Waco, TX) operates a "Camp Teen Challenge" for students with visual impairments in grades 6-12. It is designed to offer opportunities for recreation, social interaction, and mastery of daily living activities. It also sponsors a Technology Olympics for students with visual impairments in grades K-12.

2. Parent support groups. Parents of children with severe handicaps often find it helpful to get professional advice about how to help their children at home and find interacting with parents similarly situated as a source of good ideas as well, for example, how to address the special problems they face at home in assuring nondisabled children they will get adequate parental attention.

3. Pinal County Office of Education (Florence, AZ). Special needs students are one of the main foci of the Therapeutic Equine Academy for Children. The school operates during the regular school day. The curriculum includes grooming and tacking horses, leading horses in an arena, and side walking horses.

Prevention

One of the newer efforts of ESAs to serve local districts in the area of special education is prevention. Nationally 80 to 85 percent of students referred to special education for evaluation end up placed in special education classes (Jones 2002). ESAs in Iowa use a model that calls for immediate assistance from the service agency to classrooms of students who give early evidence of some deficit without a referral or an Individualized Education Plan (IEP). Because of this model of early intervention in the early grades only about 25 percent of referred students are placed in special education (Jones). For example, the El Dorado County Office of Education (Placerville, CA). The county office provides a part-day preschool for children ages 3, 4, and 5. A developmentally appropriate curriculum is emphasized as well as parent education and involvement.

Service agencies in a number of states have for many years been required by statute to assume responsibility for the operation of an educational program for incarcerated youth.

Regional nature centers and outdoor education centers have been a staple in the program enrichment efforts of a number of service agencies for several years. For example:

1. Kent Intermediate School District (Grand Rapids, MI) operates the Howard Christensen Nature Center that offers educational programs for kindergarteners through seniors; the center is located on a 134-acre nature preserve having miles of nature trails.

2. San Joaquin County Office of Education (Stockton, CA) has operated the County Resident Outdoor School for over 45 years, and approximately one-third of a million elementary school students have participated in the program since its founding; two sites are maintained where the focus of the program is on natural science and environmental education.

3. Multnomah Education Service District (Portland, OR) has sponsored an outdoor school since 1966. A comprehensive natural science and environmental science curriculum is offered.

VOCATIONAL/TECHNICAL EDUCATION

Categorical (specifically targeted) federal funding for vocational education for secondary school students began in the United States in 1917 with the passage of the Smith-Hughes Act (P.L. 347). The legislation calling for this categorically focused additional money grew out of a recognition that the country's future was becoming dependent on an industrial economy. The value of vocational education at the higher education level had been recognized as early as 1862 with the passage of the Morrill Act whereby states were given land that could be either sold or leased to raise money for establishing at least one college in the state. In this college liberal and practical education studies were to be combined into a curriculum that "was vocational without being viewed inferior to a purely academic education" (Old Dominion University, Lesson 5 2003).

Smith-Hughes provided categorical aid only within narrowly defined limits, but it required that states create boards to supervise vocational education in cooperation with a federal board. This initiated a federal-state-local partnership that has lasted to this day. Equally important, the legislation required states to bear half the cost of salaries for vocational education teachers.

What this legislation did not provide was money to equip classrooms or build special facilities for this type of education. Then and now local school districts did not have and do not have sufficient funding to adequately provide the specialized, and expensive, laboratories and equipment needed to train an industrial work force in adequate numbers. However, vocational education took on growing importance as the 20th century progressed.

There were few service agencies in America at the initiation of federal funding for vocational education. However, the population boom that started after WWII pressed local districts to find the money to build schools at an accelerating pace. The Vocational Education Act of 1963 reaffirmed the importance of vocational education to the nation and, for the first time, allocated federal dollars that could be used for the construction of area vocational schools. The Carl D. Perkins Vocational and Applied Technology Education Act of 1990 reinforced this "bricks and mortar" component of vocational legislation (P.L. 101-392). States and local districts with the highest concentrations of disadvantaged students were given additional funds to improve vocational education facilities and equipment.

The possibility of using federal dollars to build area vocational schools introduced another curriculum area where economies of scale pointed to the educational service agency as a natural locus for developing programs to serve a number of local districts, and for quite the same reasons that special education programs migrated to service agencies:

- ♦ Vocational education programs were expensive, requiring specialized equipment.
- ♦ The supply of vocational education teachers was limited. Most practitioners of skilled trades could make more money in their fields of expertise than in teaching. State regulations regarding teacher certification made it difficult for trades people interested in working in schools to get the necessary licenses to get full-time positions that paid as much as other classroom teachers, further limiting the supply of these teachers.
- ♦ The number of students interested in individual vocational programs in any single district is limited. Aggregating a class of students from several school districts make specialized programs cost efficient.

Some states, in recognition of the special challenges of providing vocational education, authorized regional taxes to help to cover costs beyond the small share of building costs that could be covered by federal dollars. The educational service agency in some states was given authorization to seek public approval for and levy extra taxes for vocational education on behalf of the region as had been done to increase funding for special education. In the state of Michigan, for example, 30 of the 57 regional service agencies have been able to pass vocational education tax levies to build facilities and thereby operate regional vocational centers. The concept of regional centers serving vocational students was probably initiated by provisions of Title VIII of the National Defense Education Act of 1958. This section of the act:

> . . . created the area school concept and provided funds for the operation of postsecondary area schools in each state. The intent of Congress was to extend vocational education to residents of areas inadequately served and to encourage the development of postsecondary vocational programs that emphasized a combination of manipulative skills and related technical knowledge . . . that would enable graduates to work effectively as technicians— aids to engineers and scientists. (Old Dominion University, Lesson 5 2003)

It should be noted that, for reasons beyond the scope of this publication to summarize, the term "vocational education" developed a number of invidious connotations among parents and students as the 20th century drew to a close, including judgments that this form of education was inferior to other, more "academically-focused," forms of education. The public perception was that vocational education was focused on inculcating skills that were growing irrelevant to an economy increasingly based on information rather than hard goods production. Thus, both as a reflection of the reality of newer programs that were more in tune with the needs of a 21st century economy and the need to reorient the public perception of skills-based education, the more modern term for this form of instruction has become "technical education," or "vocational/technical education." This changing nomenclature was reinforced by some of the manpower training legislation passed as the century came to a close, especially the School-to-Work Opportunities Act of 1994. This legislation called for schools, businesses and industry to cooperate in preparing students with the knowledge, skills, abilities, and information about occupations and the labor market that would enable those who chose to go in this direction to make a seamless transition into post-school employment. Today's vocational education is not, as the saying goes, "your father's vocational education." It is "characterized by a curriculum based on the need for students to demonstrate mastery of rigorous industry standards, high academic standards and related general education knowledge, technology and general employment competences." The Tuscola Intermediate School District in Michigan, one of the 30 service agencies in the state operating a skills center, provides 27 programs including some that offer national skill standards certifications to make graduates employable in state-of-the-art environments. In the evening center programs are offered to local business and industry. Many of the programs that they offer can be found in vocational/technical centers throughout the country and include: advertising design and production; auto body repair; diesel equipment maintenance and repair; carpentry where in some environments students actually build a house as a course project; cosmetology where students meet standards for professional certification upon completion of the program; culinary arts where students learn both cooking skills and the business aspects of running a restaurant; machine and metal trades; electricity; and, welding.

Other popular programs offered through vocational/technical centers around the country include the following offerings: heating, ventilation, air conditioning; horticulture/landscaping; computer graphics; radio and television broadcasting; child care; and, floral arts.

A sample of the more unique programs include the following: criminal justice (Monroe #1, Fairport, NY) students may earn college credit in this two-year program; aircraft maintenance technology (Western BOCES, Dix Hills, NY); and, animal science.

The above list of programs is only suggestive. Program offerings are constantly changing at service agencies in order to keep up with a rapidly changing marketplace.

One of the more promising educational trends has been the development of partnerships between school districts and other entities in the community—

businesses, unions, non-profit agencies, civic organizations, and citizens who do not have children in schools. Some of the energy for partnerships comes from business itself, realizing that it is good business to have good schools in the community for their employees and a wise use of resources to help the schools prepare a workforce that would not need additional training when initially hired. Some fields have become especially alarmed about their ability to attract a cadre of competent workers and have joined in collaboration with voc/tech centers to develop programs targeted to their specific employment needs.

The St. Clair ISD (Port Huron, MI) offers a half-time Academy of Plastics Manufacturing Technology in cooperation with companies in the plastics industry. This same service agency offers a Health Career Academy, a Hospitality Academy, and an Information Academy, at the main campus of the ISD and all in collaboration with their respective industry representatives.

The General Motors Academy (GMA) at Oakland Schools (Pontiac, MI) is a collaborative effort between the General Motors Corporation and the service agency in Oakland County, Michigan, to provide an instructional program "designed to introduce 11th and 12th grade students to the skills for a career as a validation technician/engineer."

The St. Lawrence-Lewis BOCES (Canton, New York) and ESU #10 (Kearney, Nebraska) are two of many ESAs that offer the Cisco Networking Academy, which trains students to becomes certified network associates.

Education for immediate employment is not the only focus of ESA-sponsored career education. For example, the Wayne-Finger Lakes Bureau of Cooperative Educational Services (BOCES) in Newark, New York offers a study of the health care industry, a one-year program for college-bound seniors. Students completing the course receive two credits in Health Occupations, one credit in English, and one credit in social studies. Students report to a hospital setting for classroom work and rotate throughout the various departments. They also offer an Animal Science course that involves internships with veterinarians and kennels.

ALTERNATIVE EDUCATION

Some children and young adults are not able to adjust to the way learning is delivered in the traditional school. It has been argued that schools and classrooms were really designed for students who are passive learners and who learn by watching and listening and then manipulating abstract theories and concepts. Young people who learn best by manipulating their environment, verbally interacting with teachers on a continuing basis, and changing activities frequently are often unsuccessful in traditional schools. This lack of success may lead to a number of possible unpleasant consequences for these students. Such students have become an increasingly larger clientele for services offered by or through educational service agencies. The academic program provided is equivalent to that of a student's home school. Though many such schools are run by local school districts, a few have been established by service agencies. The ESA-sponsored alternative schools have been especially useful for smaller districts, which often cannot afford to run separate schools on their own. ESA-managed alternative schools are quite common throughout the country. Offered here are but a representative selection of such schools.

1. Educational Service Unit No. 13 (Scottsbluff, NB). The agency, serving a largely rural area, sponsors the Valley Alternative Learning Transitioning School. It was established to serve students at risk of not graduating from high school. The school enrolls 45 students each quarter, with one-half attending either a morning or afternoon schedule of classes in a core curriculum. Elective credits are available for students who work at least 20 hours per week.

2. Clark County Educational Service Center (Springfield, OH). This service agency sponsors the Clark County Academy. The school provides classroom instruction for middle school students having unsuccessful educational experiences in their home districts.

3. Greater Lawrence Educational Collaborative (Methuen, MA). The alternative school provides a co-educational program for students ages 14 through 21 having significant behavioral or psychological problems in their home district. A core academic curriculum is offered in addition to a vocational education program. A 45-day diagnostic placement is also available as needed.

4. The Helensview High School is one of four alternative schools sponsored or co-sponsored by the Multnomah Educational Service District (Portland, OR). The school serves students who have already dropped out or one experiencing difficulty in their regular school. Students receive a comprehensive educational program and social services, including that of the service agencies' Pregnant and Parenting Student Services.

5. The Education Cooperative (Wellesley, MA) sponsors TEC School, a facility designed to provide secondary students who are able to achieve academically but are failing to do so in their home schools. The school offers a comprehensive educational program, including extensive out-of-school enrichment experiences.

6. Wayne-Finger Lakes Board of Cooperative Educational Services (Newark, NY) maintains two alternative schools open to secondary school-age students of average to above average abilities recommended by their home school.

7. The Program for Alternative Comprehensive Education (PACE), managed by the Nassau (New York) BOCES is operated at an outdoor education site. This agency also runs a late afternoon/evening program (Positive Alternatives Twilight High School, or PATHS) for students who prefer this type of school schedule.

8. CESA 9 (Tomahawk, WI) established a virtual high school program for at-risk students. It was so successful that it evolved to become the Wisconsin Virtual High School.

9. Though not the norm, the involvement of the Maricopa County Regional School District (AZ), serving metropolitan Phoenix, warrants special comment because of its extensive immersion in the provision of special schools. In 2001 the Regional School District operated 10 schools throughout the county that provided alternative educational services to school districts. These include: sec-

ond-chance high schools for students who have dropped out of their regular high school, or have been expelled and a school for pregnant pre-teens.

Court-Involved Students

For reasons that may or may not be related to the inadequacies of many traditional schools, some students find themselves in legal trouble because of their own actions or they suffer from family problems that require they be removed from the home. Service agencies are frequently called on to provide educational programs for children who must remain in protective custody while their cases work their way through the courts or who must remain under the jurisdiction of the court even though they are not held in jail. Courts will often contract with ESAs to provide educational services to young people held in juvenile detention centers or who are court-assigned to special programs where they may receive special counseling in addition to educational programs. There are many examples similar to the following.

1. Appalachia Intermediate Unit 8 (Edensburg, PA) provides educational programs for serious juvenile offenders from across the state at a maximum-security juvenile facility for as long as students are incarcerated there. They are but one of many service agencies serving as the educational provider of choice for incarcerated youth.

2. Educational Service District 101 (Spokane, WA) serves youth placed on electronic monitoring who are court-ordered to attend an alternative school setting.

3. Ventura County Office of Education (Camarillo, CA). The county office of education maintains the Marguerite McBride School. This is a short-term educational program housed in a maximum detention facility, located in the county juvenile hall, for minors awaiting adjudication proceedings or placement.

4. Multnomah Education Service District (Portland, OR). The agency sponsors the Donald E. Long School, a facility located at the Multnomah County Juvenile Justice Complex. Students awaiting hearings or trials are provided a full-day educational experience.

5. Colusa County Office of Education (Colusa, CA). The county office provides the educational services for court-adjudicated males ages 14-18 who are placed at the county detention center at Fonts Springs Ranch. Both an academic core curriculum and a vocational curriculum are provided.

Agency-Involved Students

Still other young people find themselves involved with outside agencies not because they are criminals but because they have become parents while still teenagers, or are victims of one or another kind of chemical dependency, are homeless or suffer some other kind of problems so serious that they cannot be safely returned to their parents without support. The Berks County Intermediate Unit 14 (Reading, PA) provides basic instruction to students who have been placed in the Caron Foundation due to chemical dependency. Allegheny IU 3 (Pittsburg, PA) sponsors an initiative that works with homeless children.

Migrant Children

Educational Service Districts 105 (Yakima, Washington) and ESD 189 (Mt. Vernon, Washington) are but two of the many service agencies that play a key role in educating migrant students, who move frequently from school district to school district. All ESCs in Texas provide comprehensive services to migrant children, their families, and the educators who service them. For example, ESD 5 (Beaumont, TX) secures and trains recruiters who identify eligible migrant students and their families, coordinate services to local districts serving this population and provide staff development and instructional assistance to local school districts. ESC 12 (Waco, TX) serves as fiscal agent for 42 Migrant Shared Services Arrangement Districts in their region. Eight migrant service coordinators provide coordinated services to local districts. They assess student and family needs of instructional and support services.

Charter Schools

Service agencies in a number of states have in recent years assumed sponsorship of charter schools. Some examples include the following.

1. Cooperative Educational Service Agency #1 (West Allis, WI). This agency serves the larger Milwaukee metropolitan region and has designed and implemented a Charter Middle School for at-risk students in 10 school districts and a charter proficiency-based high school for at risk-students in five school districts.

2. Lucas County Educational Service Center (Toledo, OH). For several years this service agency has operated five charter schools.

GIFTED AND TALENTED EDUCATION

Just as there has been a crescendo of debate about what proportion of available education dollars should be spent on schooling for disabled students, especially those with severe handicapping conditions, there has been a somewhat more muted public disagreement about whether students deemed to have special intellectual and/or artistic abilities should be entitled to special, and more expensive, programming. It is probably more accurate to say that the bulk of the argument has taken place among professionals and parents of so-called gifted and talented students, many of whom feel that regular education programs are pitched to the middle levels of achievement and their children, when challenged at all in the classroom, are called on to be assistant teachers to the other students in the classroom, a role which limits their ability to learn new material.

As a matter of public policy the issue of whether gifted and talented students ought to be objects of special concern, and funding, has had an up-and-down history. The federal government seemingly paid no attention to this subject until the Soviet Union put Sputnik into orbit in 1957. Soon thereafter Congress passed the National Defense Education Act, designed to foster significant growth in achievement in math, science, and foreign language. This act, for the first time, set aside money for gifted and talented education. Soon states were allocating dollars for this special purpose as well. However, once the United

States began to show progress in its own space programs, interest in educating the intellectually gifted began to decline as did the difficult economic times of the 1970s.

As categorical funding for this purpose began to decline, the onus for finding money for these students fell to local school districts. This gave rise to many disputes about whether providing challenging and accelerated and separate programs for gifted and talented students was undemocratic and unfair. Local districts have resolved these disputes in a variety of ways. Some ignored the presumed special needs of these students or argued that the needs of all children were being met in the regular classroom. Others created "pull out" programs where children left their regular classroom for special instruction with like children from other classrooms for one or more sessions a day or week. A small number accepted the local cost of designing special full-time programs for elementary students, with the expectation that no such programs were necessary in higher grades since the growing differences in curriculum opportunities would take care of the needs of gifted students automatically.

However, state interest in this issue did not entirely die in most places. More and more states opted to create special schools for intellectually gifted students, whether full-year residential programs such as one in Illinois or special summer programs sponsored by the state. The educational service agencies have frequently had a role to play in these programs, whether by simply helping to screen candidates for these programs or by actually being a site for such a program. Other service agencies worked with their constituent districts to set up and operate programs for gifted and talented students on behalf of interested districts. Listed below is a very modest list of such programs around the country that have been created through some kind of efforts of the regional service agencies.

1. Oakland Schools ISD (Waterford, MI) created a special choir for students in grades 4-7 throughout the county and then took over from a private agency an orchestra serving middle school and high school students in the 28 school districts in the county.

2. Montgomery Intermediate Unit 23 (Norristown, Pennsylvania) identifies "mathematically precocious youth" in the eighth grade and teaches all of their pre-calculus mathematics in the ninth and tenth grades in special classes held at a centrally located county community college.

3. ESU 8 (Neligh, Nebraska) operates academic quiz bowls.

4. The St. Lawrence-Lewis BOCES (Canton, NY) sponsors Odyssey of the Mind competitions, an activity which emphasizes the development of individual creative skills and problem solving as a member of a team.

5. Nassau BOCES (Garden City, NY) Cultural Arts Center is an arts and academic high school program that offers course work in dance, drama, music, musical theater, visual arts, and theater technology. Students may attend full or part-time. The service agency also offers a Summer Arts Academy, a four-week enrichment opportunity for students in grades 6-12.

6. Kane County Office of Education (Illinois) has created a network for all

local district gifted and talented program coordinators to share ideas, initiatives and challenges. They also provide assistance in identifying gifted children and in training teachers to meet the needs of teachers working with gifted children in mixed ability classes.

7. The Trumbull County Education Service Center (Warren, OH) offers a special Saturday program for students in grades 2-6 who are recommended for this experience.

MAGNET SCHOOLS

While some magnet schools are created to meet the needs of children with special gifts and/or talents (e.g., performing arts schools, accelerated academics), many are established for other reasons: (1) to add variety, whether in presentation ("back to basics" instruction) or form (all students wear uniforms) to what is usually a homogenized form of education in all schools in districts shaped by district-adopted curricula and textbooks; (2) to offer opportunities for children to study areas that are particularly meaningful to students and their families (e.g., African-American studies, science, math) either not discussed in the regular curriculum or not developed sufficiently to meet the needs and interests of some students; (3) to create smaller schools, which research shows are likely to increase student behavior and achievement.

Here again the opportunity to draw on populations from the service agency region makes it possible to aggregate enough students to create a cost efficient entity.

OTHER PUPIL PERSONNEL SERVICES

A number of states, including Illinois and Michigan, require educational service agencies to employ a truant officer. This person is required to identify the whereabouts of chronically absent students, counsel the parents/guardians of such students, and may file court petitions affecting the child and/or the parents/guardians. This same student clientele is a focus of a program offered by the Clark County Community Truancy Project located at ESD 112 (Vancouver, WA). Upon referral by the juvenile court students attend life skills classes and are offered service learning experiences to encourage academic success.

Many educational service agencies provide training for school personnel in suicide prevention, violence prevention, and alcohol and drug abuse prevention. Often these programs are cooperative efforts with medical institutions and mental health and other social service agencies and rely on federal and state funding from a variety of sources.

SUMMARY

Educational service agencies have many admirable characteristics. The ability to respond quickly and flexibly to emergent needs are among the most important of these traits. ESAs have played an increasingly important role in helping local school districts to educate children with very low and very high cognitive abilities. They help to challenge very talented students and those who are not succeeding in traditional programs. They partner with local districts to prepare students who wish to move immediately into the workplace and those who are still searching for the most suitable of the traditional professions. They respond to the needs of children who sometimes seem to belong to no educational agency, most particularly the children of migrant workers and homeless children. They support the needs of the ill (e.g., those who are chemically dependent) and those who are in the best of health. And they do all this constantly proving to their constituent districts, state departments of education and, most significantly, state legislatures that they are the most cost-effective, cost-efficient option to help serve these varying constituencies.

REFERENCES

Education of All Handicapped Children Act. 1975. Retrieved from http://asclepius.com/angel/special.html.

Gardner, H. 1983. *Frames of mind: The theory of multiple intelligences*. New York: Basic Books.

Jeffords, J. 2002. Keeping our promise on special education{Electronic version}. *The Hill*. Retrieved from http://www.hillnews.com/090402/ss_jeffords.shtm (accessed January 21).

Jones, S. Personal communication, 21 October 2002.

Levine, E. L., and Wexler, E. M. 1981. *PL 94-142: An Act of Congress*. New York: Macmillan Publishing Co., Inc.

Old Dominion University 2003. Foundations of Career and Technical Education, Lesson 5. Retrieved from http://www.lions.odu.edu/org/deca/oted401/lessons5.html.

Chapter 7

Improving School and School District Infrastructure

INTRODUCTION

Another critical role assumed by educational services agencies is the provision of programs and services that strengthen the infrastructure of local schools and local school districts and that enhance the infrastructure of the state system of elementary-secondary education as well. For purpose of this discussion, we define the **infrastructure** of a local school and local school district more broadly than some. For example, in a treatise on rural community economic development, Sears, Rowley, and Reed (1990) limit the term to mean "the permanent physical installations and facilities supporting the socioeconomic activities in a community, region, or nation" (p. 1). Similarly, the American Society of Civil Engineers focuses on physical facilities in a recent comprehensive report on the condition of the nation's infrastructure (2001). This traditional view would include such basic facilities as roads, bridges, water and sanitation facilities, civic centers, libraries, parks, police and fire protection, and other public works buildings and equipment necessary to produce and deliver public services.

We prefer to extend the definition to include factors beyond the presence or absence of service and production facilities. In doing so, we share Cigler's (1987) position that, in the case of human services organizations, it is particularly critical that the organizational and management capacity of such entities also be acknowledged as a vital component in any effort to address the infrastructure issues of these types of organizations (p. 27).

Our position is that an understanding and assessment of the ways that educational service agencies contribute to the infrastructure needs of schools/school districts and, by extension, to the infrastructure of the state system of elementary-secondary education must give consideration to two major dimensions of the construct infrastructure when applied to a school/school district:

    Dimension 1—the adequacy of the physical facilities needed to meet the requirements of a comprehensive educational program for all students, including its technology infrastructure

    Dimension 2—the adequacy of the organizational and management capacity to meet the requirements of a comprehensive program

In advancing this broader definition we share Baldwin's (2000) keen observation that "infrastructure can be hard to define, but you know it when you don't see it—that is, you may not notice its presence, but you can't help noticing its absence or inadequacy" (p. 3). The availability of adequate and safe facilities for all students and the need for specialized facilities to enrich the educational experience of special populations of students seem indisputable. So, too, is access to needed management services essential for the optimum of the performance of the educational program.

The poor condition of many school facilities, especially those of large urban and rural districts, has been well documented in the past, including two relatively recent reports by the U.S. General Accounting Office (2000). Furthermore, many, both within and outside the profession, have serious concerns about the organizational and management capacity of many schools to fulfill the public expectations held for them. Moreover, the increased pressures resulting from the current accountability movement will likely add to the particular difficulties of schools and school districts serving urban and rural small communities, that frequently lack the fiscal and human resources to function in the most efficient and effective way. The stringent requirements of the latest chapter in the accountability movement, passage of the No Child Left Behind Act of 2001, are likely to add to the burden of many schools and school districts of this type.

ORGANIZATION OF CHAPTER

The remainder of the chapter is organized into four sections. In the first section, comments are offered about some of the principal ways that service agencies across the country address the special physical facility needs of schools/school districts, Dimension 1 in the conception of infrastructure used here. This is followed by a section with illustrations of the many ways that educational service agencies provide assistance in strengthening the organizational and management capacity of schools/school districts, the second dimension in our view of the more meaningful way to think about the infrastructure requirements of an educational organization. A number of broad patterns in the activities of service agencies in this programming area are presented in the third section. In the final section, we provide a discussion of the role played by service agencies in addressing the infrastructure needs of schools/school districts, and, by extension, we stress, again, the role played by these agencies in addressing the infrastructure requirements of the state system of elementary-secondary education.

ASSISTANCE IN MEETING SPECIAL
PHYSICAL FACILITY NEEDS

The major way that educational service agencies address the physical facility needs of schools/school districts is usually through the management and operation of a special facility created to meet the needs of special populations of students enrolled in schools/school districts located in the catchment or area of the service agency. Special schools administered by a service agency are usually of eight major types, as shown in Figure 7.1.

Of the eight major types of regional schools administered by a service agency, the most common appear to be regional schools that serve special needs students. Regional vocational/technical schools operated by service agencies are

Figure 7.1
**Major Types of Special Facilities
Sponsored/Administered by Educational Service Agencies**

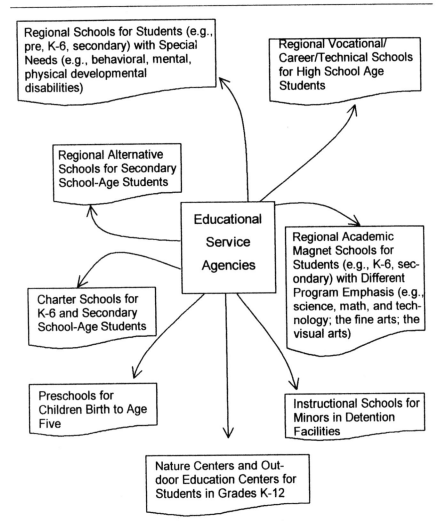

also a common programming effort, especially in the two states of Michigan and New York. Illustrations of these two types of schools were provided in Chapters 5 and 6. These chapters also demonstrated other special facility initiatives sponsored by service agencies. Such initiatives include alternative schools, magnet schools, schools in detention facilities, outdoor education centers, preschool programs, and other unique efforts to meet the needs of special populations.

ASSISTANCE IN ADDRESSING
ORGANIZATIONAL AND MANAGEMENT
CAPACITY ISSUES

Educational service agencies contribute in numerous ways toward enhancing the organizational and management capacity of schools and school districts, the second half of our view of the infrastructure equation as this is being developed here. The types of programs and services offered by service agencies across the country would be a very long list since they are based on a wide variety of locally determined needs. An indication of the variety of offerings is provided in Table 7.1. This listing, which should be viewed as very conservative, nonetheless represents the results of the most recent national survey of the general nature of service agency involvement in programs and services designed to strengthen the organizational and management capacity of schools and school districts. The survey was conducted by the Association of Educational Service Agencies (AESA) and identifies the categories, but not in all cases the specific nature, of programs or service offerings. A total of 438, or 86 percent of the member organizations of AESA, participated in the survey. These agencies were located in 30 different states and represent what is generally regarded to be some of the most comprehensive individual and statewide networks of service agencies in the nation.

Forty-three agencies, or 9.8 percent of the respondents, identified a type of management service not specifically listed as a choice in the survey. In order to illustrate the range of programming efforts engaged in by service agencies, we have listed the "other" responses in Table 7.2. Also used to construct the table are examples cited in a sampling of the web sites and the current annual reports of individual service agencies and those referenced in the composite annual reports of an entire state network of service agencies. Here, again, this list should be regarded as conservative.

The examples of program and service areas shown in both Tables 7.1 and Table 7.2 provide only a partial view of the depth and breadth of the particular areas cited. For example, the AESA survey instrument requested respondents to merely indicate whether or not they provided a cooperative purchasing program (280, or 63.9 percent reported that they did). Our review indicates that, in fact, a number of service agencies at the present time apparently limit their efforts here to the sponsorship of a single product cooperative. However, a much larger number administer cooperative purchasing programs that include a wide variety of products. Some of the most common products included in either single or multiple cooperative purchasing programs include: audiovisual supplies and equipment, computer components and peripherals, copiers, office and school supplies, custodial equipment and supplies, and school cafeteria commodities and equipment. Some ESAs have ventured into purchasing utilities such as electric power on a regional basis. These examples provide some insight into the extensive involvement of service agencies in efforts to enhance the organizational and management capacity of schools and school districts in their service region.

Table 7.1

*Results of AESA Survey of Member Agencies Offering
Administrating/Management Services, 1999-2000*

(N = 438)

Program/Service[1] Category	Number of Agencies Offering Services	Percent of Agencies Offering Services	Rank
Cooperative purchasing services (product not specified)	280	63.9	1
Computer services	263	60.0	2
Fiscal planning	234	53.4	3
Audiovisual repair services	193	44.5	4
Personnel recruitment and screening services	186	42.5	5
Special needs student transportation services	153	34.9	6
Insurance planning	152	34.7	7
Teacher/administrator credentialing services	147	33.6	8
Shared staff planning and administrative services	141	32.2	9
Safety risk planning	135	30.8	10
Fingerprinting services	132	30.1	11
Management planning	110	25.1	12
School district organization planning	110	25.1	12
Energy management planning	104	23.7	14
Maintenance management planning	102	23.3	15
Program auditing services	101	23.1	16

Source: Membership Survey, 1999-2000, Association of Educational Service Agencies. Arlington, VA (unpublished).
Note
[1]The 16 program/service categories were established in the survey instrument that was finalized after two rounds of field-tests. A small number of respondents identified a program or service not included in one of the 16 categories. Forty-three respondents identified "other" (see Table 7.2).

Table 7.2

Illustrative Examples of Programs and Services That Address the Organizational and Management Capacity of Schools/Districts

- Planning Programs/Services
  - Food services planning
  - School-community strategic planning
  - School communications planning
  - Facility heating/cooling planning
  - Management systems analysis and design planning
- Financial Programs/Services
  - Financial accounting services
  - Budget analysis services
  - Property inventory/accounting services
  - Workers' compensation claims adjudication services
  - Disbursement of state aid services
- Cooperative Purchasing Programs
  - Consumable paper products
  - Audiovisual supplies and equipment
  - Technology supplies and equipment
  - Art, music, science, and athletic supplies and equipment
  - Natural gas, electric, and fuel oil products
  - School lunch commodities
- Other
  - Drug/alcohol testing services
  - Crisis intervention services
  - Bus routing services
  - Home school permit services
  - State and federal legislative monitoring services
  - Enrollment projections
  - Legal services
  - Medicare/Medicaid reimbursement services
  - Printing and production services
  - Adjudication of school district boundary changes
  - Acquisition of school building construction, repair, and demolition permits
  - Operation of school elections
  - Regional substitute teacher pool
  - Scheduling regional interscholastic, athletic events and assignment of officials for these events
  - Data processing services (e.g., student scheduling and attendance, fiscal management, property inventory)
  - Regional special students transportation services
  - Coordination of business-education alliances

Examples of Support Programs

A brief description of some promising organizational and management support programs and services follows. The examples cited were selected from a large potential candidate pool and are included to illustrate several key points, including:

♦ Ways by which service agencies in both metropolitan and non-metropolitan settings strengthen critical school and school district management support systems, and the role played by the state in providing incentives to engage in such efforts;

♦ Ways that a service agency, whether serving either a metropolitan or nonmetropolitan area, has enhanced the ability of its clients and customers to leverage their existing financial resources;

♦ Ways that a state network functions in a systemic manner to provide management support services to assure a degree of equity for students in all districts.

The decision to make use of these three categories to organize the programming description was clearly an arbitrary one. So too is the placement of an illustration in one category as opposed to another. For example, cooperating purchasing can be used as an illustration of how a program activity enhances the management support system of schools/school districts (e.g., the likely greater ability to develop detailed and accurate bid specifications, one of the critical steps for the purchase of products), but also serves as an example of how an ESA-provided service contributes to the ability of schools/school districts to better leverage existing financial resources.

The examples cited include individual service agency programs and services and those of an entire state network as well. The brief descriptions were taken from either the 2000-01 or 2001-02 annual reports of the agencies.

Strengthening Management Support Systems

Educational services agencies are deeply engaged in the provision of programs and services designed to strengthen the management support systems of schools/school districts. In some cases their involvement in a program area is mandated by statute or administrative rule. In other cases, it represents a response to the decisions reached by advisory groups representing schools/school districts served by the agency.

Eight different examples of ancillary services are described below. Together, they illustrate the diverse ways that service agencies provide assistance in strengthening the management support systems of schools/school districts that they serve.

1. Otsego Northern Catskills BOCES (Stamford, NY) collaborates with another BOCES in the provision of a Policy Update Service to schools/school districts in the two service regions. The program has three major components: the provision of abstracts of the latest state and federal mandates, state and federal laws and regulations; sample policy statements; and, technical assistance for those districts interested in crafting their own policy statements based on the experience of others.

2. Educational Service District 112 (Vancouver, WA) provides at-cost construction management services to school districts, serving as the school district's representative on construction projects. The ESA also provides comprehensive business management services to small and rural districts in its service area. A school district can purchase up to three days on-site services per week.

3. Jefferson-Lewis-Hamilton-Herkimer-Oneida BOCES (Watertown, NY) offers a Field Service Negotiations service whereby the BOCES will provide local school districts a range of technical assistance on various phases of the negotiation process, as well as serving as spokesperson for the school district's negotiating team through the process.

4. Grant Wood Area Education Agency 10 (Cedar Rapids, IA) offers local districts a communications audit, a comprehensive assessment of the ways that a district provides information to and receives information from its public.

5. Region IV Education Service Center (Houston, TX), through its Financial and Administrative Services Department, provides comprehensive financial services to 17 charter schools. These services include: accounts payable, payroll, general accounting, federal funds and grants accounting, and budget planning. Professional development training for charter school financial administrators is also provided.

6. First District Regional Educational Service Agency (Brooklet, GA) features an Environmental Services Program. Included in this program are: asbestos awareness training, assistance to districts in complying with provisions of the Americans With Disabilities Act, testing of underground storage tanks, radon and lead testing, and sick building syndrome testing.

7. Mid-Ohio Educational Service Center (Mansfield, OH) provides a variety of printing services to its member districts, including: production of newsletters, brochures and miscellaneous forms, lamination services, and poster printing.

8. Arrowhead Area Education Agency 5 (Fort Dodge, IA) offers a Data Management Program designed to improve the management and use of data in all areas of decision-making. Every administrator, teacher, and student in its service region has 24-hour access from school or home, or other remote locations, to over 10 online databases. In addition, the agency provides $500 for each school facility toward the purchase of any other online database product that is included in the statewide cooperative purchasing proposal.

We repeat an often-stated qualification to these examples. It is not suggested that these are the only service agencies providing these services. They are identified merely as illustrations of the wide range of administrative services provided by ESAs throughout the country.

Leveraging Financial Resources

Service agencies assist schools/school districts not only in the provision of programs and services that strengthen their management support systems, but also in their ability to have a direct impact on the financial resources available to constituent districts.

Presented in Table 7.3 are examples of the publicly reported cost savings for management support services provided by an individual educational service agency. The method used by each agency to compute the cost savings is not established. However, it is to be stressed that the savings are reported in the annual

Table 7.3

Examples of Publicly Reported Annual Cost Savings on Management Support Services Provided by Individual ESA Cooperative Purchasing Programs

State	Educational Service Agency and Reporting Period	Publicly Reported Cost Savings to Schools/Districts	Principal Product(s) or Service(s)
KY	Kentucky Educational Development Corporation, Ashland (1996-2001)	$2,000,000	Workers' compensation premiums
NY	Ulster County BOCES, New Paltz, (2000-01)	60,601	Custodial supplies
PA	Bucks County Intermediate Unit 22, Doylestown (2001-02)	720,064	Cafeteria food items, audiovisual supplies, fuel oils, unleaded gas & diesel oil
WV	Regional Educational Service Agency II, Huntington (2001-02)	60,000	Instructional, custodial, computer supplies/ equipment
NE	Educational Service Unit 14, Sidney (2001-02)	15,800 18,800	Custodial supplies Food products
PA	Colonial Intermediate Unit 20, Easton (2000-01)	149,000	Duplicating paper & janitorial supplies
IN	Region 8 Educational Service Center of Northeast Indiana, Markle (2001-02)	6,500,000	Cafeteria supplies
IA	Arrowhead Area Education Agency, Fort Dodge (2000-01)	124,334 80,359 437,379 108,078 991,753	Food products Media materials Computer software Computer hardware Miscellaneous products
TX	Region IV Education Service Center, Houston (2001-02)	2,400,540	Furniture, office supplies, technology equipment

reports of the agencies, a document ordinarily disseminated to member local school districts, the media, and to the state education agency. Pressure for credibility of these claims to be accurate seems assured. Individual service agencies also use other approaches to illustrate how they assist schools/school districts in leveraging their existing resources and in realizing economies in other ways. In contrast to the reports of the examples cited in Table 7.3, some annual reports of service agencies establish the formula used to compute how these savings, or what is commonly referred to as "value-added" benefits, are arrived at.

For example, the East Central Educational Service Center (Connersville, IN) first identifies the total dollar value of all of its services, then subtracts the total membership fees paid by member schools/school districts. The difference of these two figures is called net value and/or savings. In 2001-02 the net value and/or savings to the membership totaled $2,859,575.84. This figure covers all programs and services of the agency for that school year, instructional as well as management support.

Region IV Education Service Center (Houston, TX) has for several years provided each of the districts in its service region an annual report on the added-value each district gains from the participation of its teachers and administrators in Region IV professional development activities. The formula used in 2001-02 to compute district savings was as follows:

Estimated cost to participate in a Region IV professional development training (average training period of 3 days):
Registration $75, travel $54, meal(s) $30—total $159
Estimated cost to participate in a commercially produced professional development training (for the same average training period of 3 days):
Hotel $210, registration $600, travel $200, meal(s) $75—total $1,085

The difference between the estimated cost to participate in a Region IV training program and that of a commercially produced program is then computed for each district's participation.

Using this method, Region IV estimated that its professional development training in 2001-02 provided $52,202,324 in added value to the school districts in its service area. Of interest, the very smallest enrollment district, one with only 117 students, received $48,152 in added value through the participation of its eight staff members in Region IV professional development activities. The largest district, Houston Independent School District, with 210,993 students, received over eight million dollars ($8,271,958) in added value as a result of the participation of staff members in the professional development efforts of Region IV.

The formula used to compute cost savings to schools and school districts through participation in Region IV's cooperative purchasing program is similar to that employed by other service agencies. Here the agency reduces each product purchased 25 percent over the average catalogue price for the product, then adds an additional one percent savings accruing to a school and school district resulting from Region IV's assumption of a number of the management functions (e.g., development of specifications, development of bids, review of vendors) that would ordinarily be assumed by the participating organizations in the cooperative.

Still other service agencies across the country chose to emphasize the financial benefits of their programs and services in other ways. Two strategies are of interest:

♦   Educational Service Agency 112 (Vancouver, WA) established in its 2002 annual report that each dollar the state invests ($490,000) in the service agency generates $80.22 in services to schools.

♦   The Education Cooperative (Wellesley, MA) established in its 2001-02 annual report that its student programs alone saved participant districts $3,039,287. The method used to compute this cost-saving was straightforward: number of students enrolled in a program times the difference between the service center's tuition costs and the average cost of a similar private program.

A number of state network service agencies have established a statewide cooperative purchasing program. Examples of five such efforts are presented in Table 7.4. The principal items of most include products for use in the instructional program of a school as well as items used in the noninstructional components of a school.

Relatively current data on the total dollars saved through the cooperative purchasing activities of an entire state network are available for the Iowa Area

Table 7.4
Examples of Statewide Cooperative Purchasing Programs
Sponsored by a State Network of Agencies

State	Title of Cooperative	Principal Product(s)
IA	Cooperative Purchasing Program Sponsor: Area Education Agencies	Media & technology resources (materials, equipment & supplies), food commodities, office supplies
NE	Statewide Cooperative Purchasing Program Sponsor: Educational Service Units	Technology equipment & supplies, office-school furniture, school lunch commodities, paper supplies
PA	Pennsylvania Energy Consortium Sponsor: Pennsylvania Association of Intermediate Unit Administrators	Energy (electricity)
PA	Pennsylvania Education Joint Purchasing Council	Classroom consumables, food, maintenance supplies, heating supplies
WA	Washington School Information Processing Cooperative Sponsor: Eight of the nine Educational Service Districts in the state network	Computer equipment (notebook, printers, servers, desktop software)

Education Agencies in 2000-01. All 15 agencies in the network were requested to submit to the state dollar savings for six cooperative purchasing programs. The results were: food cooperative, $124,334; media materials $80,359; computer software $437,379; computer hardware, $108,078; reference materials $2,945,083; and other products $991,753. Total dollar savings publicly reported for 2000-01 for the state totaled $14,202,958 (*Iowa AA Cooperative Purchasing, 2000-01*).

Some service agencies offer a cooperative purchasing program that serves both school districts and other governmental entities such as public and private schools and postsecondary institutions, municipalities, and county and state government agencies. One such cooperative is the Texas Cooperative Purchasing Network (TCPN), administered by Region IV Education Service Center. Many of the state's 20 service agencies reportedly make use of the TCPN in the administration of their individual cooperative purchasing initiatives.

Another recent development is the formation of the Association of Education Purchasing Agencies (AEPA). This organization, formed in 2001-02, is made up of representatives of cooperatives from 20 states, most of them staff members from educational service agencies in their respective states. All multi-state vendors must be fully bonded and meet the bidding requirements of the respective states. Participating vendors include several manufacturers of large-scale products not generally included in cooperative purchasing programs, such as vehicles, playground equipment, and modular buildings and portable classrooms.

Activities of Statewide Networks

A number of statewide networks of service agencies are also active in the provision of management support services, other than the previously cited sponsorship of a statewide cooperative purchasing program. Descriptions of the programs that are for the most part of a single agency in the network are provided below. While the specifics of other agencies in the same network might vary somewhat, all tend to include the core features cited.

1. Region IV Education Service Center (Houston, TX), like the other 19 centers in the state, offers a service to address a state requirement that all local school districts periodically be subjected to a DEC, a district effectiveness and compliance on-site review by an external panel. The DEC is a process used by the Texas Education Agency to review a local district's compliance with state and federal requirements for special programs that in 2002-03 numbered 17. A DEC on-site review assesses whether or not a district's procedures are in compliance and also examines whether the programs are effective.

Technical assistance provided by Region IV includes: provision of training on the DEC process and programs, review of student folders and district self-analysis documents, and the conduct of mock interviews with district personnel and parents who are likely to be interviewed during the site visit.

The 20 service centers in the state were assigned this role as part of the decentralization of the state education agency, a process that began in the mid-

1990s and moved a number of former field operations of the state agency to the service centers.

2. Regional Education Service Agency IV (Summersville, WV) is one of the state's eight service agencies serving as a central player in the state management information system. RESA IV makes the following eight products available to the county school systems in its service area: Office Vision, Student Management System, Financial Management System, Employee Management System, Human Resources Management System, Warehouse Inventory Management System, Substitute Tracking System, and Fixed Assets Inventory System. Agency staff also provide technical assistance to the county school systems in the use of the various data systems.

3. Region 19 Education Service Center (El Paso, TX) serves as the liaison between the local school districts and the Texas Education Agency for implementation of the Public Education Information Management System (PEIMS). PEIMS is the state's primary program for the collection of data on all school districts in the state, such as: student attendance and enrollment, staff certification, staff positions, staff salaries, and financial information. The data stored in PEIMS are combined with data contained in other data systems to determine the standing of each local district, and each campus, relative to the state's accreditation system and funding eligibility. For each district and campus, Region 19 also disaggregates student performance data on the state's testing program. It also provides technical assistance in the interpretation of student performance data and the use of data to improve teaching and learning.

The role played by Region 19 and the other service agencies in the state with regard to PEIMS is another outgrowth of the mid-1990s decentralization of selected field operations of the state agency and their assignment to the service centers.

4. Washington School Information Processing Cooperative. The WSIPC is a cooperative composed of eight of the state's nine Educational Service Districts. WSIPC provides a number of products that enhance the management support systems of the state's local districts. One of these is the Human Resources and Payroll System, a system that tracks employee payroll and personnel information (e.g., salaries, deductions, and benefits). The system is fully integrated with another of WSIPC's products, its Fiscal System. In addition, employee data can then be transferred electronically to the state retirement system and the state education agency. The second WSIPC product cited is the Student Information System, which allows local school officials to enter and access student information (e.g., demographics, schedules, grades, special programs).

5. Southern Westchester BOCES (Rye Brook, NY). This service agency is part of the Lower Hudson Regional Information Center (LHRIC). The LHRIC is one of 12 centers in the state that are configured around the boundaries of the state's system of educational service agencies. Each center provides both educational and administrative services to local school districts. The administrative services include school district student and financial data and test scoring services.

6. Grant Wood Area Education Agency 10 (Cedar Rapids, IA), like all other service agencies in the state network, functions under a state accreditation system. One of the accreditation standards that must be met is the requirement that the agency provide technical assistance to school districts in school-community planning. One of the major efforts undertaken by the agency in this area is assistance provided to rural school districts and the rural communities with ongoing technical support to school and community leaders that encourages them to engage in strategic planning for the future of the school district and community.

BROAD PROGRAMMING PATTERNS

Virtually all educational service agencies across the country, irrespective of type, Type A: Special District ESA or Type C: Cooperative ESA, are engaged in programming activities that address the infrastructure needs of schools/school districts in their service regions. Some of the more comprehensive service agencies offer what amounts to a smorgasbord of programs and services. This characterization would especially hold for those activities designed to enhance the organizational and management capacity dimension of the infrastructure of schools/school districts.

However, a number of board patterns or tendencies appear to be present regarding service agency involvement in infrastructure support and improvement. Some of the most significant of these fall into three areas:

♦ Differences in the nature of service agency involvement in the typical phases of program development
♦ Variations in the recipients of programs and services
♦ Variations in the financing of programs and services

It is to be noted that in these three areas, some differences exist in the tendencies of Type A: Special District ESAs and those of Type C: Special District ESAs. However, as cautioned regularly on these pages, care should be exercised here and elsewhere in placing too much emphasis on the type of service agency. That is, there is no pure type A or type C but rather certain types of agencies that tend to exhibit certain governance, organizational and programming patterns.

Differences in Involvement in Program Planning and Implementation

Substantial variations are present in service agency involvement in the typical phases of programs and services designed to enhance the infrastructure requirements of schools and school districts. Moreover, the nature of service agency involvement not only varies by type of program, but along a host of other factors as well. Additionally, and also complicating the difficulty of profiling service agency practices, it is a common practice for an ESA to initially assume all start-up and implementation activities associated with a program only at some later time to then spin off one or more or all aspects of program planning and development to schools and school districts, at their request and as preplanned, once a program is fully operational. For purposes of this discussion, we define program planning and development as consisting of the six conventional phases shown in Figure 7.2.

The previously described illustrative examples of promising practices of service agency involvement in addressing both dimensions of the infrastructure issue—the adequacy of physical facilities and the adequacy of the organizational and management capacity of a school and school district—were presented in part to provide a limited description of differences in the nature of service agencies involvement. Certain tendencies can be identified concerning this important role played by service agencies.

Sponsorship of specialized facilities. A number of tendencies or patterns concerning service agency involvement in the sponsorship of specialized facilities (e.g., schools for students with special needs, regional vocational/technical schools, regional alternative secondary schools, and regional academic magnet schools) appear to be evident. The functions of these facilities have already been discussed in previous chapters.

Service agency involvement in specialized facilities typically means that these agencies have primary responsibility for the administration of all six phases of program planning and development—from the conduct of need assessments through the evaluation phase.

However, it is a common practice that program planning and policy development be shared between the governing board of a service agency and a separate advisory committee established to provide guidance and oversight for the specialized facility. In the case of a specialized school for students with special needs that typically is financed in part by federal and/or state funds, the composition of an advisory committee must, by state and/or federal regulation, include parent representatives. Advisory groups appointed to help set policy and program direction for a regional vocational/technical school, almost always the recipient of federal and/or state funds, must also include noneducators in order to be in compliance with federal and/or state regulations.

Involvement in management support programs. Discernable patterns are clearly present in the nature of service agency involvement in the provision of management support programs and services. Though here again it is to be stressed that while there are usually variations among individual service agencies in a given state and between one state and another, certain tendencies appear to hold.

Service agencies tend to assume primary responsibility for all phases of program planning and development for many of the illustrative examples of the management support programs and services cited in Table 7.1. This is especially true where a program or service consists of the employment by the service agency of a specialist in a particular area who then either provides technical assistance to schools and school districts which request assistance (e.g., food service planning, school-community strategic planning) or actually conducts the program or service on behalf of participating schools and school districts (e.g., bus routing services, state and federal legislative monitoring services).

Service agency involvement in some of the more highly specialized programs and services that are ordinarily outside the field of education (e.g., legal

Figure 7.2
Conventional Phases of Program Planning and Development

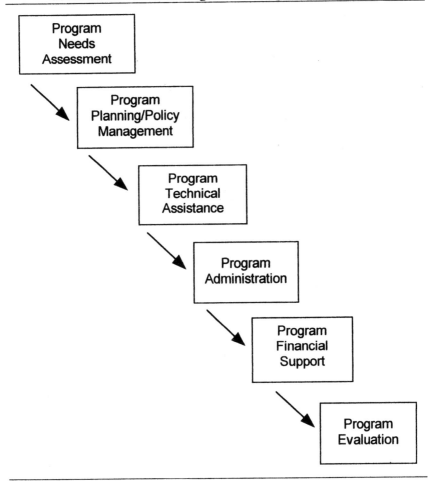

services) or, in addition, requires both specialized knowledge and facilities (e.g., drug/alcohol testing) is typically limited to contracting with a third-party who then provides the service.

Variations in the Recipients of Programs and Services

A number of patterns appear to be present in this, the second of the three approaches used to distinguish some of the programming patterns in the diverse educational service agency population in the United States.

If there is one pattern that is more pronounced than any other, it is that rural and small, and small suburban schools and school districts clearly have been and continue to be the major participants, and thus the principal benefactors, of efforts by service agencies to enhance the infrastructure of schools and school districts. Rural and small school districts (generally defined by the U. S. Department of Education as having fewer than 600 pupils) frequently lack the fiscal resources and/or number of appropriate students to justify creating a specialized facility for students with special needs. They also frequently are in need of both the fiscal and human resources to enhance the capacity of their management support system that is critical for a strong instructional program. Likewise, small suburban district participation is ordinarily driven by a realization that both lower costs and quality of programs and services are possible by joining neighboring systems in collaborative approaches to common needs.

While rural and small schools and school districts and suburban systems have historically been most active in their participation in most of the management support programs and services offered by educational service agencies, larger enrollment size districts increasingly are more prone to participate in those programs and services where significant cost savings can be realized (e.g., cooperative purchasing) and/or where they have had a loss of a management support service due to a reduction-in-force that caused the elimination of an existing management staff specialization.

Variations in the Financing of Programs

Financing special schools. Most service agencies do not posses independent taxing authority. As established in Chapter Two only a small number of state networks, most of them Type A: Special Districts ESAs, are statutorily authorized to levy a tax for support of their programming and capital improvement requirements. It follows, then, that a significant number of two of what have been in the past the most prevalent of the six types of special schools—those for students with special needs and those for students pursuing vocational/technical programs—are to be found in three of the states where the service agencies have the statutory authority to independently levy taxes:

♦ The California County Offices of Education
♦ The Michigan Intermediate School Districts
♦ The Oregon Education Service Districts

Another state network, the 38 New York Boards of Cooperative Educational Services (BOCES) is also deeply engaged in the administration of these two types of special schools. Though without the power to tax, the BOCES, subject to approval by component districts and the state commissioner of education, may purchase or construct facilities. The governing board of the service agency and those of component school districts may enter into an agreement with the State Dormitory Authority to acquire facilities. Costs for the acquisition are shared between the component districts and the BOCES, with the costs of the latter reimbursed by the state (Article 40.11 and 13, pp. 397-398).

Also, those agencies that are the recipients of state financial assistance for operational purposes do not receive funds for capital acquisitions or improvements. It should come as no surprise, then, that the result of these two conditions means that the financial support for the acquisition of a majority of special facilities ordinarily administered by a service agency without taxing authority comes from the approval of a special assessment on participating schools for a program offered by the service unit. Membership fees for this purpose, where used, are ordinarily nominal and are generally used to help offset administrative costs for the agency, not underwrite programming costs.

Financing Management Support Services

A number of patterns and tendencies are also discernable with regard to how service agencies are able to fund organizational and management support programs and services.

The Type C: Cooperative ESAs, almost without exception, rely on local funds to cover programming costs, generally in the form of service contracts with schools and school districts that participate in a particular management support program or service. Though not in a majority, some agencies of this type also assess a membership fee as a condition of eligibility to participate, irrespective of enrollment size. The use of a wealth factor, or other measures of ability to pay, to set the membership fee is not a common practice.

As established in Chapter Two, the Type A: Special District ESAs clearly function under a set of more prescriptive statutory guidelines than do Type C: Cooperative ESAs. This situation certainly holds with respect to the funding of most organizational and management support services. A majority of statutes authorize agencies of this type to offer what is frequently referred to as discretionary programs that might be requested by school districts. However, another frequent qualifier is that programs of this type must be self-supporting.

Some service agencies of both types also make use of a number of alternative methods for covering costs for the sponsorship of a management support service, particularly for some of the highly specialized programs. A base fee for participation may be required based on the enrollment size of a school or school district, or an equal assessment of each school district, regardless of size, may be required. As cited earlier, operating costs for two types of special schools in particular—for students with special needs and for students interested in the vocational/technical education—are typically derived in part from targeted federal and/or state funds that a service agency would be eligible to receive by virtue of its assumption of this responsibility formerly assumed by a local school district.

DISCUSSION

What follows are observations concerning the roles played by service agencies in enhancing the two dimensions (physical facilities, human capacity) of the infrastructure requirements of schools and school districts. These are organized around five major themes:

- ◆ Programming changes for the period 1979 to 1999
- ◆ Two primary foci of programs and services
- ◆ Programming consistent with mission
- ◆ The critical role of the state
- ◆ Potential multiple benefits

Programming Changes 1979-1999

Both constancy and change seemingly characterize the programming efforts of service agencies designed to strengthen the infrastructure requirements of schools and school districts. This proposition is supported in part when comparing the results of the two known major attempts to profile the programming activities of service agencies that were undertaken over the past several decades:

♦   The 1979 report by Stephens (*Education Service Agencies: Status and Trends* 1979) that included a description of the facility practices and management support services, as well and other programs offered, and the governance and organizational features of 326 agencies operating in 26 states

♦   The previously cited 1999 unpublished survey conducted by the Association of Educational Service Agencies that also reported on the programs and services offerings of 438 member organizations located in 30 states

A service agency can perform a critical service for its component schools and school districts by assuming responsibility for the administration and operation of special schools if doing so can result in both educational and economic benefits. However, there have also been significant changes in the nature of special schools maintained by service agencies. For example, in the late 1970s, many service agencies sponsored special schools for several categories of the students with less severe special needs. In more recent years, changes in federal and state regulations (e.g., the movement to teach handicapped students in a regular classroom) have meant that service agencies are more likely to serve the most severely physically and mentally handicapped students. Moreover, the other major types of special schools currently administered by service agencies are the outcome of new policy pressures facing schools and school districts that were generally not major priorities several decades ago (e.g., alterative schools, charter schools, math/science magnet schools, preschools).

Constancy and change also seemingly hold true for management support services offered by service agencies over time. Some of the more consistent program areas include: cooperative purchasing, data processing services, financial consulting services, certification services, and federal and state legislative monitoring services. These staple programming areas have been expanded to include a heavy emphasis on the provision of technical assistance in a range of areas designed to assist schools and school districts in their own capacity building competencies and skills. Other changes are also the direct result of new pressures that simply did not loom large on the radar screens of school and school district decision makers in the late 1970s. Examples here include: computer repair services, safety risk planning, fingerprinting services, and crisis intervention planning.

Two Primary Foci

It is useful to view the various activities of service agencies being of two types, and, further, that it is important to distinguish the two. On the one hand, many of the efforts to address both dimensions of the infrastructure requirements of schools and school districts are intended to result in an enhancement of the organizational capacity of schools and school districts. The construct organizational capacity has of course been defined in numerous ways by scholars in organizational studies. We define the construct here to mean that *a school or school district possesses the human and fiscal resources necessary to fulfill local, state, and federal expectations held for them.*

This broad definition of organizational capacity is consistent with the prevailing perspective in the literature that there are several critical dimensions of a school and school district's capacity that must be present if effective teaching and learning are to occur. These include fiscal capacity, commonly defined to mean an educational organization's access to sufficient revenues to carry out its obligations to its students and parents, staff, and the public. Certainly another critical dimension of capacity has to do with teacher capacity, itself multidimensional, a point stressed by Massell (1998) who, based on a study of how eight states have developed strategies for building local district capacity, argued that the capacity of educational organizations that are critical for supporting improvements in teaching and learning are of seven major types that she then grouped into two categories. The first of these focused on classroom-level capacities: teacher knowledge and skills; student motivation and readiness to learn; and, curriculum materials for students and teachers. The second group stressed school, district, and state organizational capacities such as: quantity and types of people supporting the classroom; the quantity and quality of interaction within and among organizational levels; material resources such as adequate facilities and access to technology; and, organization and allocation of school and district resources.

Therefore, it is important to view service agency involvement in infrastructure improvement efforts that enhance the capacity building capabilities of schools and school districts. The construct capacity building is another of those popular terms used in different ways in the professional literature in various disciplines. Here we define the term to mean:

The ability of the staff and policy and decision makers of a school or school district to acquire the competencies and skills that are essential to deliver a quality educational program.

The principal ways that service agencies function in addressing both the organizational capacity of schools and school districts, and how they assist in capacity building efforts are summarized in Figure 7.3.

Programming Consistent with Mission

At first glance one could view the diverse programming activities of service agencies that are intended to assist in strengthening the infrastructure of schools and school districts as an example of a type of educational organization that is undisciplined, one lacking a "north star" to guide its programming decisions. It is true that great diversity certainly characterizes service agency programming, particularly in the second dimension of the construct infrastructure, management support services. However, such an assessment would be incorrect.

Figure 7.3
**Distinguishing the Two Primary Foci of ESA Programs
and Services That Address the Infrastructure Requirements
of Schools and School Districts**

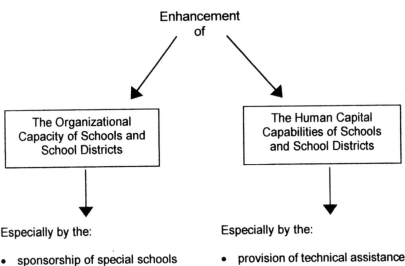

Enhancement
of

| The Organizational Capacity of Schools and School Districts | The Human Capital Capabilities of Schools and School Districts |

Especially by the:

- sponsorship of special schools

- direct delivery of programs for special needs students

- direct provision of cost saving management support programs and services

Especially by the:

- provision of technical assistance in planning needed management support service areas

- provision of training in needed management support service areas

This is so for several interrelated reasons.

As discussed in Chapters 2 and 3, statutory authorization for the creation of Type A: Special District ESAs, the dominant form of service units, almost without exception includes certain common expectations. Though the language may vary, the expectations of the state call for the service agencies to: (1) promote efficiency in the delivery of services by the service agencies; (2) promote the efficiency of school district programming; (3) deliver programs that are effective; and, (4) promote equity in the state system of elementary secondary education. Most Type C: Cooperative ESAs have been established by general state statutes that authorize intergovernmental agreements between two or more school districts with the intent that granting such authority would facilitate the achievement of policy goals of efficiency, effectiveness, and equity in the programming efforts of schools and school districts. As a general rule, intergovernmental agreements that have been sanctioned in most states for several decades allow schools and school districts, as well as other governmental jurisdictions, to jointly offer programs, use facilities, and employ staff. There-fore, it can be argued that the involvement of service agencies of both types in delivering numerous management support services merely represents one more way that these organizations attempt to address state expectations held for them.

Relatedly, though less common, a fairly significant number of service agencies also must be in compliance with statutory requirements that they be re-sponsive to requests from schools and school districts. These are frequently called "discretionary" programs and services, or in some cases by individual agencies, "enterprise" services that are beyond statutorily prescribed core ser-vices. Some statutory pronouncements of this sort are general in nature. For ex-ample:

- ◆ Texas Regional Education Service Centers—may offer any service re-quested and purchased by any school district or campus in the state (Chapter 8.053. Additional services, p. 3).
- ◆ Georgia Regional Educational Service Agencies—may provide any additional service and assistance to its member school systems as de-termined by the board of control (HB 1187. A plus Education Reform Act of 2000, p. 83).

Statutory pronouncements in some other states concerning how a service agency is to respond to requests for a management support service, as well in some cases, to any other type of service, are more directive. For example:

- ◆ Iowa Area Education Agencies—shall provide services for costs re-quested by 60 percent of districts or districts representing 60 percent of enrollment (Chapter 273.7. Additional services, p. 2329).
- ◆ New York Boards of Cooperative Educational Services—in addition to providing specified "aidable" core services, they may offer other ser-vices if requested by two or more districts and approved by the state commissioner (Article 40, Boards of Cooperative Educational Ser-vices, p. 375).
- ◆ Oregon Educational Service Districts—all optional programs, called resolution programs, can be offered when approved by 2/3 of compo-nent districts that shall enroll at least a majority of students (Senate Bill 259, Section 5(41), p. 3).

Critical Role of the State

The critical role that the state can play in facilitating the provision of pro-gramming efforts by service agencies that are designed to enhance the infra-structure requirements of schools and school districts is indisputable. Those states like Michigan and New York that make provisions for their state network of service agencies to acquire resources for the acquisition of specialized schools to serve the educational needs of special populations of students, other than by an added special assessment placed on school districts, have experienced what would appear to be great success. For example, surely there is little argu-ment that the quality of the educational experiences of the thousands of students who have passed through the regional special education schools administered over the years by the Boards of Cooperative Educational Services in New York have been enhanced because of the actions taken by state and local interests to insure that a definite funding process was in place. Similarly, the thousands of students over the years who have attended regional vocational/technical schools administered by the service agencies in Michigan have benefited because of the foresight of the policy communities in that state in granting the agencies the ability to levy a tax to support the acquisition and maintenance of the facilities upon approval of the voters in the area.

Unfortunately, most service agencies do not possess taxing authority for the acquisition of facilities, for capital improvements, or for any purpose. Moreover, as cited earlier, capital improvement funds are not part of most state aid formulas for those service agencies that receive state aid.

One possible explanation for the practice of most states in limiting the ways that a service agency can ordinarily acquire resources for capital improvements is that historically most states have also not been active in providing state resources for the capital improvement programs of local school districts. Though this tradition is beginning to change, it is still not widespread. Rossmiller (2001) cites as an encouraging recent development that bodes well for local districts, the practice of some state legislatures appropriating funds for constructing new facilities or retrofitting existing facilities in especially poor districts in response to existing or potential finance litigation. He cites as examples both Abbot v. Burke, a 1998 decision handed down by the New Jersey Supreme Court that required the state to pay for needed facilities in 28 low wealth districts; and, Roosevelt Elementary School District v. Bishop, an earlier 1994 decision by the Arizona Supreme Court that required the state to formulate a program of aid that would assure all districts in the state have adequate facilities (p. 20).

Whether or not the handful of successful state legislation or judicial decisions will become a major trend is uncertain. However, should this occur it is highly likely that this would first result in the appropriation of funds for basic facilities to support the general student population, not for the acquisition of specialized facilities for special needs students.

Another possible explanation that is particularly germane to state networks of Type A: Special District ESAs is that state interests in many states over the years have regularly raised concerns regarding the efficacy of the number of units in the state network. This is particularly true for state networks formed in the 1960s and 1970s that replaced older county offices of education. One of the main arguments commonly advanced by those who raise questions along these lines is that the state network needs to be realigned to conform to changes that have occurred since the initial formation of the units (e.g., declining rural population in many parts of most states, the development of a statewide technology infrastructure). Realignment generally has come to mean a reduction in the number of units in a state network. The erection of a special school could potentially complicate this policy goal.

The general lack of state incentives that would facilitate greater service agency involvement in the provision of management support services is in many ways an even greater puzzle. Clearly the state has a vital interest in the organizational capacity of every school and school district in the state system of elementary-secondary education. So, too, does the state have a similar vital interest in promoting the capacity-building capabilities of every school and school district. Though service agencies are only one resource state interests can utilize in any strategy designed to strengthen schools and school districts, they are generally more accessible to local schools and districts than other policy options, an increasingly recognized important consideration in any meaningful state intervention strategy. Moreover, many examples are available, some of which have been demonstrated here in Figure 7.4, that illustrate the cost savings that flow from service agency programming in the provision of management support services.

It is positive that some states have made it legally permissible for service agencies to engage in management support services. However, it is also necessary that states subsidize, not every program or service that school A or school B might possibly want, or possibly even be in need of, but those programs identified by consensus as critical for the support of an effective educational program. The current widespread practice that forces service agencies to provide all of their management support services through fees and assessments can result in economies of scale for those who participate. However, a fee assessment for services frequently hurts the very schools and school districts that might benefit most from participation, especially the rural and small districts and fiscally poor urban and suburban systems.

The requirement that some Type C: Cooperative ESAs charge a membership fee to cover administrative costs of a service agency in addition to a service fee can also be a hardship on the very type of school and school district that can benefit most from participation. A 1998 report by the Colorado State Auditor's Office of the administrative fee structures used by the state's 18 Boards of Cooperative Educational Services (Boards of Cooperative Educational Services: Performance Audit 1998) revealed that five different approaches were used:

- ◆ five charge each member a flat fee;
- ◆ seven charge a flat fee to cover up to 75 percent of their administrative costs with a per pupil assessment for the remaining portion;
- ◆ two charge their administrative costs based on current or historical pupil counts;
- ◆ one splits its administrative costs evenly among participating districts; and,
- ◆ another secures funds from special education grants and district special education assessments (pp. 39-40).

In a comparison of a sample of six BOCES, those that charge a flat fee to cover all or a majority of their administrative costs penalized school districts with smaller enrollments in that they are required to pay a disproportionate share of the costs, as shown in Figure 7.4.

Figure 7.4
COLORADO BOCES
Per Pupil Administrative Charges for Fiscal Year 1998

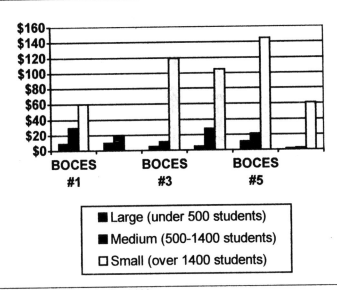

■ Large (under 500 students)

■ Medium (500-1400 students)

□ Small (over 1400 students)

Source: Office of the State Auditor 1998.

Potential Multiple Benefits

It is important to stress that many individual management support services offered by service agencies potentially result in multiple benefits for schools/ school districts. One example is used to illustrate the point that a single program or service can produce more than one benefit.

As established previously, the sponsorship of one or more cooperative purchasing programs is one of the dominant program functions of service agencies across the country. This holds true regardless of type, Type A: Special District or Type C: Cooperative. The comprehensiveness of the products offered varies from one service unit to another, although the management support programs and services included in a cooperative under the auspices of a statewide network tend to be uniform. There are also variations in the nature of service agency involvement in the six conventional phases of program planning and development used here to establish patterns in the practices of the agencies.

The potential multiple benefits occurring to schools and school districts that participate in a management support program or service offered by a service agency-sponsored cooperative would likely realize, at a minimum, two major advantages, cost-savings and enhanced quality of the program or services.

The claim that cost-savings are highly likely for individual schools and districts is supported given the obvious financial gains that are to be realized through bulk purchases of, for example: school lunch commodities, instructional supplies and equipment; consumable paper products, or the employment of specialists in, for example, workers' compensation adjudication. The claim that involvement in a cooperative results in the likely enhancement of the quality of a product for many participating schools and school districts is based in large measure on the manner in which most cooperative purchasing programs are typically administered. Local school and school district staff members are ordinarily involved in all phases of the purchasing cycle, particularly the critical phases of needs assessment, development of a product or service specifications, and the evaluation of a product or service. It is generally acknowledged that the quality of decisions arrived at through the deliberations of multiple stakeholders sharing a common need is ordinarily superior to those that involved only one or limited viewpoints.

SUMMARY

One of the major missions defined for service agencies in the 1960s and 1970s years was to work with local districts to secure, staff, and equip special facilities for disabled students. In more recent decades the number of special populations has continued to grow: adolescents interested in vocational/technical education, students with high interest and capacity in math and science, preschool age children, adjudicated youth and others. In some instances the service agency serves these young people directly; in others the agency trains staff who do work with a special population.

Another early responsibility of educational service agencies was to coordinate the bidding, purchase, and distribution of products commonly used in all schools, such as paper, pencils, office supplies, buses and food products. These functions have continued to evolve and increase. Now products and services as diverse as insurance coverages of various kinds, energy products, and legal services are now subject to collaborative purchase. Service agencies are also providing expertise to local districts in many areas of school operations including construction, administrative data processing, testing services (data collection, processing, and interpretation), public relations, and other nonacademic functions.

REFERENCES

American Society Civil Engineers. 2001. *Renewing America's infrastructure: A citizen's guide.* Washington, DC: Author.

Association of Educational Service Agencies. *Membership survey: 1999-2000.* Arlington, VA: Author. Unpublished.

Baldwin, F. D. 2000. Infrastructure: Foundations for development. *Appalachia* 33, no. 2(May-August):3.

Cigler, B. A. 1987. Rural infrastructure: Research needs. *The Rural Sociologist* 7, no. 1(January):18-34.

Georgia General Assembly. 2000. HB 1187—A Plus Education Reform Act of 2000.

Hummell-Rossi, B. and Ashdown, J. 2002. The state of cost-benefit and cost-effectiveness analysis in education. *Review of Educational Research* 72, no. 1(Spring):1-30.

Iowa AEA Cooperative Purchasing, 2000-01 Annual Report.

Iowa General Assembly. 1997. Chapter 273.7 Area education agencies.

Levin, H. M. 1983. *Cost-effectiveness: A primer.* Beverly Hills: Sage Publications.

Levin, H. M. and McEwan, P. L. 2002. Cost-effectiveness and education policy, Chapter 1. In *Cost effectiveness and education policy: 2002 yearbook.* American Education Finance Association. Larchmont, NY: Eye On Education, Inc.

Maricopa County Superintendent of Schools. 2001. Retrieved August 10, 2001 from http://www.maricopa.gov/schools/bio.asp.

Massell, D. 1998. *State strategies for building local capacity: Addressing the needs of standard-based reform* (July). Policy Brief RB-25, University of Pennsylvania, Graduate School of Education. Consortium for Policy Research in Education.

New York General Assembly. 1959. Article 40.7d(1). Boards of Cooperative Educational Services.

No Child Left Behind Act of 2001. Pub. L. No. 107-110.

North Central Educational Service District. 1991. *Program cost savings study: July, 1990-June, 1991* (July). Wenatchel, WA: Author.

Office of the State Auditor, State of Colorado. 1998. *Boards of Cooperative Educational Services: Performance audit* (May). Denver, CO: Author.

Oregon Legislative Assembly. 2001. S.B. 259. §5(4).

Pennsylvania Association of Intermediate Unit Executive Directors. 1992. *Report to the Pennsylvania legislature* (November). Author.

Puget Sound Educational Service District 1992. *Cost-benefit study: 1990-1991* (April 11). Burien, WA: Author.

Rice, J. K. 1997. Cost analysis in education: Paradox and possibility. *Educational Evaluation and Policy Analysis* 19, no. 4(Winter):309-317.

Rossmiller, R. A. 2001. Funding in the new millennium. In S. Charkind and W. J. Fowler (Eds.), *Education finance in the new millennium: 2001 yearbook.* Larchmont, NY: American Education Finance Association/ Eye on Education.

Sears, D. W.; Rowley, T. D.; and Reed, J. N. 1990. Infrastructure investment and economic development. In *Infrastructure investment and economic development: Rural strategies for the 1990's* (November):1-18. Washington, DC: United States Department of Agriculture, Economic Research Service, Agriculture and Rural Economy Division.

Southeast Service Cooperative. 1996. *1995-96 annual report.* Rochester, MN: Author.

State of Washington, Legislative Budget Committee. 1995. *Educational service districts: Report 95-8* (February 15):1-16. Olympia, WA: Author.

Stephens, E. R. 1979. *Education service agencies: Status and trends* (June). Burtonsville, MD: Stephens Associates.

Stephens, E. R. 2000. *On the design of the AEA annual progress report and other accreditation-related recommendations* (October). A report to the Iowa Department of Education – AEA Design Team.

Stephens, E. R. and Harmon, H. L. 1996. Cost-analysis studies of programs and services of state networks of ESAs. *Perspectives,* 2(September):7-21.

Texas Education Code. 2001. Chapter 8.053 Regional education service agencies.

U. S. General Accounting Office. 1995. *School facilities: Condition of America's schools* (February). Washington, DC: Author.

U. S. General Accounting Office. 2000. *Condition of America's public school facilities: 1999* (June). Washington, DC: Author.

West Virginia Regional Educational Service Agencies. 1994. *Cost savings programs provided by regional educational service agencies: A report to the state legislature* (pp. 106): Author.

Chapter 8

Strengthening Schools Through ESA Partnerships

The term "partnership" can have several meanings. In a legal sense it refers to a contractual relationship between those engaged in a common enterprise. Metaphorically it can mean a joining of purposes, interests and actions that bind people together in a manner that can be even more energizing than a legal partnership. Such "partnerships" are perhaps more properly defined as collaborations, which Bardach has defined as "any joint activity by two or more agencies that is intended to increase public value by their working together rather than separately" (p. 8). People work together because they want to work together and because they can see the resulting synergy of their joint actions.

Partnerships in the educational environment can be either legal or informal. Sometimes commitments between agencies can be both legal and "spiritual," rooted in the sense of mission that partners may share. The focus in this chapter will be on partnerships that include participation of educational service agencies, whether they serve as the "managing partner" or merely as a participant.

In order to fully understand the complexity of the relationship between educational service agencies and their partners, this chapter will look at both the theory and practice of partnerships. We begin with a history of partnerships between educational institutions and major societal agents (businesses, unions, community agencies). We then look at the research about how successful partnerships are built and sustained as well as weaknesses that are inherent in any partnership. We conclude with summaries of partnerships between educational entities linked by service agencies as well as partnerships with other community groups.

HISTORICAL ROOTS OF PARTNERSHIPS

Hillary Rodham Clinton touched a nerve in the American psyche when, in 1999, she entitled a book with the African expression that "it takes a village" to educate a child. However, this idea had been a core concept of public policy for a long time before her book was published. Schools had a long history of involvement with other entities in the community, often for good, occasionally for ill.

Education's Partnerships with Business

The role of business as a partner of education seems essentially a fresh idea since there have been so many new educational initiatives started by business leaders in the late 20th century as well as newer federal and state-initiated programs that sometimes encourage and occasionally require partnerships between business and educational institutions. It is not. Business has had a role in education practically since the founding of the republic. Horace Mann, in his Herculean effort to bring about common schools for all, argued that business leaders should support publicly funded schools for very practical reasons:

> Finally, in regard to those who possess the largest shares in the stock of worldly goods, could there, in your opinion, be any police so vigilant and effective for the protection of all the rights of person, property and character as such a sound and comprehensive education and training as our system of common schools could be made to impart; and would not the payment of a sufficient tax to make such education and training universal, be the cheapest means of self-protection and insurance. (Cremin 1965)

Business in its largest sense—unions, farmers, tradesmen, and others—have tried to shape education to their own purposes for over a century. Karier (1973) has stated that "American education in general has provided an effective service function to the business community in the training of both producers and consumers. It has also served as the vehicle through which the basic values of a commercial culture are transmitted from generation to generation" (p. 20).

The historical relationship between business and education has not been a one-way street. Since business needed trained workers and since schools needed a place to train young men and women without costly expenditures on facilities and equipment, business sites became a logical training ground for young people seeking the skills to make a living. Karier (1973) asserted that "American industry operated the largest vocational technical-training school in the world" in the 1920s and 30s" (p.20).

The role of business in policy development for elementary and secondary education became far more direct in the last two decades of the 20th century. There is probably no one explanation for the furor that was created in 1983 upon publication of *A Nation at Risk*, the national report on the state of public education commissioned by then Secretary of Education Terrell Bell. However, the economic tribulations that beset America throughout much of the 1970s and early 1980s were undoubtedly a significant contributor to the universal expressions of concern that America's public schools were failing its students and the needs of the country.

The American economy was beset by many difficulties at this time. Perhaps the triggering event of the trauma was the oil crisis precipitated in 1973 by the reduction in oil supplies initiated by the oil producing countries that were members of the OPEC cartel. Reduced supplies of oil and gasoline lead to a sharp increase in the cost of petroleum products, as well as grievously inconvenient long lines at gasoline stations. Since oil and its byproducts are at the core of many commercial services (airlines), manufactured goods (roofing materials), and other essential materials (home heating oil), price increases rippled throughout the economy. This phenomenon had a deadly double barrel effect: a slow-down in economic activity (recession) and inflation because of the competition for scarce energy supplies. This period of "stagflation" was almost unprecedented in American economic history. Prices were going up while increasing numbers of people were losing their jobs and thus were unable to afford the consumer purchases that had been driving the American economy since World War II.

Beset by gasoline shortages, the automobile industry searched for ways to increase productivity and maintain profits. This led them to build a larger number of smaller cars, which were less profitable per unit but at least there was a market for them, and to reduce capital costs by using fewer platforms for their varying car models. Though this latter strategy may have reduced manufacturing costs in the short run, it led to a public perception that all model cars looked alike. Foreign-built automobiles, with a growing reputation for quality and more distinctive designs for their vehicles, began to erode the domestic share of the American automobile market.

Similar stories could be told about many industries in the United States during this period. American industry was becoming less and less competitive because it became increasingly incapable of competing with foreign manufacturers on two fronts: quality and cost. It was very difficult for American industry to compete with foreign manufacturers on costs since wage rates are much lower in Europe and especially Asia; this latter area was fast becoming a significant competitor in the global economy. The only hope for American manufacturing was to substitute "smart machines" for costly workers. Automation and computer-managed operations began to appear on the plant floor.

Smart machines needed educated people to operate them. Business leaders rapidly reached the conclusion that American schools were not supplying sufficient quantities of computer literate, autonomous, problem-solving workers needed to operate successfully in this new manufacturing environment, the worker clearly described in the report of the Educational Task Force of the Business Roundtable (1992).

Concurrently, and somewhat paradoxically, it became clear that the one aspect of American education that seemed highly regarded throughout the world was higher education. American colleges and universities were producing a larger number of highly educated graduates than anywhere else in the world, exactly the kind of worker the "new economy" was calling for.

For eons the major focus of economic life had been the growth of life-sustaining food (the agricultural age). By the 19th century the development of artificial power (the steam engine and the like) made it possible for fewer workers to produce the amount of food necessary to feed the world, and these newer technologies absorbed these excess workers in the processes of mass manufacturing and distribution of goods (the manufacturing age). As circumstances in the late 20th century were forcing industry to redesign production processes so as to use fewer workers, newer technologies (the computer, the Internet) were now positioning society to make information the key product of the 21st century and beyond. With information as the "new frontier" of the American economy, the public concluded that only well-educated workers would be able to function successfully in this new environment.

The symbiotic relationship between business and society was now entering a new phase. Either business and education would be successful together or the purposes, form, and functions of public education would need to be reconceptualized.

Education's Partnerships with Unions

Unions have also played an important role in the development of public schools. Generally, they were supportive of the development of common schools in the first half of the 19th century as part of a conceptual commitment to choke off the advantages of special privilege and to provide "all youth with an equal chance of advancement." However, they cooled in their enthusiasm as a result of factionalism and an increased need to focus on issues of wages and hours when the economy stalled (Kaestle 1983). They did not become champions of public education again until the beginning of the 20th century, this time because keeping children in school helped to manage the labor pool and keep students from competing for jobs and driving down wages. Newly passed compulsory attendance laws required students to stay as full-time students until various ages as determined by each state.

Education's Partnerships with Community Agencies

The formal involvement of schools with other entities does not have so long a history. Relationships between schools and municipal and county governments, the criminal justice system, health and human service providers and the nonprofit sector are relatively recent phenomena. Though legislation passed by state and national government in the last two decades of the 20th century began to foster if not require cooperation and collaboration among educational institutions and one or more of these entities, about which more will be said later, early efforts in this regard appear to have been the result of recognized mutual need.

Courts which incarcerated young suspects pending trial or took responsibility for young children after removing them from a neglectful or dangerous home needed to provide educational programs for their charges and often turned to school districts to provide this service. Recent state and federal efforts to eliminate "welfare as we know it" required the identification of providers of adult basic education for clients government was threatening to cut from regular payments unless they found a job. Many of them could not realistically seek a job when they were unable to read or add and subtract. Such situations engendered solicitations for the provision of educational services for the clients of the welfare agency.

Sometimes the need for assistance was recognized by school districts. Children who were failing in school because their home life was chaotic could not be significantly helped by regular school personnel working exclusively in schools. The etiology of the child's dysfunction might be substance abuse by one or both of the caregivers, poverty so complete that inadequate nutrition was provided, severe illness of a parent or grandparent, or some combination of these and other pathologies. It is understandable that school officials would reach out to other agencies to provide assistance that they were incapable of offering.

CONCEPTUAL BASES FOR PARTNERSHIPS

Building formal partnerships among agencies where none existed before can be a daunting task. Witness the many small municipalities in metropolitan areas that insist on maintaining their own tiny police and fire departments though an enlarged department serving several communities would be more effective and efficient. An anecdote from the school environment suggests the many issues that are involved in creating new partnerships.

About 20 years ago two school districts in Michigan agreed to jointly serve their students more effectively and efficiently by making use of newer building facilities in both communities. The two boards of education decided that all the children in the two communities were to be served by one community's newer middle school while high school students from both areas would go to the new high school located in the second district. The program lasted about three years, disintegrating in community objections to the loss of one high school football team.

Creating an effective interagency collaboration is hard work, even when individual agency autonomy is maintained. The process challenges the comfortable momentum of individual organizations acting alone. It changes interactions among people within the organization and requires the creation of new relationships with people from other organizations, in effect, undermining the existing authority structure (Hacker and Wessel 1998). It requires a rethinking of financing structures and sources. Bardach (1998) has noted that "every effort at interagency collaboration involves a veritable ecosystem of people proposing to one another that they do things differently and better—and of course disagreeing profoundly, often bitterly, about what 'better' means and whether or not the other person's better might actually be worse" (p. 6).

Core motivations for collaboration can spring from a variety of sources. Some agency leaders act from the desperate knowledge that they cannot survive financially without the human and financial resources that will arise from joining efforts with other agencies. Still others have higher motivations, acting out of a pre-existing sense of positive opportunity to build something better (Moore 1996). A common motivation is the desire to move away from the fragmentation and underutilization that impacts clients when they are served by multiple agencies that know only one piece of a person's or family's problems. Not uncommonly, the same or similar corrective strategies are undertaken by multiple agencies (McMahon, Browning, and Rose-Colley 2001).

It is clear that state and local government authorities are encouraging partnerships and collaborations through funding mechanisms that require collaboration to qualify for government grants for no other reason than the recognition that effectiveness and efficiency require joint action. "The financial, public relations, and political costs of institutional aloofness are becoming too steep to bear" (Russell and Flynn 2000).

REQUIREMENTS OF SUCCESSFUL COLLABORATIONS

Basic Characteristics

The rapid evolution of collaborations between and among business, general government agencies, educational institutions, and nonprofit organizations around the world, especially as opportunities for government to redesign services through the synergies of collaboration, led to a two-year study in the United States, Canada and Europe to identify the characteristics of successful collaborations that transcend cultural and national boundaries. Several key themes emerged.

1. Each collaboration depends on an understood though not always articulated working philosophy. Whether the collaboration occurs out of a desire to reduce costs, expand markets, improve services, avoid duplication of services, become eligible for state and/or federal grants, or some other purpose, partners need to have a congruent sense of why they are working together and the values that will sustain their partnership.

2. Collaborative relationships are dynamic, not static. The world never stops changing. Economic circumstances change, sociopolitical environments evolve, dominant political philosophies change election by election. Effective partnerships are fluid, responding to changing circumstances. This may mean adding to or subtracting from the membership of the partnership as originally designed, altering the way the collaborative does business, recalibrating financial and staff contributions, or making other alternations to the partnership.

3. Multi-organizational collaboratives need an institutional framework. Good will and good intentions do not assure a successful collaboration. A clarified manner for doing business, including allocation of authority within the partnership is essential (Dawes and Prefontaine 2003).

Rees and Gardner (2003) note three ways in which members of a collaborative might create a framework for effectiveness: (1) create contractual relationships that spell out duties and obligations of partners; (2) impose an authoritative integrating and supervisory structure, in effect, bureaucratize the operation; (3) create a "network governance" in which participants are able to identify complementary interests. In the network structure the binding factors are trust, loyalty, and reciprocity.

Beyerlein, Freedman, McGee and Moran (2003) have identified the basic principles of successful joint human endeavors such as collaboratives. Knowledge about the importance of each characteristic provides leaders the basis upon which to assess unsuccessful partnerships. They are as follows: (1) focus on mutually desired results; (2) align organizational systems to achieve ownership by all parties; (3) articulate, and enforce, a "few strict rules"; (4) exploit the rhythms of convergence and divergence; (5) manage complex tradeoffs on a timely basis; (6) create high standards for dialogue and discussion; (7) foster personal accountability; (8) align authority, information, and decision-making; (9) treat collaboration as a disciplined process; and, (10) design and promote flexible organizations.

Camino and Heidrich (2003) have identified six characteristics that were found in successful collaborations between universities and nonprofit organizations: (1) team members perceived a good reason to work together; (2) team members were acquainted; (3) teams were supported by formal structures; (4) team members respected each other; (5) team members had experience in each other's domains; and, (6) team members brought complementary strengths as well as the need to have common purposes and values.

Jane Arsenault (as cited in Grubbs 2000) calls for the establishment of definitive language about the desired outcomes of the partnership at the very beginning of the process, the level of integration of the partner organizations necessary to achieve defined goals, and the necessary steps for achieving this integration. To the extent possible she suggests that all levels of partner organizations be part of the organizational discussion so that ownership for the partnership can be created at all levels.

Personal Characteristics of Collaborative Leaders

Though much has been written about successful and unsuccessful collaborations among public, private, and nonprofit entities, there is still no definitive recipe for assuring successful collaborations. This is undoubtedly true because not all collaborations, even among similar partners, have similar goals, structures, values or personalities among key members. Research does seem to suggest that different types of collaborations require different behavioral patterns and management techniques (Mandell 2002-2003). Other research has demonstrated that, at least among nonprofit sector leaders, certain characteristics of leadership, contribute to successful collaborations, including expectations of a successful collaboration, high role ambiguity, and low stress about organizational boundaries on the part of leaders of collaborative projects (Goldman and Kahnweiler 2000).

Sarason and Lorentz (as cited in Grubbs, 2000) paint a darker picture of public sector organizations as good candidates for collaboration. They see public organizations as stuck in an "organizational chart mentality" (p. 276). They suggest that the private sector offers better models for successful leadership concepts and behavior. They see the ideal promoter and leader of collaborations as someone who has "a capacity for appreciating organizations in their broader social context, for scanning the environment to build connections across organizational systems and for focusing on strengths rather than seeing only weaknesses in individuals and groups" (p. 276).

The Weaknesses of Collaboration

Though interorganizational collaboration has proven so necessary in contemporary times that it enjoys considerable cultural sanction, it is not a panacea for every problem. The drawbacks are conspicuous. Bruce Gladrud (1999) has identified four major drawbacks of collaboration:

- ◆ Collaborations aren't very agile. When you can't make decisions quickly, you lose valuable opportunities.
- ◆ Collaborations are time-consuming. As frequently practiced, collaborations require meetings, meetings, and meetings. Managers who come from the business sector are driven to distraction by the way nonprofits over-emphasize the process of collaboration.
- ◆ Collaboration is based on consensus building. Work products built on consensus are rarely visionary or revolutionary. Without transformational shift you can't truly build for the future.

Major Conclusions Regarding Successful Collaborations

It is very clear that research conclusions are converging in several domains:

- ◆ It is necessary to have well-designed structures which manage the work of the collaborative.
- ◆ Common goals and values are essential.
- ◆ The human side of the enterprise is as important as the goals of the partnership, the structure within which work is accomplished. Members of the organization need to understand and respect the values and motivations of others.

SUSTAINING EDUCATIONAL PARTNERSHIPS

The Governance of Partnerships

Certainly two of the major criticisms of bureaucracy are its inflexibility and its preoccupation with drawing boundaries to circumscribe work. The boundary issue acts in two ways to mitigate progress: (1) "bureaucrats" are given firm boundaries of responsibility in the accomplishment of work so that they will do only what they have been assigned to do; (2) they will not share assigned responsibilities with any other person or department, no matter how long a delay may be involved in acting on their own. Though government agencies are thought of as the quintessential bureaucracy, to a large extent all large organizations have a bureaucratic infrastructure. The bureaucracy is an almost essential component of quality control for the organization. If knowledgeable people handle similar problems in similar ways, quality and consistency can be assured. Waterman (1990) has noted that "Bureaucracy gets us through the day; it deals efficiently with everyday problems. The trouble is, change ignores conventional bureaucratic lines. The real action in organizations occurs outside 'the proper channels'" (p.17).

It is therefore not remarkable that establishing governance structures for partnerships among multiple agencies can be a challenge. It is hard enough to overcome bureaucratic structures in one's own organization for the organization's own purposes. Challenging the bureaucratic structures to achieve the purposes of a partnership can be an intimidating task.

Problems of governance become acutely difficult when partnerships require the expenditure of dollars from different funding streams. Whether expending dollars from state or local governments or donated dollars from nonprofit organizations, each partner feels accountable to its funding provider. Thus, successful partnerships usually depend on the participation of individuals who are patient, broad-minded, and flexible in analyzing problems and inventing solutions.

The Durability of Partnerships

Interagency partnerships are usually brought together for one of two reasons: compelling need or the opportunity to use state or federal funds when a partnership is encouraged or required by the legislation. For state or federal agencies there is no more efficient way to achieve multidimensional solutions to social problems than to require cooperation among disparate agencies as a condition of achieving funding. It is efficient for the same reason that local collaborations are efficient. The state/federal agency needs to deal only with personnel from the fiscal agent on behalf of the partnership, and no money gets spent until strategies to achieve the goals of the program have been designed and implemented. State and federal agencies are recognizing that dealing with the educational service agency is an effective and efficient method of marshalling all school districts, or at least all appropriate districts in an area, in the effort to solve a common problem or achieve a state-designated purpose.

The most fundamental test of the quality and viability of a partnership occurs when outside funding disappears and partner agencies must use their own resources to continue the project. Research does not yet appear to have a definitive answer to how to maintain interagency partnerships when they are initiated as a result of funding opportunities. Those initially created out of real need seem to have more staying power, but evidence is more anecdotal than empirical.

ESAs AS THE LOCUS OF PARTNERSHIPS

The Convenience of the ESA as Partner

There are over 15,000 school districts in America. Though districts organized around county boundaries, by definition large districts, are common in the south, they are uncommon in much of America. Many American districts are too small or too rural or both to have sufficient resources to provide for all of their needs in curriculum, instruction, and administrative support. This situation was one reason for the creation of service agencies.

Conversely, in some large metropolitan areas it is not uncommon to find 50 to a 100 school districts within an hour's drive of the core city. It is simply impractical for a business willing to offer on-site training opportunities for high school students or an agency willing to provide placements for students to meet a community service work obligation to deal with such a large number of school districts individually. Of course the path of least resistance is to work only with the school district in which the business or agency is located, and this is not an uncommon occurrence. However, very often the business/agency needs to draw from a larger pool to find students who have the interests and burgeoning skills to make a good fit with the opportunities that are available at the business. It is also good public relations to serve a larger cohort of students since businesses and agencies almost always see themselves as offering products and/or services to an audience beyond the boundaries of one municipality. Therefore, the educational service agency has become a natural partner for working with these many school districts.

TWO TYPES OF EDUCATIONAL PARTNERSHIPS

It is possible to define two types of partnerships involving educational service agencies: those that are created within the education profession and those that involve education agencies and entities representing other state and municipal governments, businesses, nonprofit organizations and others.

Intra-Education Partnerships

Obviously the earliest partnerships between school and community were formed between teachers and the families of children. This "partnership" is so obvious that it is often overlooked or at least underemphasized in the history of education.

Also, almost by definition, the relationship between an educational service agency and its constituent districts might be described as a true partnership. As noted elsewhere some service agencies are almost completely dependent on selling programs and services to the districts they are chartered to serve and, increasingly, to other interested school districts. Local school districts need the service agency to be successful so they can acquire the assistance necessary to operate a successful educational program. The service agency needs revenue from the districts to maintain its very existence. This is a partnership of need where both agencies are mutually dependent on the success of the other. Interlocking governance structures whereby service agency board members are elected from constituent district boards or selected from among district chief executives complete the partnership picture.

Local districts also recognize that some common needs are best met by working collaboratively with a small number of other districts within the larger ESA service area. Some services are best rendered in a narrow geographical area; for example, shared bus repair facilities. Such collaboration may also be beyond the scope of services offered by the service agency. Propinquity also may be useful in serving teachers and administrators within a narrow geography since teachers and administrators will have only a short journey to navigate in order to get to training programs.

The core work of schools understandably drives the focus of partnerships that school districts are likely to develop. Districts are driven to collaborate on common problems for several logical reasons:

◆   The solution to a problem is expensive, and the solution is more attainable if districts pool their resources to acquire a solution that might benefit the partners. For example, deaf children are relatively rare yet require expensive equipment in their educational program to maximize learning. It makes sense for districts to pool resources (finances, facilities) and aggregate such students for quality programming.

♦ Expertise is scarce in the area. It is more efficient and cost-effective to bring high-quality expertise into the area than to have each district settle for expertise that is less than adequate. Teachers of the deaf are rare as are teachers of children with autism. It would be impossible for every district to acquire sufficient teachers for these low-incidence handicaps. Colleges of education are simply not producing enough of them.

♦ School districts with a recognized common interest are satisfied to work with others who share that interest. Districts interested in offering the Jason Project as a science enrichment activity can pool resources to make this program available.

The number of partnerships is far too large to capture completely in this chapter. In fact many of them have already been discussed in Chapters 5 and 6, which discussed the different populations that are served by educational service agencies. We have particularly noted the partnerships with business and unions, in designing and delivering vocational/technical programs. Education and training programs for adults seeking to get off welfare programs, educational programs for young people in the criminal justice system, classes for those who need to learn the English language and other special populations frequently represent partnerships between schools and other government and nonprofit agencies. These relationships are sometimes formed directly with the service agencies; at other times they are a joint project of the service agency and constituent local districts. The goal here will simply be to describe some programs that are more representative of the variety of partnerships that are often initiated by the service agency or by a state agency that recognizes the unique position that service agencies hold in coordinating services within a region.

The following descriptions are not intended to attempt to identify the best partnerships in the country, but to illustrate the variety of collaborations among school districts and to illustrate how educational service agencies can be the catalysts for cooperation among districts. It should also be noted that many partnerships involve projects between service agencies and state departments of education that are not the result of a higher authority (the state department) telling a lower echelon agency (an ESA) what to do but a natural outgrowth of synergy between skilled professionals at both levels who see needs and spontaneously set about to design programs to meet these needs.

It should be noted that the categories "school improvement," "technology," "professional development" and "special education" are not discrete. Some school improvement projects include professional development and some of that professional development may be in the uses of technology for instruction. A special education initiative may have professional development and so forth. The categories only loosely define the differences in emphasis among the projects.

For purposes of this discussion partnerships that include institutions of higher education with local school districts will be included under this rubric.

School Improvement

1. Bringing about Whole School Change—A program of the San Mateo County Office of Education and the California School Leadership Academy. Participants are six regular high schools and one alternative high school.

2. Galileo Project—A program initially funded by the Kellogg Foundation that attempts to develop classroom teachers who will return to their districts prepared to create communities of learners. Participants include two service agencies, two community colleges and eight school districts. One service agency is the project manager and fiscal agent.

3. Project Accelerate—A program designed to provide online professional development in connection with New York State's standards and assessment programs. Participants now include 12 service agencies and their constituent districts after initiation by one of them.

4. Testing Initiative—A project started by service agencies within one of the four zones within which Oregon's service agencies work together. Under a contract with CTB McGraw Hill, the service agencies developed assessment tests in reading and math for use in the grades (4, 6, 7), which are not included in the state testing program.

5. Online Advanced Placement Courses—Two Pennsylvania service agencies combined to develop online courses for students as preparation for taking the Advanced Placement tests.

6. Partnership for Educational Excellence Network (PEEN)—This is a partnership between the Pennsylvania Department of Education and the Pennsylvania Association of Intermediate Units. It is intended to provide products and training to enable all state students to meet state academic standards. It has produced training manuals, assessment planning guides, and online professional development.

Technology

1. Middle Michigan Network for Educational Telecommunications (MMNET)—A partnership of two service agencies and eight local school districts whereby financial resources were pooled to build a 200-mile fiber optic network. Initial contributions were $439,000 per participant.

2. Washington State Information Processing Cooperative (WSIPC)—A consortium of seven service agencies to develop software and establish a delivery network for school districts to do reporting and to provide statewide bidding and purchasing of technology equipment.

3. Technology Collaborative—Illinois has a statewide telecommunications network with 11 geographical regions. The five educational service agencies (called regional Offices of Education in Illinois) in Iroquois/Kankakee represent one of the hubs of the system. It is designed to achieve a complete sharing of staff and technical resources among K-12 districts, institutions of higher education and eventually museums and other entities for public education.

Professional Development

1. Online Professional Development—Three California service agencies,

operating under grant funds and with university partners as well, have been developing online professional development for teachers and administrators.

2. Professional Development Alliance—Two Illinois regional offices of education pooled their funds to create a center to provide professional development for their combined constituency.

3. Staff Development Cooperative—Two service agencies in Iowa jointly employ a staff development coordinator. Together they were able to offer 430 courses in the 1999-2000 school year.

4. Northern Michigan Learning Consortium—Eleven service agencies, five community colleges, and five universities collaborate to offer what they call "state of the art" professional development. Service agencies provide considerable funding and activity is supported by grants as well. Colleges rebate 50% of the tuition collected for courses offered under the auspices of the consortium.

5. Online Professional Development—Two Pennsylvania service agencies collaborate in the training of ESL teachers. Actually one agency provides the training but another also accesses it at defined costs.

6. South Central Academic Alliance—This is a cooperative venture between the South Central Service Cooperative (Camden, Arkansas), its 20 member public school districts, private schools in the area and Southern Arizona University. It supplies coordination for curriculum planning, staff training, and grant development.

7. The Tri-State Graduate Center is a unique intergovernmental agency that offers graduate education programs serving three states (Iowa, Nebraska, and South Dakota). The present governing board consists of university officials, state college representatives, two Area Education Agencies (educational service agencies) and business leaders.

Special Education

1. Autistic Programming—Two Iowa service agencies pooled resources to create a demonstration center to model exemplary practice in the education of children suffering from autism.

2. Transition Fair—A joint project of two service agencies in Michigan to provide a special experience ("Transition Fair") for high school juniors and seniors with disabilities to help them prepare for adult life and work.

3. Deaf Education—Four service agencies in Texas collaborate to provide technical assistance and training in local districts through cooperative programs. Training is provided in various sign languages. The program also certifies interpreters.

Business Affairs

As noted in Chapter 7 educational service agencies provide all kinds of assistance to local districts in building and supporting school infrastructure. These services include assembling purchasing cooperatives for all kinds of products including energy supplies.

The 36 BOCES in New York represent an ideal form of partnerships arrangements. Any service not available in one BOCES may be accessed if feasible via contract with another BOCES. Some of the services made available to other service agencies in the state include drug and alcohol testing, purchase of natural gas and electricity, negotiations, printing, and policy manual development.

Inter-Agency Partnerships

Partnerships with Business. For reasons stated earlier in this chapter, partnerships between schools and businesses are among the most recent and the most exciting focus of joint efforts between education and other agencies. Listed below is only a sample of some highly successful business/education partnerships.

1. Many educational service agencies have formed local partnerships to train young people in trades that will provide employment upon graduation. CESA #9 in Tomahawk, Wisconsin has apprenticeships in health occupations and a carpentry apprenticeship program for juniors and seniors. Such programs are popular all over the country where service agencies have a role in vocational/technical education.

2. The Central Savannah River Area Regional Educational Service Agency (Dearing, GA) established apprenticeships in the areas of computer technology, graphic arts, and construction as well as other fields. Business partners agree to expose students to the various tasks and duties outlined in the training plan. A heating, ventilation, air conditioning, and refrigeration (HVACR) program was established among local district students, a technical college, several businesses in the HVACR field and the service agency. Students completing the program receive certification in their field.

Chapters 5 and 6 summarized several projects that involved higher education institutions, health care institutions, businesses and museums.

Partnerships with Human Services Agencies. An example of a service agency's partnership with another human services provider is the work of Education Service Center VI (Huntsville, Texas) in providing job placement for clients who are studying in adult education programs under the Temporary Assistance to Needy Families legislation (936-295-9161). Also under this legislation, the agency works in partnership with a local college under a grant from the Texas Workforce Commission to address personnel shortages in the areas of bus driving, food services, maintenance and custodial care for schools. The agency conducts criminal history checks, assists interested people in application skills and trains, as needed, those hired.

Partnerships with General Government Agencies. Though fiscally independent of each other, the office of the Kern County Superintendent of Schools (Bakersfield, CA) and the general government officials of Kern County built the Southeast Bakersfield Community Services Center. This building houses multiple agencies that provide services to children and their families including mental health and physical health services. Funding came from county agencies occupying the building. In 1997 the office of the Kern County Superintendent of Schools was approached by the Kern County Museum about a partnership to continue the museum, which was facing severe financial difficulties. The partnership allowed a more structured educational component to be added to museum offerings.

SUMMARY

Because of their coordinative roles on behalf of the state and as a result of their defined mission to provide cost-effective and cost-efficient programs and services to their constituent districts, educational service agencies are uniquely positioned to serve in this capacity within their jurisdictions. As all businesses, government agencies, nonprofit organizations and educational institutions struggle to meet their goals within fixed or declining resources, there has been a natural growth in partnerships between and among all of these entities to share resources and expertise. In addition, there has been a growing recognition that most human problems are complex and no agency is staffed to respond to all the factors that contribute to the problems each agency is trying to remediate. In effect, all contributing factors to a problem must be addressed simultaneously if significant progress is to be made in alleviating the problem. Also, as resources continue to shrink, organizations that provide a duplication of services within a particular geographic area are going to be forced out of business. However, if agencies can disaggregate the components of a social problem and attend to discrete elements of the problem, all can survive and perhaps thrive.

Most state departments of education have experienced declining resources in recent years because of declining legislative appropriations. They simply cannot play a significant role in assisting local districts without help, the type of help educational service agencies are able to provide. The entrepreneurial spirit of ESAs largely sustains their financial resources. Districts are willing to pay the ESA for quality programs that they need. In a few cases ESAs have independent taxing authorizations granted by citizens over the years and are not as dependent on legislative appropriations as either local districts or the state department of education. For these reasons the role of ESAs in fashioning multiagency solutions to educational and human problems is likely to grow.

REFERENCES

Bardach, E. 1998. *Getting agencies to work together: The practice and theory of managerial craftsmanship.* Washington, D. C. Brookings Institution Press.

Business Roundtable Education Task Force. 1992. *The essential components of a successful education system.* Washington, DC: The National Alliance of Business.

Clinton, H. R. 1996. *It takes a village: And other lessons children teach us.* New York: Simon and Schuster.

Cremin, L.A. 1965. *The republic and the school.* New York: Teachers College, Columbia University Bureau of Publications.

Cutshall, S. 2001. Facing tomorrow: The future of school to work funding. *Techniques* 76:26-28.

Dawes, S. S., and Prefontaine, L. 2003. Understanding new models of collaboration for delivering government services. *Association for Computing Machinery. Communications of the ACM.* 46:40.

Glasrud, B. 1999. The dark side of collaboration. *Nonprofit World* 17(6)(December):20-

21.

Goldman, S., and Kahnweiler, W. M. 2000. A collaborator profile for executives of non-profit organizations. *Nonprofit Management and Leadership,* 10, 4, (check pages)

Grubbs, J. W. 2000. Can agencies work together? Collaboration in public and nonprofit organizations. (Review of the books *Forging nonprofit alliances* and *Crossing boundaries: Collaboration, coordination and redefinition of resources*). Public Administration Review 60(3):275-280.

Hacker, K., and Wessel, G. 1998. School-based health centers and school nurses: Cementing the collaboration. *Journal of School Health* 68:409-414.

Holt, D. G., and Willard-Holt, C. (2000). Let's get real: Students solving authentic corporate problems. *Phi Delta Kappan* 82:243-246.

Joyce, P. J. 2001. The slothfulness quotient. *School Administrator* 58:24-26.

Kaestle, C . F. 1983. *Pillars of the republic: Common schools and American society 1780-1860.* New York: Hill and Wang.

Karier, C. J. 1973. Business values and the educational state. Eds. C.J. Karier, P.C. Violas, and J. Spring, *Roots of crisis: American education in the twentieth century*. Chicago: Rand McNally.

Mandell, M. P. 2002-2003. Types of collaborations and why the differences really matter. *Public Manager* 31(4):36.

McMahon; Browning; and Rose-Colley. 2001. A school community partnership for at-risk students in Pennsylvania. *Journal of School Health* 71(2):53-55.

Moore, M. 1996. *Creating public value: Strategic management in government*. Cambridge, MA: Harvard University Press.

Rees, P., and Gardner, H. 2003. Best value, partnerships and relationship marketing in local government. *International Journal of Nonprofit and Voluntary Sector Marketing* 8(2):143-152.

Russell, J. F., and Flynn, R. B. 2000. Commonalities across effective collaborations. *Peabody Journal of Education* 75:196-204.

Waterman, R. H., Jr. 1990. *Adhocracy*. New York: W.W. Norton & Company.

Chapter 9

Holding Service Agencies Accountable: Concepts and Practices

INTRODUCTION

The accountability of service agencies has been in the past and continues to be a fiercely debated topic in many state and local policy circles across the country. A number of factors that are unique to a given state and to a particular state system no doubt help explain the seemingly unending controversy associated with many service agencies. However, there also is another, more generic, explanation. Most educational service agencies were created through action of the state legislature or by administrative rule. They operate under a state charter to, among other roles, provide programs and services to schools/school districts, and also receive funding from state and/or local sources. As such, they are a classic example of an organization having multiple stakeholders. One clear finding and conclusion of the now increasingly extensive literature on organizational effectiveness of human services providers is that different stakeholder groups are likely to have vastly different world views of how this concept is to be defined and then measured. It should come as no surprise that there are frequent disagreements on this matter between state and local interests and even frequent disagreements among the principal stakeholder groups of a single service agency—large and small enrollment size districts, central city and suburban and rural districts, wealthy and poor districts. Differing stakeholder interests then, it is argued, are the principal source of the regular controversy surrounding many service agencies. This is not to suggest that there are also not other contributing factors that might be state-specific.

CONTEMPORARY NOTIONS OF ACCOUNTABILITY

The concept of accountability of public sector organizations like educational service agencies has undergone several evolutions during the past few decades. In the 1960s and 1970s, for example, many observers (e.g., Emerson 1989; Pipho 1997) noted that the focus was on the efficient operation of a public sector educational agency. This emphasis on efficiency reflected the strong advocacy and support at that time on the application of private sector management techniques to the operation of public sector organizations, including educational entities. Prominent examples of management techniques championed during these two decades included: function-object budgeting; planning, programming, and budgeting systems (PPBS); management-by objectives (MBO); zero-based budgeting (ZBB); and zero-sum budgeting.

Beginning in the mid-1980s and continuing to this day, the newer emphasis in discussions of the accountability of public sector educational organizations has clearly been on the demonstration of results produced by agencies. Though the processes used to produce results are still of interest, the attention of members of both state and federal policy circles is clearly now much broader and centers on performance measurement; that is, how consistent are the results of an organization's work (i.e., its outputs and outcomes, especially the impact of its work) with its program intentions (i.e., its inputs and activities).

Moreover, it should now be abundantly clear that there will be no wavering from the commitment of federal as well as state interests in the continuous development of more effective strategies that will result in greater accountability for public sector educational organizations. For example, at the elementary-secondary level in the year 2001-02, 49 states had adopted standards in one or more subjects, all 50 have in place a requirement that there be an assessment of student achievement, 43 require a form of annual report card, 30 rate schools based on various data, with student test scores given prominence, and a fairly significant number of states have enacted legislation authorizing the use of a form of sanctions (school closure or reconstitution, student transfer, withholding of funds) for persistently low-performing schools (*Quality Counts* 2002). Provisions of the No Child Left Behind Act of 2001 (Pub. L. No. 107-110) calling for annual student testing in reading and mathematics in grades 3-8 and holding schools accountable for annual student progress, among other features of this legislation, will solidify the new conceptualization of a state accountability system.

When applied to educational service agencies, the concept of a state accountability system is defined here as *the cumulative set of state rules, regulations, and policies that are expressions of the state's intent to provide oversight of educational service agencies to ensure that they further the achievement of some prized state policy(ies).* Various approaches are employed by the states including the use of fiscal accountability measures, legal compliance accountability measures, and accreditation standards that focus on the processes and procedures used by the agencies and the measurement of the outcomes and impact of their efforts.

Rationale for the New Focus

It is important to note that inclusion of standards that establish performance expectations, and the establishment of meaningful ways to demonstrate results in the newer accountability systems for educational organizations in many respects merely parallel these same features as imposed on contemporary general government. Virtually all of the most significant advocacy groups in the field of public administration have for many years supported the use of performance measurement in local and state government. Also in recent years, Congress has seemingly been very active in the passage of legislation designed to increase the accountability of federal departments and independent agencies that it co-funds. The most significant federal initiative in this area in recent years is arguably the Government Performance and Results Act of 1993 that, as stressed by the Government Accounting Office, "forces a shift in the focus of federal agencies—away from such traditional concerns as staffing and activity levels and toward a single overriding issue—results" (United States General Accounting Office 1996, p. 1).

The convergence of a number of major factors in the 1990s in large part explains the widespread, accelerated quest for more meaningful strategies for use in measuring the performance of public education entities. Some are long-standing, but seemingly have gained a new urgency in recent years. Others are of more recent origin, or at least seem to have gained most of their momentum in the past several years. It is the coming together of old and new that has created what is generally regarded as an unprecedented, powerful vortex for change and improvement.

The major precipitating causes for the intense interest in accountability center on the following major themes. Some, however, appear to be more prominent in explaining the insistence on policy action at one level of government than another, at least at this time.

1. The claim of some that the productivity of (especially) public elementary-secondary education has been in a state of decline for several decades.

2. A growing consensus in the policy communities, and in the education communities as well, that many of the earlier accountability systems only stressed input and process characteristics with little attention given the products of educational organizations.

3. A growing consensus, again, both within and outside the professional community, that meaningful indicators should be used to measure the health and performance of educational institutions, especially those that are grounded in the effective schools research literature.

4. The emergence of a consensus that the systemic reform movement of the early 1990s offers a much better conceptual and analytical framework for the development of a comprehensive strategy for affecting improvements in education than was true of earlier reform concepts that frequently lacked coherence.

5. The pressure placed on policy makers to broaden the historical commitment to pursue equity issues in education to include the requirement that educational opportunities must pass the test of adequacy (the increasingly used judicial language) or implement opportunity-to-learn standards (the political and professional language) that assure all students of fair access to needed resources.

These five themes capture the main motives prompting the widespread interest in strengthening state accountability systems by incorporating meaningful standards and performance measures in an assessment of public sector organizations. The convergence of many of the themes, especially when combined with a seemingly renewed awareness of the claimed benefits of performance auditing, suggest that the standards and performance measurement movement of the 1990s is not likely to dissipate soon.

Potential Benefits of Performance Measurement

A summary of the more important gains attributed to the use of performance measurement in assessing the efforts of organizations, whether public or
private, is presented below.

Typical of the earlier statements regarding the major benefits to be realized
by measuring the quality of public sector services are the claims of Hatry
(1974), who argued that doing so offers the possibility that problem areas can be
better identified; feedback on the performance of both programs and policies is
enhanced; priorities in the allocation of funds and personnel can be improved;
management and employee incentives will be improved; and, community involvement in establishing priorities is greatly facilitated (p. 41). Similar rationales were offered by many other earlier advocates of more rigorous systems for
assessing public sector performance (e.g., Balk 1975; Levin 1983; Ross and
Burkhead 1974).

In the General Accounting Office (GAO) 1996 report to Congress on recommendations for the implementation of the Government Performance Results
Act of 1993 (Pub. L. No. 103-62) the GAO argued that a federal agency that
typically reports only on the amount of funds it expends, or staff employed, or
activities completed "has not answered the defining questions of whether these
programs have produced real results" (United States General Accounting Office
1996, p. 7). The GAO correctly asserted that the public is beginning to insist that
the federal government be "accountable less for inputs and outputs than for outcomes, by which is meant the results of government programs as measured by
the differences they make" (p. 7).

There appears to be general agreement with the assertion made in another
GAO report published soon after passage of the Government Performance and
Results Act of 1993 that federal data requirements have significant impact on
the practices of state governments anxious to be in compliance with federal requirements (United States General Accounting Office 1994).

Also capturing much of the contemporary rationale for the use of performance measures in human services organizations are the gains to be realized that
have been asserted by Martin and Kettner (1996). In addition to facilitating accountability, the use of performance measures, according to these authors, has
three major added benefits.

1. They have the potential to improve the management of human service
programs in that they help provide answers to eight basic questions: Who are the
clients? What are their demographic characteristics? What are their social or
presenting problems? What services are they receiving? In what amounts? What
is the level of service quality? What results are being achieved? At what costs?
Martin and Kettner conclude by citing still other potential benefits: their use
promotes making client outcomes prominent in all programming planning; their
use provides a common language in making evaluation judgments; their use facilities monitoring program performance; and, staff morale is improved (p. 9).

2. The second major benefit of the use of performance measurement advanced by Martin and Kettner is its potential to improve the allocation of re-

sources; that is, their use holds the promise of not only affecting the "politics of the human service budgetary process" but, in addition, "the politics of human service funding in general—and perhaps, the overall politics of government budgeting and funding as well" (p. 10).

3. The third major benefit, and perhaps the most important, for the use of performance measurement put forth by Martin and Kettner is the growing pressures at all levels of government to do it. Governments will have no option but to follow this path (p. 18).

Given prominence by the United Way of America in an earlier report (*Measuring Program Outcomes: A Practical Approach* 1996) are several additional potential benefits of performance measurement that are particularly relevant to educational service agencies. Data that demonstrates that programs make a difference in the quality of life for people can, for example, attract new participants in a program, attract new collaborators, foster recognition as a model or demonstration site and gain support for innovative programs (p. 4).

STATE ACCOUNTABILITY PRACTICES

Individual states make use of a variety of accountability practices in their desire to achieve oversight of the efforts of educational service agencies. Some of these practices are long-standing, having been introduced early in the formative years of the agencies. Other, more stringent accountability practices, have been implemented in recent years in a number of states, a reflection of the growing support for stronger performance accountability measures for all public sector organizations. An overview of the approximate time period when major state accountability initiatives were introduced for Type A: Special District ESA state networks, where state oversight is most prominent, is provided in Figure 9.1

Traditional Features

One useful way to establish the general direction of state accountability systems for the ESA networks is to view these from the perspective of the locus of control or authority enjoyed by the networks. Portraying ways in which the state tends to maintain some oversight over the operations of the network provides important information and insight on efforts by the state to create meaningful checks and balances on what the ESAs do and cannot do. From this perspective one can develop a sense of the degrees of freedom and discretionary authority provided the ESAs to set policies that govern their own affairs, as well as the nature of state intervention in ESA matters.

Presented in Table 9.1 is an overview of common state practices that are designed to promote the accountability of service agencies. Not all of the most common practices cited are exercised by every state, though several states make use of a significant majority of these practices. As expected, the examples cited tend to be most comprehensive for Type A: Special District ESAs but some of these examples apply in some states to Type C agencies as well.

A fairly substantial number of the state oversight activities cited would likely appear on most lists of meaningful accountability measures that ought to

Figure 9.1
**Overview of the Time Period When State Accountability Initiatives
Governing the Work of Type A: Special District State Networks, 2001-02
Were Established**

1960s	Submission of <u>annual financial report</u> and <u>annual audit report</u> required of all 13 established state networks	
1970s		Requirement in a strong majority of states for a <u>general advisory group</u> other than specific advisory groups required to be in compliance with federal and state special education vocational programs
1980s	Requirement in minority of states that the general advisory committee and/or local district member boards <u>approve all or part of annual budget</u>	
1990s		Development in minority of states of an <u>accreditation system</u> that generally included: standards, an on-site evaluation, and expanded reporting requirements such as: a multi-year comprehensive plan, an annual progress report, and a self-evaluation report
2000s	The inclusion of <u>performance measures</u> in minority of state accreditation systems and the use of <u>sanctions</u> against poorly performing agencies	The adoption in minority of states of provisions <u>allowing local districts to purchase services</u> from <u>any</u> agency in the state network
	Completion of a state sponsored <u>customer satisfaction</u> survey on the work of the agencies in minority of states	Publication of an <u>annual report card</u> on the work of the state network in minority of states

<u>Definitions</u>:	strong majority	= 10 of 13 state networks
	majority	= 7 of 13 state networks
	minority	= less than 7 state networks

Table 9.1
Major Traditional State Oversight Practices From the Perspective of the Locus of Authority for ESA Policy Development

---

Policy Development Categories and
Examples of State Oversight Practices

---

1. Method of Establishment, Alteration, or Dissolution of an Agency

✶ state guidelines for establishment, alteration, or dissolution ✶ state guidelines allowing a school district to join another agency ✶ periodic state assessment of the efficiency of the number of service agencies

2. Governance Practices of an Agency

✶state-required procedures for establishment of a governing board ✶ roles and responsibilities of board established in statute ✶ state mandate for the establishment of an advisory committee composed of school/school district staff ✶ state-required granting of budget review authority to advisory council or to component school district governing board

3. Staffing Practices of an Agency

✶ applicable state certification required ✶ applicable state/federal employment/dismissal requirements

4. Financial Practices of an Agency

✶ state-required budget format and accounting practices ✶ state-required annual audit ✶ state prescribed limit on administrative costs as a percent of total operating costs ✶ state restrictions on revenue generating sources ✶ state restrictions on expenditures for capital improvements ✶ state funding for categorical programs and services only ✶ state prohibition on tax levying authority

5. Programming Practices of an Agency

✶ state-required core programs and services ✶ state requirement for an agency to offer programs and services requested by school districts ✶ state requirement that certain classes of programs and services be only offered on a no-cost basis to the agency

6. Acquisition of Facilities of an Agency

✶ state prohibition on acquisition of facilities through bonded indebtedness ✶ state guidelines on facility acquisition through purchase or lease-purchase

7. Planning, Evaluation, and Reporting Practices of an Agency

✶ state-required submission of compliance reports on state/federal funded programs

---

be used as a check on the activities of a type of organization designed to provide programs and services to local school districts. Certainly the use of a required advisory council composed of representatives of local education agencies would be one of these. It comes as little surprise, then, that a significant majority (defined here to mean three-fourths or more) of the service agencies work under such a state requirement. Moreover, this practice not only impacts the governance prerogatives ordinarily assumed by an ESA governing board but shapes decisions in many other policy categories as well, as intended in the adoption of the state practice in the first instance. Another popular state oversight provision that would likely be supported in state and local circles as a meaningful check-and-balance on ESA practices vis-à-vis local district practices is the near universal prohibition on ESAs against levying taxes to support the agencies (only three networks can). This practice likely has its rationale grounded, at least in part, in the position that the service agencies ought not to compete with local districts for taxpayer support.

As might be expected, state oversight is most complete in influencing the fiscal policies and practices of the service agencies given the tradition of a strong state presence in the fiscal affairs of public education entities. Campbell, Cunningham, and McPhee (1965) reached this conclusion over three decades ago in one of the early assessments of the role of the state in the decision processes of local districts. This conclusion not only holds true to this day but rather is undoubtedly even more pronounced given the improved technical ability of most states to manage large databases.

State interest in keeping many of the Type A: Special District state networks on a relatively short leash is also evident in the frequent use of other oversight practices. One prominent example is the periodic assessment of the appropriate number of agencies to maintain in each state network. Probes of this kind, where these have occurred, have nearly always been initiated by the state. Another example of how the state's desire to closely monitor the efficacy of a state network relates to the generally limited options available to most service agencies for the acquisition of operating space, e.g., the frequent prohibition on bonded indebtedness.

THE NEW GENERATION OF STATE ACCOUNTABILITY PRACTICES

States continue to retain their long-standing accountability measures to the present day. However, beginning in the mid-1990s, a small number of states initiated steps to begin the challenging tasks inherent in the design of a more rigorous accountability system, one with a priority on the performance measurement of the network.

Several states have adopted and implemented a state accreditation system for their network of service agencies that compels the agencies to meet certain requirements for their continued operation. The nature of these existing requirements during the 2002-03 year varies. Most include a set of common core programs and services that each agency must offer. These core programs and services are typically closely aligned with a state's school improvement strategy. Some accreditation systems not only identify a set of common core programming requirements but also establish performance measures for each requirement. Other provisions of the existing accreditation systems require the agencies to develop and submit to the state a multiyear comprehensive plan and an annual progress report detailing progress toward achievement of the goals identified in the comprehensive plan. Still other requirements of one or more of the existing accreditation systems specify that the state is to conduct an annual statewide customer satisfaction survey.

Several state accreditation systems include provisions for the state to levy a sanction against a service agency judged to be negligent in the achievement of the state's expectations for the network. A variety of other requirements have also been incorporated into one or more of the existing accreditation systems.

A description of the current designs of several of the new generation of state accountability practices that have as their centerpiece a state accreditation system is provided in the next chapter. Special emphasis is given to an overview of the requirements of the current accreditation systems covering seven state networks. As expected, all but one are Type A: Special District ESA networks. An overview of the latest proposals in the emerging new accountability practices in several states, including the requirement that the state publish an annual report card on the work of the network, is also provided in the next chapter.

DISCUSSION

The widely acknowledged goal of holding an educational service agency accountable is to ensure that an organization of this type is effective in achieving expectations held for it by those who, in one way or another, support the work of the agency. We clearly are in agreement with this overriding goal. However, there are a number of major issues that need to be acknowledged at the onset of a discussion of the accountability of service agencies. One of these clearly relates to the goal of attempting to establish the agency's organizational effectiveness. As noted by Cameron and Whitten (1983), the construct organizational effectiveness is a concept that organizational theorists have wrestled with for a very long time, and as many observers note, has produced an inordinate number of conceptual and analytical frameworks for the study of organizational effectiveness. Cameron and Whitten's earlier conclusion is seemingly just as valid today as when it was issued nearly two decades ago as is their observation that "there cannot be one universal model of organizational effectiveness" (p. 262). This is so in part because "all general theories of organizations have built into them implied criteria for measuring effectiveness" (p. 262), and in part because,

> The impossibility of circumscribing a single set of criteria for organizational effectiveness . . . prohibits a single model of effectiveness from being developed. The construct space is so broad, and it accommodates so many indictors, that there would be little utility in any model that tried to encompass them all. (p. 265)

The continued validity of Cameron and Whitten's earlier conclusion notwithstanding, organizational theorists have continued to struggle with the issue of whether or not a single theoretical perspective or multiple theoretical perspectives are necessary to assess organizational effectiveness, and, if so, what are these to be? In answering this question Alter and Hage's (1993) position is that there are four major theoretical models that can be combined for assessing the effectiveness of an interorganizational network similar to what most educational service agencies should in many important ways be classified. The four models, which are adaptations of earlier work by Cameron (1981), are shown in Table 9.2.

The work of Alter and Hage is instructive and is supported by many. However, it should now be quite apparent that the answer to the question of how to define organizational effectiveness given by members of the policy communities at the state and federal levels is to determine how effective an organization is in achieving results, and whether or not it does so with efficiency and high quality.

Nevertheless it seems clear that there is substantial support in the literature for the position that multiple goals should be pursued in the establishment of accountability practices to assess the performance of public sector organizations, and in the design of an accreditation system. Further, priority ought to be given to the three major perspectives—the efficiency of the organization's efforts, the quality of its efforts, and the effectiveness of its efforts. Indeed, most of the support for performance measurement stems from the fact that this focus forces one to address, simultaneously, all three perspectives.

The position of Martin and Kettner (1996) on this issue is helpful. These authors, who are two of a fairly large and growing number of students of human service organizations, argue for support of the inclusion of all three perspectives

Table 9.2
Four Models of Assessing Interorganizational Networks

Theoretical Model	A Network System Is Effective to the Extent That	When Useful
Goal Model	It accomplishes its consensual goal(s).	Goals are clear and measurable.
System-Resource Model	It acquires needed resources.	Inputs can be specified and measured.
Internal Process Model	It has an absence of internal strain; it exhibits smooth internal functioning.	There is a clear causal connection between internal processes and desired output.
Strategic Constituencies Model	All strategic constituencies are at least minimally satisfied.	Constituencies have powerful influence.

Alter and Hage 1993, p. 186. (Adapted from Cameron 1981, p. 5).

by asserting that this approach:

> enables performance . . . to be viewed by different stakeholders holding different opinions about the nature of accountability. . . . Performance measurement implies no hierarchy of preference among the three perspectives but rather assumes that all three . . . are important to at least some stakeholders. (p. 3)

That the service agencies have multiple stakeholders seems indisputable. That these stakeholder groups frequently have divergent views concerning the performance of the agencies also seems indisputable. Furthermore, and compounding this issue, there are even frequent substantial differences between stakeholder groups within a single catchment area.

A schematic that illustrates Martin and Kettner's position is shown in Figure 9.2.

Organization of Discussion

We have organized the discussion of accountability issues as these relate to educational service agencies around six themes. The first two are directed at

Figure 9.2
The Expanded Systems Model and Performance Measurement

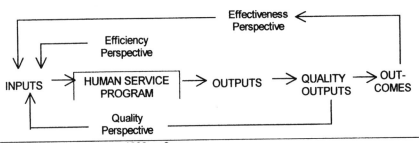

Source: Martin and Kettner 1996, p. 8.

Where:
- *Inputs* are anything a system (or human service program) uses to accomplish its purpose. More specifically, inputs can be thought of as the resources and raw materials (e.g., funding, staff, facilities, equipment, clients, presenting problems, etc.) that go into a human service program.
- *Process* constitutes the actual treatment or service delivery (i.e., the human service program) during which inputs are consumed and translated into outputs.
- *Outputs* are anything a system or a human service program produces.
- *Outcomes* can be thought of as changes in the condition of participants as a result of the activities of the human service organization.
- *Feedback* can be thought of as information about the performance of a system, or a human service program, that is reintroduced into the system as an input. (p. 8)

state networks of Type A: Special District ESAs. The last three are pointed toward all agencies, irrespective of type:

- ♦ More state adoptions of a performance-based accountability system are needed for any state network that has adopted a state accreditation system.
- ♦ More state adoptions of a policy-relevant annual report card on the work of the state network are needed.
- ♦ Programs and services benchmarking efforts are needed.
- ♦ The need for costing-out studies.
- ♦ Greater commitment to engage in voluntary accountability practices must be forthcoming.
- ♦ The imbalance in the accountability practices of a school and school district, a service agency, and the state needs to be repaired.

State Adoptions of an Accreditation System: A Growing Phenomenon

Progress, albeit slowly, is being made in the introduction of state performance accreditation systems across the country. However, we take the position that it is imperative that state interests and supporters and practitioners of service agencies in many states must be more aggressive in working toward the design of a meaningful system that will help ensure that there is continued support for this type of organization. Described here are some of the design challenges present in the development of a state performance accreditation system and the outline of the preferred features of such a system.

Design challenges. The design of a state performance accreditation system poses numerous theoretical, research, technical, and political issues that ordinarily involve choices to be made among frequently competing alternatives. Stephens and Harmon (1998) organized the issues into eight categories: (1) purpose of the state performance accreditation system; (2) theoretical issues; (3) implementation issues; (4) performance standards; (5) performance measures; (6) data collection and analysis; (7) use of results; and (8) monitoring processes. Most of the eight categories were further broken down into a number of sub-issues, or design challenges. The authors stressed there are no right or wrong answers for most of the issues, although in some cases the choice made for a specific issue must be consistent with the choice made for a related issue. Further, the choices made for all issues must be consistent with the very first one raised—what is to be the overriding purpose of the performance accreditation system, or are multiple goals to be pursued, and, if so, what are these (p. 16).

The authors also discuss what they regard to be essential action that should take place prior to a consideration of design challenges. They argue that the state, in collaboration with the service agencies and other stakeholders, must have in place a strategic plan for the state network that, at a minimum, includes what they regard to be three absolute requirements: (1) a vision statement that expresses the values and beliefs regarding how the ESA network contributes to the state system of elementary-secondary education; (2) a comprehensive mission statement that flows from the vision statement, explaining why the network exists, and stating the expectations for the network in results-oriented terms;

and, (3) a statement of the long-term strategic goals for the network, also in re-sults-oriented terms.

The absence of these three essential prerequisites virtually assures that the potential benefits of a state performance accreditation system will not be real-ized. There is little use, for example, for engaging in a discussion of the overrid-ing goal(s) of the system without benefit of the results of these three critical de-liberations. Further, it surely would be counterproductive for all interests—the state, the ESA community, and the principal stakeholders—if an attempt were to be made to establish annual performance standards absent long-term strategic goals from which short-term goals ought to flow. Moreover, if ambiguity, con-fusion, or disagreement is present in the development of performance standards, it follows, then, there will be similar concerns and issues raised regarding the development of the all-important performance measures.

Preferred Features of an Accreditation System. There are, of course, a number of defensible positions that can be held regarding the ideal system com-ponents of an accreditation plan. We take the position that the centerpiece of a comprehensive accountability plan ought to be a state performance accreditation system that will provide timely, policy-relevant information on whether or not the state network and its constituent individual agencies meet, exceed, or fail to meet the expectations held for them. Our recommended design includes 16 fea-tures, as shown in Table 9.3.

Taken together the 16 recommended features facilitate achievement of the apparent consensus conclusions of service agency leaders regarding what ought to be the essential objectives of a rigorous performance measurement and report-ing strategy. The achievement of these common objectives will benefit the two principal stakeholder groups of a state network: local school districts/schools and the state itself. Obviously there also are benefits for the individual agencies and the network of agencies as well. To accomplish the recommended compo-nents, a service agency must do the following:

(1) Determine an objective way to assess, in a timely, cost-efficient man-ner, progress toward achieving the mission, goals, and objectives of the organization.

(2) Make resource allocation decisions that are based on valid and reli-able data.

(3) Engage in the practice of benchmarking exemplary operational and instructional practices and to subsequently establish benchmarks or performance targets.

(4) Collect comparative data to measure the performance of the organiza-tion over time.

(5) Continuously and systematically align planning decisions to ensure that the state's expectations for the organization are realized.

(6) Include explanatory information in the periodic, policy-relevant re-port that will help the consumers of the report better understand the data provided.

The 16 features represent the broad framework of a preferred state per-formance accreditation system. Their implementation in each state will, of

Table 9.3

Recommended System Components of a State Performance Accreditation System, State Network of Special District ESAs

1. The accreditation period is specified and is the same as the one for districts/ schools.
2. Standards are established and, at a minimum, include required core services to be performed by each agency in the network.
3. Performance measure(s) are established for each core services standard.

Each ESA is required to:

4. Submit to the state a periodic, multiyear comprehensive improvement plan, first approved by districts/schools, and then by the state.
5. Submit to the state an annual progress report.
6. Submit to the state an annual budget, aligned with comprehensive/annual reports.
7. Submit to the state an annual self-assessment report.
8. Submit to districts/schools, and the public in the service region an annual report card, with both aggregated and disaggregated data.

The state is required to produce:

9. An annual statewide customer satisfaction survey of core services.
10. A periodic statewide cost-analysis study of core services.
11. An annual report card on the network, with both aggregated and disaggregated data that features comparison with past performance and having a required broad dissemination schedule.

The state is also required:

12. To schedule an on-site re-accreditation review by an external panel.
13. To provide for public disclosure of the report of the on-site re-accreditation review.
14. To allow a service agency to file a rejoinder to the review report.
15. To levy sanctions for a poor accreditation report.
16. To provide a reward for an exemplary accreditation report.

course, need to be customized to reflect the context of a particular state. All 16, however, should be addressed in some meaningful way.

State Adoptions of a Policy-Relevant Annual Report Card

Here, again, the focus of the discussion is on state networks of Type A: Special District ESAs. At this present time, few states produce a report card regarding the work of their ESAs, though this situation is likely to change significantly in the near future. This is so for several reasons. The focus thus far has seemingly been on the implementation of annual report cards for K-12 education, and, to a lesser degree, on post-secondary education as well. This will undoubtedly be redirected to assure that the work of all public sector organizations is reported on regularly. Moreover, many state networks of service agencies have in the recent years been assigned major supportive roles in state school improvement initiatives, a movement that will result in greater visibility in state policy circles.

Several of the few existing state-sponsored annual reports do provide policy-relevant information on several aspects of the work of the state network. Selected financial data on both revenues and expenditures that is both aggregated for the network as well as disaggregated for each agency is the one common feature of the current state practices. Also included in at least one annual report card, that of the Texas ESCs, is a variety of other descriptive data, such as aggregated and disaggregated staffing data, programs and services offered, and selected participation data.

The required report of the Texas Education Agency to the state legislation is possibly the most comprehensive current annual report card currently in operation. A recent Regional and District Level Report (1998) contains important data that would likely be viewed by most in the state policy community as information that helps inform discussions about the work of the state network, including, as previously described, financial, staffing, and programming data. What is especially significant, however, is the inclusion of data that directly links each service agency to high priority state improvement efforts directed at local school districts. Regional service agency data for the year 2001-02 are reported on three areas of state policy significance: (1) the percent of students in the region passing reading, math, and writing state assessment exercises; (2) the drop-out rates for each region; and, (3) the attendance rates for each region. The percent of superintendents, principals, and teachers who rated service agency services as "satisfactory" or "unsatisfactory" on the most recent annual statewide client satisfaction survey is also included in the report card, though these data are aggregated for the state network.

The specific content of a state-sponsored annual report card will, of course, continue to reflect the individual needs of a particular state at a particular point in time. Nonetheless, having acknowledged this requirement does not negate the need for information about relatively universal objectives that ought to be pursued in the design of an annual report card.

Universal Objectives of a System of Report Cards. We argue for three overriding objectives: (1) to provide timely, policy-relevant information on whether or not the network, and its component parts, meet, exceed, or fail to achieve progress in achieving the state's expectations held for it; (2) to give priority to a "vital few" core activities on what ought to be first among equal state expectations for the network—its progress in impacting those variables thought to enhance teaching and learning and improvement in the efficiency of the state system of elementary-secondary education; and, (3) to make provision for periodically supplementing the "vital few" core data items with data about the network's performance on other current high-interest aspects of the state school improvement agenda.

Guiding Principles for a Report Card. We argue further for the close adherence to a number of guiding principles for use in the design of the annual report card:

(1) Report with aggregate (network) as well as disaggregated (individual agency) data.

(2) For the first few years, until meaningful benchmarks can be established, compare performance with past performance.

(3) Use multiple year, not single year, data.

(4) Give adequate consideration to the organizational capacity of the network and parts thereof to address state expectations by including appropriate explanatory information about the meaning of the data.

(5) Always focus on the outcomes of the work of the service agencies that are under the reasonable control of these agencies.

(6) Always acknowledge that the work of the service agencies unquestionably results in different levels of outcomes, depending on local conditions.

(7) Give adequate consideration to the non-quantifiable benefits that service agencies provide schools and school districts and the state.

Preferred Design Features of an Annual Report Card. Our preferred design of an annual report card on the activities of a state network of service agencies is provided in Figure 9.3. As noted, the recommended design incorporates multiple theoretical perspectives for addressing the construct organizational effectiveness, in deference to the differing interests of stakeholder groups. Definitions and illustrative examples of several of the key components of the design are provided in Table 9.4.

Not all of the key components (i.e., inputs, activities, outputs, outcomes, and impact) need to be reported on annually for all programs of a service agency. Rather the focus should be on programs and services directed at the provision of assistance to school districts and schools in their school improvement efforts with particular emphasis given to a "vital few" programs and schools designed to enhance teaching and learning. The inclusion of data on inputs, activities, outputs, outcomes, and impact addresses the measurement of program effectiveness approach argued for by supporters of the use of a program logic model, such as: the United Way of America (*Measuring Program Outcomes: A Practical Approach* 1996), the W. K. Kellogg Foundation (*Logic Model Development Guide* 2000), and the Division of Research, Evaluation, and Communication, National Science Foundation (*The 2002 User-Friendly Handbook for Project Evaluation* 2002).

Figure 9.3
Recommended Design of an Annual Report Card

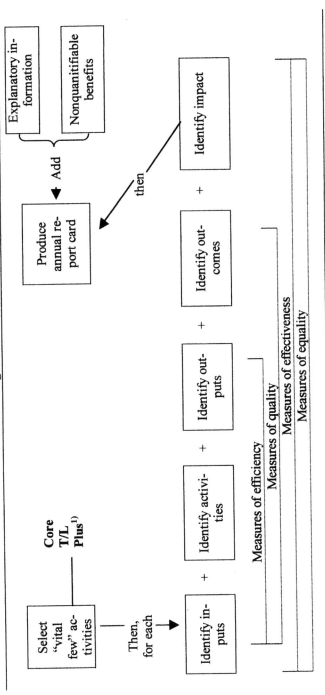

[1] Core activities related to teaching and learning.
<u>Source:</u> Stephens, E. R. 2000.

Table 9.4
Illustrative Examples of Inputs, Activities, Outputs, Outcomes, and Impact Data

Data Type	Definitions	Illustrative Examples
Inputs	The resources, financial and non-financial, invested, used, or spent for a program, activity, or service.	• Funding • Staff FTE • Facilities, equipment • Technology
Activities	What the program does with the inputs to fulfill its mission; the actions through which program purposes are carried out.	• Sponsor staff development activities • Provide support services to the disabled student • Provide technical assistance in curriculum planning • Provide comprehensive technical assistance to low-performing schools • Provide differential services to less wealthy districts
Outputs	The direct products of program activities.	• Number of classes taught • Number of educational materials distributed • Number of participants in staff development programs
Outcomes	The results of a program (e.g., client benefits or program consequences) compared with its intended purpose; the goods, products or services produced (amount, quality, quantity or other activities).	• New knowledge • Increased skills • Changed attitudes or values • Cost-savings from cooperative } altered status, improved condition
Impact	Direct or indirect effects or consequences; outcomes that would not have occurred in the absence of the program; the net impact due to program.	• Ability of clients/customers to enhance teaching and learning • Ability of clients/customers to improve school/district planning • Ability of clients/customers to leverage cost-savings

The Need for Benchmarking Activities

We make a clear distinction here in our call for more serious benchmarking efforts on the part of individual service agencies, state networks, and the national professional association representing the service agency community, the Association of Educational Service Agencies (AESA). Benchmarks are measurements used to establish whether organizational *processes* represent best practices that can be found in the field and *results* accomplished by the unit meet some predetermined targets of excellence that are being achieved by one or more comparable organizations. Moreover, it follows that a disciplined period of investigation of what other comparable organizations are achieving and how they are achieving these results should precede the establishment of a benchmark on which to judge the performance of a service agency on a particular program or service.

Our judgment is that there are few existing examples of an individual service agency that has engaged in systematic benchmarking. Clearly the past efforts of state networks represent a commitment to improve existing practice and are to be commended. However, similar to the benchmarks that are to be found in some state accreditation systems, there is little evidence to suggest that both are based on the systematic search for best practices that produces excellent performance.

Rather, in most cases of an individual agency, the state network acting upon its own initiative, or state leaders acting to establish benchmarks, use is made of one or more of the conventional approaches for the development of standards of performance. Hatry, Fountain, Sullivan, and Kremer (1990) provide a useful classification of approaches that have tended to be favored by public sector organizations and include: (1) comparisons with other times/places; (2) the use of absolutes; (3) use of judgment; (4) normative goal-centered judgment; (5) improvement judgment; (6) comparison with the private sector achievements; and, (7) judgment of professional organizations (p. 441). For the latter, we add the caution that the judgments be grounded in research, not merely in self-serving position criteria.

Our position is that some of the conventional approaches have merit and of necessity need to be used, absent the time and resources to engage in a systematic process of identifying and closely assessing best practices for an external service provider like an ESA. Much better, though, would be for the service agency community in a state, in conjunction with state officials, especially in the case of networks of Type A: Special District ESAs, to engage in collaborative, on-going, benchmarking exercises. So, too, would the efforts of an individual agency or a state network of service agencies benefit from the involvement of the one national professional association positioned to be of assistance, the AESA.

The main advantage of a statewide approach is that it facilitates successfully addressing a number of challenges in benchmarking exercises. Ammons (2001) gives emphasis to the challenge of data availability and the identification of comparable organizations. One of the major advantages of involving the national organization, AESA, is that it is in perhaps the best position to identify benchmarking partners.

The benefits for an individual service agency resulting from the on-going processes of uncovering best practices wherever they may be found are many. Bogan and English (1994) stress a number of these, including the following: (1) improved organizational quality; (2) motivation for change; (3) exposure to new ideas and the creation of a culture for new ideas; (4) catalyst for learning; (5) increased employee satisfaction through involvement, empowerment, and a sense of ownership; (6) increased level of maximum performance; and, what they regard to be of most importance, (7) instruction in new lessons in competitiveness (p. 14).

The benefits for a state network, working in collaboration with other state interests, are also significant in that this process will better assure that the debate and final decisions concerning benchmarks on which to judge the performance of the network will hopefully be informed by educational, not political, rationale.

The Need for Costing-Out Studies

Costing-out methodologies are increasingly being used by the states to determine the amount of money needed by a school district to provide each child an opportunity to meet all applicable standards established by the state. Three major approaches are now in use: the successful schools approach; the professional judgment approach; and the expert judgment approach.

While all three methodologies are of potential value in examining the work of educational service agencies, at this time the first two would be particularly useful in establishing benchmarks of successful efforts by service agencies that meet not only state accountability standards but professional standards that may exceed standards as well. The third methodology, the expert judgment approach, is highly dependent on the availability of research-based literature. As has been stressed regularly, there is at present a very limited research-based literature on the work of service agencies.

The Need for Voluntary Efforts at Accountability

The material presented in this section provides justification and a sense of urgency for all service agencies to, at a minimum, engage in the types of exemplary voluntary accountability practices previously described. For example, the technology is available for every service agency to produce an individual, customized annual summary that details the involvement of the service agency staff in the work of each school and school district in its constituency. Moreover, there are several, not too difficult to compute, ways to establish the cost-savings occurring to a school and school district by virtue of involvement of the service agency. These will be described in the next chapter.

Another voluntarily action that would enhance the accountability of not only the service agency but school districts and/or individual schools as well would be the crafting of some type of an annual letter of agreement that specifies the roles and responsibilities of each partner. The added data-burden of following this action would be more than overset by the benefits resulting in the joint planning and shared expectations of both parties.

The Need for Reciprocal Accountability

There should be little doubt of where we stand on the vital question of the need for greater accountability of more service agencies than exists at present. Moreover, much of the preceding discussion makes clear a number of ways that this can be accomplished.

However, it is also our position that while strengthening the accountability practices of service agencies should result in many benefits for the agencies, local and state interests, and the public, other steps need to be taken that will realize even greater benefits for all stakeholders and for the agencies as well. These additional steps center on the need to institutionalize a strategy that will assure that schools, school districts and state officials are also accountable to the service agencies in areas where their actions, or inaction, can impact the effectiveness of the agencies.

The call for complimentary or mutual action by local and/or state interests is seldom raised in discussions of the accountability of service agencies. Yet the accountability of both parties must be given equal consideration. Moreover, this can be done without lessening in any way the design of a rigorous accountability strategy for the service agency. Indeed, it could be argued that the design of a service agency plan is incomplete unless consideration is also given to the critical roles that local and/or state interests play in the successes or failures of a service agency.

How the needed reciprocal arrangements are arrived at for a particular state network or individual service agency will naturally be dependent on a host of factors peculiar to a state or regional context. There are, however, certain minimal universal steps that could be adopted that would help level the accountability playing field for service agencies and facilitate the achievement of the goal of creating a system of shared responsibility for the work of a service agency. Two examples are provided to illustrate this position.

Unfunded new state mandates are a particular and significant problem for service agencies. Unlike local school districts, Type A: Special District service agencies do not have taxing authority and, by definition, Type C: Cooperatives do not either. Type A ESAs are dependent on state aid for a significant portion of their operating funds. Existing state aid formulas continue to be predominately student enrollment count-driven. Little recognition is given to the added resource burden placed on smaller enrollment size service agencies as a result of the mandated core programming requirements of a state accreditation system. The problems of large enrollment size agencies that serve large metropolitan areas and that are mandated to give priority to assisting low-performing schools are similarly not acknowledged in an aid formula weighted heavily on the basis of student enrollment that assumes that the needs of all students are alike. The state is the only entity that can correct this problem. It is important that it be held accountable to do so.

State rules that allow schools and districts to obtain programs from service agencies other than from the traditional provider pose new problems. A local school district that actively participates with other districts in the planning and implementation of a new service agency program that will require a significant commitment of human and fiscal resources from constituents, then subsequently decides to secure, without financial penalty, the program from another service provider in the state can create resource problems that impact not only the service agency but local districts as well.

SUMMARY

Stronger state accountability measures are now increasingly being imposed on educational service agencies, particularly state networks of Type A: Special District ESAs. In the past, states tended to exercise oversight on networks of this type on a range of organizational and structural features, especially the funding sources available to the network and their financial practices. More recently, the emphasis in some state policy circles is on implementing practices that attempt to hold the network accountable for achieving success in the attainment of priority state school improvement initiatives. This new emphasis is usually reflected in the adoption of a state accreditation that establishes both standards and performance measures.

Both individual service agencies as well as some state networks engage in voluntary practices that attempt to be more accountable to school districts and schools. A common example of individual agencies' efforts is the extensive use of content advisory committees in helping shape the decision-making practices. Less common promising practices include: individual annual reports to each school district and schools; and, an annual letter of agreement with each school district and school that establishes the responsibilities of each party.

A deep concern is raised regarding the near absence of meaningful measures that establish the accountability of both the state and participating school districts and schools to the success of a service agency. The effectiveness of a service agency without question is a shared responsibility of the state and member school districts in the case of Type A: Special District ESAs, and in the case of Type C: Cooperative ESAs, school districts that make up the network.

REFERENCES

Alter, C., and Hage, J. 1993. *Organizations working together*. Sage Library of Social Research 191. Newbury Park, CA: Sage Publications.

Ammons, D. N. 2001. *Municipal benchmarks: Assessing local performance and establishing community standards*. Thousand Oaks, CA: Sage Publications.

Balk, W. L. 1975. *Improving government productivity: Some policy perspectives*. Administrative and Policy Studies Series. Beverly Hill, CA: Sage Publications.

Bogan, C. E., and English, M. J. 1994. *Benchmarking for best practices: Winning through innovative adaptation*. New York: McGraw-Hill, Inc.

Cameron, K. 1981. *The enigma of organizational effectiveness*. San Francisco, CA: Jossey-Bass.

Cameron, K. S., and Whitten, D. A. 1983. *Organizational effectiveness: A comparison of multiple models*. Orlando, FL: Academic Press, Inc.

Campbell, R. F.; Cunningham, L. L.; and McPhee, R. F. 1965. *The organization and control of American schools*. Columbus, OH: Charles E. Merrill Books Inc.

Emerson, E. J. 1989. Accountability in the post-Charlottesville era. In *Education Comment* (December):1-5. Los Angeles, CA: Center for the Study of Evaluation, UCLA Graduate School of Education.

Hatry, H. P.; Fountain, Jr. R.; Sullivan, J. M.; and Kremer, L. eds. 1990. *Service efforts and accomplishment reporting: Its time has come*. Norwalk, CT: Government Accounting Standards Board of the Financial Accounting Foundation.

Levin, H. M. 1983. *Cost-effectiveness: A primer*. Beverly Hills, CA: Sage Publications.

Martin, L. L., and Kettner, P. M. 1996. *Measuring the performance of human services programs*. Thousand Oaks, CA: Sage Publications.

National Science Foundation, Division of Research, Evaluation and Communication, Directorate for Education and Human Resources. 2002. *The 2002 user-friendly handbook for project evaluation*. Arlington, VA: Author.

Pipho, C. 1997. Standards, assessments, and accountability: The tangled triumvirate. *Phi Delta Kappan* 78(9):673.

Quality counts 2002: Building blocks for success. 2001. *Education Week*, 17(January).

Ross, J. P., and Burkhead, J. 1974. *Productivity in the local government sector*. Lexington, MA: Lexington Books.

Stephens, E. R., and Harmon, H. H. 1998. Standards and performance measures on the horizon. *Perspectives* 4(September):3-26.

Stephens, E. R. 2000. *On the redesign of an annual AEA progress report and other accreditation related recommendations*. Concept paper prepared for the Iowa State Department of Education – AEA Design Team, October, Des Moines, IA.

United States General Accounting Office. 1996. *Executive guide: Effectively implementing the Government Performance and Results Act*. Washington, DC, June.

United States General Accounting Office. 1994. Managing for results: State experiences provide insights for federal management reforms. Washington, DC, December.

United Way of America. 1996. *Measuring program outcomes: A practical approach*. Alexandria, VA: Author.

W. K. Kellogg Foundation. 2000. *Logic model development guide*. Battle Creek, MI: Author.

Chapter 10

Accountability and Accreditation for ESAs: Current Practices

STATE ACCREDITATION SYSTEMS

The newer state accountability efforts for educational service agencies are often encapsulated in the form of a state accreditation system, defined here as *the general statements of expectations held by the state that are applied in the decision to initially approve and/or continue to recognize that an educational service agency has complied with all existing state rules, regulations, and policies, has demonstrated that it is honoring some valued practices concerning the processes and procedures it uses, as well as meets, exceeds or fails to satisfy desired outcomes and impacts established by the state.*

The implementation of a state accreditation system that is designed to monitor the performance of the educational service agencies appears to be at the present time, the first years of the 21st century, most advanced in Georgia, Iowa, Nebraska, Ohio, Oregon, Texas, and West Virginia. As will be noted later, each of these seven states is at a different stage of development in the creation of a performance-based accreditation system. A description of the major features of the seven state accreditation practices is provided below.

Georgia RESAs

In 1997, the state board of education adopted an administrative code (O.C.G.A. 160-5-1-13) requiring each of the Regional Education Service Agencies to annually submit three items to the state education department.

1. An annual plan that includes: results of its needs assessment, agency objectives, staff assignments and a fiscal report of revenues received and expended.

2. A three-year strategic plan. In addition to a statement on goals and specific objectives, the plan should establish performance indicators that are used to measure the effectiveness in the delivery and the outcome of services provided, and also shall include intended improvement objectives, timetables for achievement of objectives, and the means by which these are to be assessed.

3. Beginning July 1, 1998, and subsequent years, each RESA has been required to submit to the department by October 1 of each year an annual report which provides specific information on the actual outcomes resulting from RESA services and programs. The report must describe how the outcomes were measured and assessed on performance in each area, including addressing the actual benefits, i.e., positive outcomes, resulting from the RESA's activities and

the costs incurred to provide such services and programs (160-5-613, p. 3).

Performance Standards. Eight performance standards for the state network have subsequently been established, several with multiple parts, as shown in Table 10.1.

Annual Progress Report. An annual progress report is required of each RESA. A standardized format for the report was developed by the state. The report is organized around performance standards and requires an agency to indicate how it assesses its current level of performance for each.

Three levels of performance are possible: (1) the agency is demonstrating satisfactory progress toward meeting the standard; (2) the agency is demonstrating commendable progress, or (3) it is demonstrating outstanding progress. Rubrics are provided for each of the three possible responses as a guide for recording an agency's assessment of where it believes it stands relative to the performance standard. Also described is an example of the progress used in the development of an annual progress report. The example relates to Standard I.B.—RESA offers professional development to support teaching and learning needs in the member school systems.

Standard I.B. RESA offers professional development to support teaching and learning needs in the member school systems.

□ **Demonstrates Satisfactory Progress**	□ **Demonstrates Commendable Progress**	□ **Demonstrates Outstanding Progress**
RESA provides and evaluates staff development offerings that match needs identified by member school systems.	RESA provides and evaluates staff development offerings that match needs identified by member school systems. RESA assures follow-up to staff development offerings with on-the-job assessment.	RESA provides and evaluates staff development offerings that match needs identified by member school systems. RESA assures follow-up to staff development offerings with on-the-job assessment. Staff development offerings are designed in collaboration with member systems and aligned to School Improvement Plans.
Rationale: Comprehensive and on-going professional development programs focused on schools' goals for improvement contribute to improved student learning as evidenced in local, state, and/or national assessments. Therefore, RESA will offer staff development to support teaching and learning pursuant to O.C.G.A. Code Section 20-2-271.		

Iowa AEAs

The accreditation system currently in place for the Area Education Agencies (AEA) was first enacted by the state legislature in a 1996 rewrite of the original legislation creating the network that was written in 1974. This statute, Chapter 273, directed the state board of education to develop an accreditation system by 1997.

Table 10.1
Performance Standards for the Georgia RESAs

Performance Standards

Standard I.
RESA provides shared services to support teaching and learning in members school systems.

Standard I.A.
RESA identifies and/or conducts research and planning to support teaching and learning needs in the member school systems.

Standard I.B.
RESA offers professional development to support teaching and learning needs in the member school systems.

Standard I.C.
RESA assists in the development and implementation of curriculum and instruction to support teaching and learning needs in the member school systems.

Standard I.D.
RESA assists in academic assessment and evaluation programs that support teaching and learning in the member school systems.

Standard I.E.
RESA assists in selection and implementation of technology that supports teaching and learning in the member school systems.

Standard I.F.
RESA provides information and training in alcohol and drug abuse education to support teaching and learning in the member school systems.

Standard I.G.
RESA assists in the development and implementation of a Statewide Mentoring Program to support teaching and learning in the member school systems.

Standard II.
RESA creates a regional plan for improvement of educational efficiency and cost-effectiveness of members.

Standard III.
RESA delivers core services to member school systems to meet local and state educational standards.

Standard III.A.
RESA trains and assists teachers in the subject areas of state-mandated testing.

Standard III.B.
RESA assists schools rated as academically failing.

Standard III.C.
RESA trains teachers/administrators/Board of Education members/school councils on site-based decision-making and control.

Continued on next page

Table 10.1—*continued*

Standard III.D
RESA assists local systems in complying with the laws and rules of the State Board of Education and the Education Coordinating Council.

Standard IV.
RESA establishes instructional CARE teams at the request of local Boards of Education.

Standard V.
RESA provides a nontraditional alternative route to state teacher certification awarded by Professional Standards Commission.

Standard VI.
The RESA Board of Control makes an annual report to the State Board of Education.

Standard VII.
The RESA Board of Control determines assistance needed by member school systems, establishes priorities from those needs, and allocates resources accordingly pursuant to O.C.G.A. Code Section 20-2-271.

Standard VIII.
The RESA Board of Control annually reviews the effectiveness and efficiency of RESA pursuant to O.C.G.A. Code Section 20-2-272.

Source: O.C.G.A. § 20-2-282.

The legislature also established a number of minimal expectations that ought to be reflected in whatever product the state board ultimately produced by administrative rule. One of these was the call for standards and the use of what was referred to as "indicators of quality" for the accreditation of the agencies. Moreover, the General Assembly made clear that the goals of the standards and "indicators of quality" were to be such that would "permit area education agencies, school districts, the department of education, and the general public to judge accurately the effectiveness of . . . services" (Chapter 273.11).

The administrative rule adopted by the state board has gone through several revisions. The most recent revised rule, Chapter 72, Accreditation of Area Education Agencies, was adopted in November, 2001. In order for an AEA to be accredited and maintain its accreditation, it must honor five major components of the accreditation system:

♦ It must provide the core services enumerated in a set of nine standards.
♦ It must establish a comprehensive improvement plan.
♦ It must submit annually a state board-approved budget.
♦ It must submit annually a progress report.
♦ It must successfully undergo a comprehensive site visit by an external review

panel. (281-72(273))

A description of the principal features of these five major components is provided below. Also described is one other practice initiated by the state education agency that is intended to serve in an important role in the accreditation process, the 2001-02 introduction of a statewide customer satisfaction survey.

Required Core Services. Each of the state's AEAs are required to provide services to all schools/school districts in their service region by addressing nine standards: (1) school-community planning; (2) professional development for instructional, administrative, and support personnel; (3) curriculum, instruction, and assessment services; (4) services that address the diverse needs of all children and youth; (5) services that support multicultural, gender-fair approaches to the educational program: (6) media services; (7) school technology services; (8) leadership development services; and (9) management services to school districts if requested (281-72.4-72.9).

Descriptors of services that shall be provided in order to establish evidence that, at a minimum, an AEA is honoring each of the nine service standards are also identified in Chapter 72. Examples of the descriptors of three of the standards are provided in Table 10.2.

Comprehensive Improvement Plan. All AEAs are required to submit a five-year Comprehensive Improvement Plan (CIP) to the state education agency. The CIP serves as a critical reference and record of improvement actions taken by an agency over time, and also as an important document for use in an accreditation site visit conducted by the state agency. The CIP must include a description of how the agency conducts on-going needs assessment and a summary of findings from agency-wide needs assessment.

The latter of these two minimal requirements is to include findings from an internal needs assessment that includes four indicators of improvement: (1) implementation of a continuous improvement model; (2) implementation of services that respond to the needs of schools and school districts; (3) a demonstration of the agency's proactive leadership; and, (4) examples of how the agency uses data to implement actions to improve student learning. Other required contents include findings from school and school district state indicator data; school and school district comprehensive school improvement plans; the department of education's comprehensive school and school district site visit reports; the AEA's comprehensive site visit report; and the statewide customer service surveys results for the agency.

Other significant content to be featured in the CIP include a description of:

♦ Agency-wide measurable goals that are based on the various needs assessment data cited above that focus on assisting schools and school districts with their school improvement processes and improving teaching and learning.

♦ Services to be provided that provide evidence that the standards are being addressed, and action plans for their implementation are available.

♦ Agency-wide resources allocation plans and staffing allocation plans.

Table 10.2

Three Examples of the Minimal Services that an Iowa AEA Must Provide in Order to Meet State Requirements for Standards of Services

---

Service Standard and Descriptors of Minimal Services Provided

---

The AEA shall deliver professional development services for schools[1], school districts and AEA instructional, administrative, and support personnel.

> The AEA anticipates and responds to schools' and school districts' needs; supports proven and emerging educational practices; aligns with school and school district comprehensive long-range and annual improvement goals; uses adult learning theory; supports improved teaching; uses theory, demonstration, practice, feedback, and coaching; and addresses professional development activities as required by the Iowa Code or administrative rules (72.4(2)).

The AEA shall deliver curriculum, instruction, and assessment services that address the areas of reading, language arts, mathematics, and science but may also be applied to other curriculum areas.

> These services support the development, implementation, and assessment of rigorous content standards in, but not limited to, reading, mathematics, and science. The AEA assists schools and school districts in gathering and analyzing student achievement data as well as data about the learning environment, compares those data to the external knowledge base, and uses that information to guide school and school district goal setting and implementation of actions to improve student learning (72.4(3)).

The AEA shall supplement and support effective instruction [for] students through school technology services.

> These services provide technology planning, technical assistance, and professional development, and support the incorporation of instructional technologies to improve student achievement. These services support the implementation of content standards in, but not limited to, reading, mathematics, and science. These services support and integrate emerging technology (72.4(7)).

Note: [1] As defined in the administrative rule, a "school" means an accredited nonpublic school. "School district" is defined to mean a public school district (72.2).

♦ The system to be used for measuring the efficiency and effectiveness of services. (281-72.9)

Of note, the five-year cycle for the submission of the Comprehensive Improvement Plan corresponds with the same time period that is required of local school districts to submit to the state their comprehensive improvement plans. The intent is to put the two agencies on the same school improvement cycle, thus facilitating closer planning and collaboration between the two.

Annual Budget. Each AEA is require to submit an annual proposed budget to the state board no later than March 15 preceding the next fiscal year. The state board must approve the budget no later than April 15th (281-72.10(1)).

Annual Progress Report. The AEAs are also required to submit an annual progress report to the state education agency. Of interest, the report is also to be disseminated to all schools and school districts in the agency's service region, as well as made available to the general public (281-72.10(2)). A description of the contents of this report is provided in Table 10.3.

Comprehensive Site Visit. All AEAs were given accreditation at the time the revised administrative rule was adopted in November, 2001. The accreditation is for a five-year period (273-10(3)). All AEAs are subsequently subject to a periodic on-site review, generally on a five-year cycle, by an external panel to establish whether or not full accreditation is to be continued, or other action is warranted. The external review panel is appointed by the chief state school officer and is to include, at a minimum, staff of the state education agency, representatives of various size schools and school districts served by the AEA, and staff from other AEAs in the state. The chief state school officer may also appoint others having expertise judged to be of value for a particular site visit.

The review panel's report to the state board must establish whether or not all requirements of Chapter 72 have been met. Upon receipt of the report, the state board can: grant continued accreditation without reservation or grant conditional accreditation. In the case of conditional accreditation, an AEA must establish a remediation plan and schedule for removal of all deficiencies.

Failure to successfully address the requirements of the remediation plan and schedule is cause for the state board to remove accreditation of an AEA. All schools and school districts in a non-accredited agency are notified of this action of the state board. The board of the non-accredited agency is required to make provisions for the continuation of services to schools and school districts, subject to the approval of the state board (281-72.11).

Customer Satisfaction Survey. The state education agency initiated a statewide customer satisfaction survey in the 2001-02 school year. The results of the survey for an individual AEA are to serve as an important data resource in addressing several of the components of the accreditation system, particularly in the development of the Comprehensive Improvement Plan, and as supporting data for the annual progress report.

The survey focuses on the services provided by an AEA. Respondents include a sampling of all instructional and administrative staff in the schools and school districts in the state. An overview of the major features of the initial survey is provided in Table 10.4.

Nebraska ESUs

The accreditation system governing the ESUs is contained in Rule 84, Title 92, Nebraska Administrative Rule, adopted in August, 1998. The current system represents a revision in Rule 84 that was first enacted in 1990.

Table 10.3
Required Contents of an Iowa AEA Annual Progress Report

Required Content Areas

Agency-wide Goals
   Progress toward meeting goals established in the Comprehensive Improvement Plan

Indicators of Quality
   Baseline data and trends over time for the following indicators of quality derived from these major sources:
   ✳ the state indicators ✳ the statewide customer service survey ✳ school and school district comprehensive school improvement plans ✳ school and school district annual progress reports

1. Targeted assistance: An AEA assists schools and school districts with specific student, teacher, and school needs evidenced in local school improvement plans by:
   ✳ addressing teacher, school and school district needs ✳ responding to student learning needs

2. Improved student learning: An AEA assists schools and school districts in:
   ✳ improving student achievement in mathematics, reading, and science ✳ reducing student achievement gaps in the above three content areas ✳ reducing dropout rates ✳ preparing students for postsecondary success ✳ planning to insure that students complete a core program

3. Improved teaching: An AEA assists schools and school districts in improving teaching in the following areas:
   ✳ mathematics ✳ reading ✳ science

4. Resource management: An AEA assists schools and school districts by determining:
   ✳ cost-efficient services ✳ timely delivery of services

5. Customer satisfaction with services: An AEA determines customer satisfaction through:
   ✳ high levels of participation ✳ high levels of customer satisfaction with quality of services (281-72.10(2))

Table 10.4
Overview of Iowa AEA Statewide Customer Satisfaction Survey, 2001-02

Major Contents

Concerning the Characteristics of Respondents

- AEA school or district located in?
- Years worked in education?
- Type of school or district employed?
- Student enrollment size?
- Educational level most time spent in?
- Main role?

Concerning General Perceptions of AEA Services

• Those received or participated in generally met my professional needs • AEA is responsive to student learning needs • AEA provides leadership to meet emerging educational needs • AEA delivers current and timely services to meet my school or school district needs	Four point Likert scale provided

Concerning Specific AEA Service Standards[1]

• School-community planning • Professional development • Curriculum, instruction, and assessment • Response to diverse learning needs of students • Support of multicultural, gender-fair approaches • Media • School technology • Leadership development	Major probes for each service standard • How often receive or participate in? • Services are of high quality? • What factors may have limited your level of participation?[2] • To what extent did services received assist in improving instruction or job-oriented practices? • To what extent did services received assist in improving student achievement? • What changes, if any, would you recommend?

Notes:

[1] A probe of the ninth service standard, management services on request, was not included.

[2] Nine possible factors were identified: (1) availability of time to participate; (2) availability of substitutes; (3) quality of services; (4) accessibility/availability—not offered when needed; (5) didn't know how to access services; (6) not aware services were available; (7) district/school provides these services; (8) services obtained from other sources; and, (9) services too expensive.

Accreditation by the State Board of Education is for a one-year period. The provisions of Rule 84 concerning how the evaluation of ESU programs and services is to be conducted is general in nature, consistent with the tradition of rule-making in the state. Each ESU is required "to conduct a comprehensive evaluation of its programs and services in every seven-year period using models approved by the Department and as scheduled by the Department" (007.01). An on-site visitation by an external review panel is also required as part of the comprehensive seven-year evaluation process.

Additional insight into the state's evaluation and assessment strategies can be gained by reviewing the provisions of Rule 84 on the subject of required core services that each ESU is to provide. Core services are defined in these ways:

1. Core services shall be within the following service areas in order of priority: Staff development, technology, and instructional materials services;
2. Core services shall improve teaching and student learning by focusing on enhancing school improvement efforts, meeting statewide requirements, and achieving statewide goals in the state's system of elementary and secondary education;
3. Core services shall provide schools with access to services that the educational service unit and its member school districts have identified as necessary services; are difficult, if not impossible, for most individual school districts to effectively and efficiently provide with their own personnel and financial resources; can be efficiently provided by each educational service unit to its member school districts; and can be adequately funded to ensure that the service is provided equitably to the state's public school districts;
4. Core services shall be designed so that the effectiveness and efficiency of the service can be evaluated on a statewide basis; and,
5. Core services shall be provided by the educational service unit in a manner that minimizes the costs of administration or service delivery to member school districts. (009.01A-E, p. 6)

Ohio ESCs

In 1995 the Ohio legislature directed the state board to establish minimum standards by which to assess whether or not each Education Service Center (ESC) has, as required, developed an acceptable plan for the provision of services to the local school districts, not city or exempted village districts, in its service region (§ 3301.07.12). The "plan of service" submitted by an ESC is to include an indication that certain minimum standards, 13 in number, have been addressed. These include assurance that the ESC governing board: (1) allows for the involvement of local school district boards in all aspects of planning; (2) has adequate and well-maintained physical facilities; (3) provides fiscal monitoring of local school districts; (4) has provided for qualified staff in sufficient numbers to implement its service plan; (5) provides classroom supervision and evaluation; (6) provides staff development for local school districts and its own staff; (7) offers specified curriculum services; (8) provides research and development services; (9) maintains regular and continuous communication among the ESC governing board, local school districts, and the community; (10) engages in continuous planning for the maximum use of existing school buildings, and the planning of new facilities; (11) monitors and enforces the state compulsory attendance law; (12) monitors record keeping practices of local school districts; and, (13) provides assistance to local school districts in the provision of special accommodations and classes for exceptional children.

The service plan is to be submitted to the state board for approval. If approved, the state board will grant a charter to the ESC. The state board is required to evaluate an ESC every five years. The state board may revoke a charter of an ESC for its failure to meet the minimum standards. An ESC may ultimately be dissolved by the state board, which has authority to transfer its territory to another ESC that is required to accept an order of the state board.

It is also to be noted that the statutory provisions addressing the accreditation plan in place do not include performance measures that would permit the state board an objective way to assess whether or not an ESC meets, exceeds, or fails to meet the 13 standards. This task has been left to the state board of education. No action has been taken in the ensuing six plus years since the state legislature added the statutory requirement that the ESCs were to be covered by an accreditation system.

This step reportedly is awaiting final action on a state board comprehensive assessment of all of the numerous regional delivery systems currently operating in the state, including the ESCs. The assessment is contained in a report completed in late 2001 by the CELT Corporation, an independent consulting firm (*The State of Ohio Independent Review of Regional Service Agencies: Key Findings and Best Practice Report* 2001).

Oregon ESDs

The state network of Education Service Districts (ESDs) has operated under an accreditation system for many years. The most recent revision occurred in 1995 with the adoption of an administrative rule by the State Board of Education, *Standards for Education Service Districts* (1995). As stated in the rule, the purpose of the accreditation system is to "determine the adequacy of services and facilities provided" and the State Board of Education "shall consider the most economic method of providing services and facilities, the quality of the services and facilities according to the best educational standards, and the needs of the students" (OGR 581-024-0210(1)).

The Oregon ESD standards are in a relative sense very comprehensive, in part because they address most of the existing statutory and administrative rule requirements relating to the processes and procedures to be followed in the conduct of their work. The accreditation standards, for example, address such topics as the role of the ESDs in reviewing local district operations, instructional services, and support services; the role of the ESDs when sitting as the district boundary board; the role of the ESDs in administering state student attendance laws for local school districts of less than 1,000 enrollment; assistance to the

State Board of Education; and the appointment, composition, and role of advisory groups.

The evaluation of a service district's compliance is obtained through a review of a required annual report that must be submitted by each ESD, and, an on-site evaluation that must be completed at intervals not to exceed five years. The standards to be focused on during an on-site visitation may vary.

The required annual report is to include a "Self-Appraisal Report" and a "Service and Performance Summary." The ESDs are to have on file documentation that will support the two required annual state reports including a description of the services provided with appropriate documentation of the quantitative data gathered; a numerical accounting of district personnel by job description and service area; and a statement of operational cost for each service provided.

The evaluation data that is to be on file in each ESD is to include: an evaluation of the assessment data as these relate to the service goals of the ESD; information obtained in the assessment activity; a summary of the reports from component local school districts regarding services provided by the ESD; and a list of deficiencies with plans for correction (OAR581-024-0226).

The format followed in the development of the mandated "Self-Appraisal Report" requires an ESD to indicate with a "yes" or "no" whether or not the ESD has on file for review evidence that it is in compliance with the standards. The chief executive officer must certify that her/his responses are true and correct to the best of her/his knowledge.

A typical annual self-appraisal report lists the different categories of ESD statutory or administrative rule requirements that have been selected by the state education agency for review for a particular school year in the five-year review cycle. Twenty-three categories of state requirements were cited for review in the 2001-02 school year. Two examples from the longer list of reporting requirements are shown below.

OAR	OARs[1] The district has evidence of the following	Yes	No[2]

581-024-0225
Planning of Services
	The District has adopted and implemented policies and procedures for planning to provide services. The procedures provide for component district involvement and include:
	
	a. District Board adopted goals for:
	   1. Instructional services if such services are offered;
	   2. Support services if such services are offered.
	b. Involving its component in determining the instructional services and support services needs.
	c. Procedures for improving instructional and support services by reducing the identified needs having the highest priority.		

581-024-0290 Advisors to the Board	The District has appointed nonvoting advisory members to the Board in accordance with OAR 581-024-0290(1), (2), (3), (4) and ORS 334.025(3). The District has assigned duties to the non-voting advisory members in accordance with OAR 581-024-0290 (5), (6).		

Notes: [1] OARs – Oregon Administrative Rules.
[2] All "no" responses must be fully explained.

The format to be followed in the development of the required annual "Service and Performance Summary" is also largely standardized for the ESDs. The following information is to be provided for each program or service: (1) a brief description of the program or service, (2) licensed and classified personnel (in FTEs) assigned to each, (3) the funding expended and source of funds for each, and, (4) the results of an assessment of both customer satisfaction with the quality of the program or service, and the need/priority assigned a program or service.

Provision is also made in the accreditation standards for an ESD to request a waiver for a standard under certain specified conditions: (1) The ESD judges that it is not feasible to comply; (2) The ESD engages in a promising "pilot or experimental service, a practice encouraged by the State Board of Education;" and, (3) The waiver request does not compromise "requirements specified in the Oregon Revised Statutes" (OAR 581-024-0212).

Upon completion of an on-site external evaluation, an ESD will be classified in one of two ways: standard ESD (meets the requirements of the standards) or substandard ESD (fails to meet the requirements). The State Board of Education may withhold state funds from a substandard ESD or may merge it with a contiguous ESD that has been recognized as a standard service district (OAR 581-024-0215).

Texas RESCs

The 20 Regional Education Service Centers (RESCs) have for a number of years operated under what is perhaps the most extensive state accountability system of the state networks of regional service agencies included in this overview. The evolution of recent efforts to put in place a more rigorous performance accountability system for the RESC is in many ways instructive, and it is for this reason that the treatment of the Texas state network is perhaps more comprehensive than several of the other profiles.

The state oversight provisions in place in 1990-91 included: an annual independent fiscal audit; an annual desk audit, including a client appraisal of the effectiveness of a center's programs and services; an on-site management and service audit conducted at five-year intervals; and, an on-site performance review at five-year intervals to establish compliance with federal and state statutes and regulations (Regional and District Level Report 1996, p. 16).

Other accountability measures taken in the ensuing years include action in 1992 by the State Board of Education that provided the chief state school officer greater authority over three areas of RESC activities: (1) approval of the selection of the chief executive officer of an RESC; (2) approval of the budget; and, (3) an annual performance evaluation of the executive officer as a condition for continued employment (Regional and District Level Report 1996, p. 8).

Legislative action in 1997, however, is clear regarding the intent of the state to establish an even stronger system for accrediting the network as part of a strengthened accountability strategy. Provisions of the new legislation (S.B. 1158) of interest here are summarized below.

1. The legislative intent is clear concerning the purpose of the network in that it establishes that the RESCs are to serve the state in three roles: assist school districts in improving student performance; enable each school district to operate more efficiently and economically; and, implement initiatives assigned by the legislature or commissioner (Sec. 8.002, p. 1).

2. The theme of improved performance is also stressed in the language describing the core services to be offered by each RESC, and how the state will exercise oversight. Each RESC must annually submit to the state for its approval a statement of how it is to improve student and school district performance, especially for campuses designated as low performing (Sec. 8.051, p. 2).

3. The legislation calls for the chief state school officer to establish performance standards and indicators that will assess whether or not an RESC is achieving the state's purpose for their operation. Minimal expectations for the system of performance standards and indicators are also established in that these must at least measure: (a) assistance to school districts in improving student performance; (b) promotion of more efficient and economical school district operations, including operations in the areas of curriculum and instruction, data processing, purchasing, staff development, technology support, and administrative services; and (c) implementation of initiatives assigned by the legislature and the commissioner (§ 8.101, p. 3).

4. The chief state school officer is also to develop a system for sanctioning an RESC deficient on one or more accountability measures. State actions, in increasing order of severity must include: (a) conducting an on-site investigation of the center; (b) requiring the center to send notice of each deficiency to each school district and campus in the center's region or served by the center the previous year; (c) requiring the center to prepare for the commissioner's approval a plan to address each area of deficiency; (d) appointing a master to oversee the operations of the center; (e) replacing the executive director or board of directors; and (f) in the case of deficient performance in two consecutive years, closing the center (§ 8.104, pp. 3-4).

5. A unique feature of the legislation is that the chief state school officer may request the legislature to provide incentive funds to encourage and reward extraordinary efficiencies in the provision of programs and services by an RESC (Texas Education Agency 1998).

In one of its latest biannual reports to the state legislature, the Texas Education Agency chose to highlight two of the measures used to assess the effectiveness of the centers:

1. The results of student performance on the same three measures used by the TEA in its accountability system for local school districts: the percent of students passing the state assessment exercises, the student drop-out rate, and student attendance rates. These same measures are applied to an RESC, and the composite results for each of the RESCs are reported to the state legislature (pp. 17-19).

2. The results of efforts underway to change the procedures used for another major measure used to assess the effectiveness of the centers, the required annual client satisfaction appraisal. Prior to 1998, the annual client satisfaction survey used a standard survey targeted on local school superintendents and administrated by each center. The 75th Texas Legislature directed the State Commissioner of Education to develop and monitor a uniform, statewide, annual client satisfaction survey. The commissioner subsequently entered into a contract with a private contractor to develop and pilot a survey of not just local superintendents, but teachers and principals from campuses judged to be low performing. The third party contractor is to manage all phases of the activity, from survey construction, to distribution and reporting. The contractor is the Texas Center for Educational Research, housed at the University of Texas, Austin.

In one of the most recent versions of the annual client satisfaction survey, conducted in May, 2002, each school district superintendent in the state, or her/his designee, was asked whether or not use was made of each core program or service of the service center in her/his region, and the effectiveness and appropriateness of the programming efforts of the service center. Space was provided for each respondent to (1) indicate whether or not he/she needed the product or service; (2) state awareness of the availability of the product or service; (3) assess the quality of products and services that were used; and, (4) indicate whether or not there were additional products and services that should be offered.

Results of the survey were sorted by size of enrollment of the school district (fewer than 3,000; 3,001-9,000; 9,001-20,000; and, 20,000 or more), as well as by the respondent's position (teacher, principal, director, assistant or deputy superintendent, or district superintendent). The survey results for each service center are presented to a center's board of directors and its regional advisory committee (Evaluation of Education Service Center Products and Services 2001-02).

Another noteworthy RESC assessment exercise warranting mention is the annual Commissioner's Performance Standards Self-Assessment Report. In this exercise, the focus is on three standards, each with a number of subparts:

Standard I: Student performance is increasing within the RESC region, as evidenced by several indicators: (1) TASS performance is moving toward the 90 percent standard of excellence in the Texas accountability system; (2) gaps in TASS performance among student groups are narrowing; (3) TASS performance is increasing; and, (4) drop-out rates are decreasing; (5) attendance rates are increasing.

Standard II: The RESC assists districts in increasing efficiency, effectiveness, and economy of operations as evidenced by the following indicators: (1) efficiency and economy are improving in districts served by the center's technical assistance, program support, and core services; (2) the center's services and regionally shared services arranged by the center are improving economy and efficiency of school operations, according to results obtained from external client surveys and other evidence; and, (3) efficiency and effectiveness of RESC operations are demonstrated in fiscal accountability through appropriately priced programs and services, according to results obtained from external client surveys and other evidence.

Standard III: The RESC advances the current statewide initiatives in the region as evidenced by: (1) support for the Texas Reading Initiative; (2) support for the implementation of the Texas Essential Knowledge and Skills; (3) participation in grant-funded projects to implement state initiatives; (4) support for the decentralization of authority and responsibility for public education through support to local school districts in the region; and, (4) demonstration of commitment to employment equity in all RESC operations and initiatives (pp. 1-5).

RESC staff are to establish where they believe their center currently is with respect to each of the subparts of each standard; that is, they are to indicate whether they are demonstrating satisfactory, commendable, or outstanding progress, and a brief statement of rationale for the self-assessment made. A uniform set of operational definitions or rubrics are provided for each subpart of the three standards. Several of these include a statistical measure (e.g., a drop-out rate of one percent or less is suggested as the benchmark for demonstrating outstanding programs in meeting the priority of providing assistance in reducing dropout rates in the region). Most of the operating definitions, however, do not include a statistical measure as a guide.

Additional information on the various features of the Texas accreditation system are provided in the next section that describes state-sponsored annual report cards on three state networks of service agencies.

West Virginia RESAs

A new legislative rule enacted by the West Virginia State Board of Education that became effective in January, 2003, (Title 126, Series 72) established for the first time a number of components of a vastly strengthened accountability system for the state's eight Regional Education Service Agencies. These include the following requirements on each agency.

1. The development of a comprehensive strategic plan of services (CSPS) that was to establish how each agency can best assist county school districts in the implementation of state board priorities, especially the provision of technical assistance to low-performing schools and school systems, and the provision of high-quality staff development designed to enhance student performance (126-72-5). The CSPS must be approved by the state board prior to its implementation, and is to be based on a three-year planning cycle.

2. A description of how the agency will contribute its expertise in building the capacity of the entire state network, especially should the state department designate one or more agencies to serve as "centers of excellence" for the provision of services to multiple RESAs, or to school districts on a multiregional basis (126-72-5.3.7).

3. The development of a performance-based self-assessment system for measuring the effectiveness and efficiency of programs and services. At a minimum, this system must address four quality standards of service:

♦ The agency's role in increasing student performance
♦ The agency's role in assisting districts in increasing efficiency, effectiveness and economy of operations
♦ The agency's role in advancing statewide initiatives of the state board and state education agency
♦ The agency's role in contributing to the capacity of the entire state network in the provision of technical assistance to districts (126-72-6.1)

4. The submission of an annual progress report, with special emphasis given to progress in meeting the four quality standards of service. Of interest, the legislative rule also encourages an agency to include in the annual report a description of the perceived nonquantifiable benefits resulting from its work. The agency's regional council must, by majority vote, verify the contents of the annual report (126-72-6.4).

The state board also directed the state education agency, in collaboration with the eight RESAs, to develop a core set of outcome measures and indicators and benchmarks for each of the four quality standards of service. These are to be developed by July 1, 2003, pilot-tested in 2003-04, and to be subsequently approved by the state board (126-72-6.2).

STATE-SPONSORED ANNUAL REPORT CARDS

The latest chapter in efforts to enhance the accountability of educational service agencies is the development in several states of state-sponsored annual report cards on the workings of their system of agencies. This development should come as no surprise in that the precedent for an annual report card on the types of public educational organizations was by the end of the millennium well established. For example, according to a recent report in *Education Week*, 45 of the 50 states in 2001 issued a report card on public local school districts (Quality Counts 2001, p. 80). This represents an incredible buildup of state interest in recent years. While developments at the postsecondary level have not kept pace, there clearly are much more serious efforts at this level in some states than previously. The accountability movement is unquestionably the great accelerator for the widespread interest in this development. It could also be argued that the use of an annual report card on the workings of public educational organizations merely reflects their now common use in virtually all other aspects of the social, economic, and political life of the nation. Report cards of one sort or another are now available for public consumption on all manner of topics such as, for example, the annual new car rankings, the ten best retirement communities, the ten best vacation sites for seniors, the ten most liberal and conservative voting records of members of Congress, to cite a few illustrations from what could be a very long list.

Presented below are highlights of state-sponsored annual report cards on three state networks of service agencies. All three networks are Type A: Special District ESA systems. As established previously, networks of this type are always subject to more stringent state oversight measures than the other major form of service agencies, the Type C: Cooperative ESAs.

The three profiles described are for:

♦ the New York Boards of Cooperative Educational Services
♦ the Oregon Education Service Districts
♦ the Texas Regional Education Service Centers

A number of considerations went into the decision to focus on the annual reporting practices for the three state networks. All three are high-profile systems and would be on most observers' lists as among the strongest networks, from top to bottom, in the nation. Moreover, all three in the past have been trend-setting networks in many programming and state oversight practices. Additionally, all three exhibit characteristics of a systemic state network.

New York BOCES

As cited by the state education agency, the statute establishing the requirement that the state publish an annual report card on the Boards of Cooperative Educational Services (BOCES) was enacted in 1994 (The University of the State of New York 2001, p. 1). The statute establishes only minimal design features, and grants the Commissioner of Education authority to develop regulations considering both the content and format of the report card. Requirements established in the statute are that the report must include measures of the academic performance of the BOCES on a school-by-school basis or program-by-program basis, and that the report must also include measures of the fiscal performance of the BOCES. Another provision of the statute is that the annual report cards be disseminated to selected members of the executive and legislative branches of state government, and to all school districts.

The chief state school officer, beginning in 1997, directed that all 38 BOCES to submit an individual annual report card to school districts in their service region. The report is to be appended to the proposed annual administrative budget that is required to be available for approval by component school districts.

Featured information in the sixth annual report card published in January, 2001 (The University of the State of New York) included background information on the history and purpose of the BOCES, selected demographic data, both individual BOCES and state totals, and in some cases, state averages for each of the major program areas offered by the agencies. Also included is both individual and composite data on expenditures. In some cases, two-year comparisons are reported.

Oregon ESDs

The Oregon Department of Education, in collaboration with the Education Service Districts (ESDs), has, for a number of years, periodically published an annual report card on the state system. The latest, covering the 1998-99 school year, is a compilation of the individual annual reports that, since 1994, must be submitted by each of the 21 ESDs to the state education agency (Oregon Department of Education 1998-99, p. 11).

The report is organized into six parts: (1) resolution services, (2) state mandated services, (3) board discretionary services, (4) contract/agreements for services, (5) review of component district operations, and, (6) the ESD self-appraisal report. These six subject areas follow requirements of the service agencies established either in statute (ORS 334.124) or in administrative rule adopted by the State Board of Education (OARs 581-024-0228 and 0228) (p. 1).

Emphasis in the report is given to five areas: (1) the composite number of services and programs; (2) expenditures for resolution services; (3) discretionary programs; (4) contracts and grants; and (5) the total full-time equivalent staff employed in the delivery of resolution services and those for contracts and agreements. These data tend to be further broken down for each of the four major service and program areas the ESDs are engaged in: special education; media and technology; curriculum, instruction, and assessment; and social services.

Texas RESCs

The annual reporting practices employed in Texas on its system of Regional Education Service Centers (RESCs) are unquestionably the most comprehensive of any state practices at this time. One biennial report targeted on the centers and three separate reports are used to provide insight on the work of the network.

Biennial report. As cited earlier this report is required by statute (§ 39. 183). Selected data on high-interest local school district operations are also included, though approximately two-thirds of the report is ordinarily devoted to the RESCs. Major information-types included in a recent biennial report (*Regional and District Level Report* 2000) included general background information on the RESC network and total state data on such topics as: total professional and support staff, and sources of financial support for both categories of personnel; sources of total revenues reported in percent; common service center programs and services funded in whole or in part from state, federal, and local revenues; expenditures by function; undesignated fund balances (for each RESC).

Information on the programming activities of the centers included a list of core services established in statute, and a list of the specific centers that offer various programs and services in the following categories: decentralized state agency functions; general education/special services; administrative support for schools; instructional support for schools; direct student instruction; and, other locally determined services.

The current accountability system for the centers is also given prominence, beginning with a listing of the five components of the system cited previously. Also included are two measures of the effectiveness of the programs and services offered: student achievement and the results of the selected data from the annual client satisfaction survey.

Student achievement data features:

♦ the percent of students in each regional educational service center passing the state student assessment exercises in reading, mathematics, and writing for the preceding two-year period

♦ the drop-out rate in each regional education service center for the preceding two-year period

♦ the attendance rate in each regional education service center, also for the preceding two-years.

A special effort is made in the report to caution the legislature to be sensitive to the diversity in the student population in the state network of service agencies. This is done by the prominent inclusion of a table that establishes for each region the following information: the average daily attendance; number of campuses; and, the percent of the student population that is African American, Hispanic, White, other, and economically disadvantaged.

The annual client satisfaction survey is the result of a state legislature's directive to develop a uniform system for the assessment of client satisfaction with the services of the centers (§ 8.102). The first survey, which was conducted by a third-party contractor, was carried out in 1997-98 and involved only local district personnel in low-performing schools. The 2001-02 version included personnel from all school campuses, as previously reported.

Academic excellence indicator system—RESC Regional Report. This is one of the special reports issued by the state education agency that provides a report card on the centers, as required by a directive of the Commissioner of Education. The report provides each center with a detailed profile on:

♦ Disaggregated student academic performance measures

♦ Other high-interest school district staffing and financial data

The data on student performance is used to rate each school campus and school district in each center. The information provided provides insight on the intent to which each center is addressing its statutory requirement that it provide services to improve student and school district performance, especially for low-performing campuses (*Academic Excellence Indicator System, ESC Regional Report, 2000-01*).

Some might question whether or not this, and the other special reports cited below, represent a report card in the conventional sense of the term. However, the information that is provided on all service centers is published, thus becoming a part of the public domain. Any interested citizen can readily ascertain the performance of each center in addressing what clearly has been established as a state priority.

Progress report on long-range plan for technology. This required state education agency report to the legislature provides a report card on the role of each center in fulfilling its responsibility to provide consultation, technical assistance, and professional development to school districts in the furtherance of the State Board of Education's strategic plan for technology.

The 2000 report emphasized: the number of educators statewide receiving technology training through all of the centers for the years 1997 through 2000; the number of campuses statewide where students received distance learning through access to their center's videoconferencing network; and, the number of educators statewide who received other training in the integration of technology into campus and school district improvement plans (*Progress Report on the Long-Range Plan for Technology, 1996-2010* 2000, pp. 20-21).

Annual statewide client satisfaction survey. As established earlier, excerpts of this report are included in the state education agency's biennial report to the legislature. The full report, which is disseminated widely, provides data on the perceptions of superintendents, principals, and teachers concerning various aspects of the operation of their service center. The report is required by a directive of the Commissioner of Education and is conducted by a third-party contractor. The data provided in the report are aggregated for all centers. Individual data are used by the Commissioner in the annual evaluation of each center's operations.

The general direction of questions pursued in the June, 2000, report asked respondents to indicate their level of satisfaction provided by their service center in meeting a state or federal requirement on local districts, such as: addressing the four content areas covered in the state assessment program; providing programs for special populations of students; operating the local district efficiently and economically; and, implementing instructional technology. The quality of performance of a center's staff is also probed (*Texas Regional Education Service Center Client Satisfaction Survey, Spring 2000* 2000).

VOLUNTARY ACCOUNTABILITY ACTIVITIES OF SERVICE CENTERS

Education service agencies also voluntarily engage in practices beyond those required in statute or administrative rule in their efforts to be accountable. Several examples of the diverse nature of these initiatives are described here. The illustrations are of two major types:

♦ Those voluntarily sponsored by an entire state network of service agencies
♦ Those voluntarily practiced by an individual service agency

Voluntary State Network Efforts

A number of state professional associations of service agencies have in the past produced, and continue to produce, reports and position papers on their respective state networks that are designed to inform schools and school districts, state interests, and the public of the work of their organizations. The examples cited are of two major types: (1) the development of a position paper that commits the state network to work toward the achievement of meaningful objectives that would enhance its accountability; and, (2) the dissemination of a statewide annual report that provides descriptive data on the work of the network.

Development of position papers. Four examples of a state professional association undertaking the task of demonstrating its commitment to be held more accountable for its work, absent a state directive, are worth noting.

1. The first example is the relatively early work of the Michigan Association of Intermediate School Administrators (MAISA) to complete a position statement on the mission, roles, and essential services of the state's Intermediate School Districts (MAISA 1989). The report, perhaps the first of its kind, established overarching goals and outcomes of the Association, as well as goals and outcomes for each of six major programming areas that represented most of the core services offered by the state network that are enumerated in statute.

It is the work of the task forces in the programming areas that is of primary interest here. Though labeled as outcomes, not standards, it is clear that the Association was committed to establishing programming benchmarks to guide the work of its individual member intermediate school districts, as well as help establish anchors that might be used by the membership in individual assessment exercises. Presented below are illustrations from several of the task force reports that represent a statement of a standard.

In the area of technology media, the Intermediate School Districts (ISDs), individually or in consortium with other ISDs, should be capable of providing 10 essential services, including: "Maintain resource files on human, material and equipment resources that can be made available to local districts addressing technology (mediate issues, computer software, textbooks, professional development programs)" (p. 34).

In the area of special education, each ISD alone or acting in a consortium, should provide 22 essential services, including the following activities: develop, with input from local education agencies and the Parent Advisory Committee for Special Education, and for ISD Board and State Board approval, a tri-annual plan that describes the special education programs and services that are provided or will be provided within the ISD (p. 40); provide leadership to local districts in conducting comprehensive needs assessments to ascertain areas for continual staff development (p. 49); provide for an administrative leadership training program to assist local district administrators in effectively addressing the major changes needed to meet the needs of the year 2000 (p. 50).

A total of 81 essential services were identified. The provision that an individual ISD can satisfy the "standards" by joining a consortium reflects an awareness of the huge diversity in the organizational capacity of the agencies. It also acknowledges an understanding that some of what were identified as essential services can best be accomplished through the pooling of resources. The diversity within the ISDs was a troublesome issue in the completion of the position paper as the membership of MAISA included one very large ISD (e.g., Wayne County that includes Detroit), as well as a number of very small agencies. The extent of diversity among the ESAs in Michigan is not usual among state networks.

2. Another relatively early effort was that undertaken by the Governing Board Council of the Iowa Area Education Agencies composed of both the chief executives and board members of the 15 agencies in the state network. In 1993, the Council completed work on a multiyear effort to develop a strategic plan for the network (AEA Governing Board Council 1993). The significance of the adoption of the plan was that all 15 AEAs publicly acknowledged, perhaps for the first time, that they were part of a state network, not a collection of 15 individual agencies. The plan committed all 15 agencies to a common mission statement:

> to lead the transformation of the early childhood, elementary, and secondary education system into . . . excellence by the year 2000, by providing quality, equitable services which meet the needs of our clients through a cooperative network of innovative regional service centers. (p. 1)

The strategic plan also established a statement of beliefs and objectives (e.g., "all clients will demonstrate student achievement relative to outcomes established within their communities" p. 4), strategies for achievement of the objectives (e.g., "we will assist our clients in developing community partnerships which work toward assuring that every student is ready to learn." (p. 5), and action plans for the accomplishment of each objective/strategy. Content specialists from all agencies were deeply involved in the crafting of the strategic plan.

3. Over the past several years the Nebraska Association of Educational Service Units, representing this state's Type C units, has worked on the development of performance measures to support the previously cited current state accreditation standards. An ESU Accountability Task force has worked on a concept paper that, at this point, focuses on core services.

A March, 1999 draft of the Task Force's recommendations described what are called "system parameters" that are being used to guide the work of the Task Force in the design of the accountability system. The system parameters include statements of both guiding principles as well as criteria selection:

- The system must align with local school improvement efforts.
- The system must be consistent with the state accountability system.
- The system must be applicable to all ESUs.
- The system must use a clear, simplified process.
- The system must use both qualitative and quantitative information. The initial efforts of the system will center on core services components, but may include general service as well, and evaluation information must be applicable to key stockholders (legislature, NDE, ESUs, LEAs) (Nebraska Association of Educational Service Unit 1999).

The draft statement establishes three accountability standards:
Standard #1.
    A. Provide for the facilitation and support of local school improvement processes.
    B. Provide support to local school improvement initiatives (action

plans) with emphasis on implementation of a standards-based system of teaching, learning, and leadership.

Standard #2. Provide high-quality programs and services focused on teaching, learning, and leadership.

Standard #3. Conduct continual evaluation measuring the effectiveness and efficiency of ESU services.

Of particular interest, the Task Force is making use of a configuration mapping planning technique to establish what would represent an indicator of the performance of an ESU in addressing each of the three accountability standards. Three levels of performance are established: the middle of the three sets forth the expected performance of all of the state's ESUs, the other two establish either a minimal or extraordinary level of performance. The purpose of the configuration map is to establish the performance expectations for each of the three accountability standards and then provide a three level continuum of services (p. 2).

Over the past few years the state association has reportedly continued to work on the refinement of the 1999 draft statement. In early 2002, the association also undertook the development of a concept paper that would establish a consensus position on the vision, mission, and goals of the state network of service agencies.

4. The recent efforts of the Ohio Educational Service Center Association, like its counterpart in Nebraska, are also focused on the development of performance measures. It is to be recalled that since 1995 the state has had in place an accreditation system having 15 standards, but no performance measures. Moreover, a 1999 report of the Legislative Office of Education Oversight (*Status Report on the Consolidation of Educational Service Centers* 1999) offered as one of its observations that the state education agency provides little oversight of the service centers, and further that if the legislature wanted to strengthen these agencies, consideration must be given to the use of performance measures as a way to enhance their accountability (p. 20).

The state association subsequently acted on the report of the Legislative Office of Education Oversight by creating a special task force to develop an accountability system. The product of the work of this group is referred to as Ohio ESC Network: Best Practice Expectations. The Best Practice Expectations focus on seven areas: (1) leadership; (2) performance results; (3) customer and student focus; (4) improvement planning; (5) information and analysis; (6) staff focus; and, (7) process management. Each of these seven areas are to be assessed using indicators. In 2001 the state association took the lead in piloting the system in two service centers. Once all service agencies have implemented the system, the plan is to assess each center once every three years (Buford 2001).

Dissemination of annual reports. The Washington Association of Educational Service Districts regularly publishes a composite report detailing the work of the ESDs. The 1999 report celebrated the 30th anniversary of the state system (Accountability Report 1969-1999). The principal information reported focused on the state network and included the following elements: mission of the Association; historical milestones in the development of the ESDs; and, an overview of the role, purpose, and services offered. A profile of each of the nine ESDs is also included. Information featured in each ESD profile included the number of public school districts, as well as information about schools, student enrollment, regional staff, county services, square miles, and ESD staff, and a brief description of programming activities. Composite financial data, such as a breakdown of statewide receipts and expenditures, is also reported.

The format used by the Kentucky Association of Educational Cooperatives in one of its latest annual reports is quite similar to that used by the Washington ESDs. One major difference is that several, but not all, of the nine individual agency profiles included selected data on the participation rates for various activities sponsored by an agency, and cost savings to schools and school districts as a result of participation in 10 agency-sponsored programs (Kentucky Association of Educational Cooperatives, no date).

The format of the third example is that of the Kansas Association of Education Service Agencies (no date) is similar to the previous two in that it includes a brief profile of each of the eleven member associations.

Individual Agency Voluntary Accountability Practices

Individual service agencies also engage in a variety of voluntary practices in their attempt to be accountable to their various stakeholders, beyond those that are the result of the work of the state network of which they are a part, and, of course, those not specified in statute or administrative rule. Examples of six different types of extraordinary accountability practices engaged in by service agencies are described below.

Joint service agreements. Loess Hills AEA 13 (Council Bluffs, IA) has for a number of years entered into a joint service agreement with each school district in its service region. Initially, the agreements were for a one-year period. More recently, they cover a five-year period, consistent with the state requirement that both the AEA and a school district develop a coordinated long-range strategic improvement plan. The agreements serve a number of major functions. On the one hand, they establish in writing the programs and services that the service agency will provide a particular school district, as well as the responsibilities to be assumed by the district in order for each program and service to be implemented effectively. Secondly, the agreements provide both entities with important documentation for use by both in annual as well as five-year assessments of the work of each in fulfilling their agreed-to commitments. Moreover, they can promote better understanding and subsequent timely agreement on any modifications that are required during the five-year period to address unanticipated developments that might impact one party, or both.

The contents of the joint service agreement with Lewis Central Community School District for the period September 2000-September 2005 included: a description of the district's priority school improvements needs, and the expected role of the AEA in providing assistance for each priority need; and, a description of how the AEA is to provide assistance in all other educational services and support services that it offers, and the district indicated it seeks such assistance.

An annual progress report is provided to each district; it is organized around each provision in the joint agreement. The date the assistance was provided, the nature of the service, and what AEA provided the service are established.

Annual profiles of services. Each school district served by the Ingham ISD (Mason, MI) is provided an annual profile, or report card, of services received from the service agency. The 2001-02 report to the Haslett Public Schools is typical. Data is provided on the number of students, staff members, and family members from the district who participated in service agency-sponsored programs. In addition, a listing is also included of service agency staff who provided direct services in the areas of Special Education Support Services (e.g., adaptive physical education teacher, audiologist, teacher consultants for hearing and physically impaired) and Administrative or Operational Support Services (e.g., attendance and truancy follow-up, property tax reporting assistance). Selected information of interest on the ISD is also included in each school district profile: role of ISD board, total revenues and expenditures, and a complete list of all ISD programs and services (Ingham Intermediate School District 2001-02).

Use of advisory committees. Region IV ESC (Houston, TX). The programming activities of Region IV are among the most extensive of any service agency in the nation. Nonetheless, the agency has created an advisory committee for each program and product offered; in the year 2001-02 the number of advisory committees totaled 74. In planning for a new school year, the superintendents of the 54 constituent local school districts are provided an opportunity to nominate one or more staff members to serve on a Region IV program/product advisory group. In 2001-02 approximately 3,200 individuals provided their professional expertise in helping to shape policies and programming decisions for the agency. Another result of the extensive use of advisory panels is the promotion of networking among members of a panel having job-alike responsibilities (Region IV Education Service Center 2002, pp. 16-17). Deliberations of individual advisory panels are then processed by the one single advisory committee required in statute, in this case, one that is composed of the chief executive officers of local school districts.

Designation of interdisciplinary teams. In the late 1990s, Grant Wood Area Education Agency 10 (Cedar Rapids, IA) completed a comprehensive redesign of the organization with the goal of improving services to schools and school districts. In the past, the organization structure, programming, and staffing arrangements carefully followed the three main state funding streams available to the agency, those for special education, media, and educational services. The result of these practices was the creation of what has been commonly referred to as "the three silos" of the 15 Area Education Agencies, where communication and collaboration among agency staff were sometimes less than needed, and where services to client groups also likely suffered. Though the three state funding streams continue to this day, Grant Wood undertook a total redesign of the agency by creating interdisciplinary teams and then assigning them responsibilities to a designated cluster of schools and school districts (Grant Wood Area Education Agency 1996).

Development of a business plan. Cooperative Educational Service Agency #1 (Brookfield, WI) serves schools and school districts in metropolitan Milwaukee. It is one of the few known cases of a service agency completing a multi-year comprehensive business plan in an effort to be more accountable in the conduct of its work. The plan for the 2001-04 period includes a description of the following major topics: business description, business environment analysis, service description, operations plan, management plan, marketing plan, and service transition strategy (Cooperative Education Service Agency, no date).

The discussion of the marketing plan adopted by the agency is especially instructive. Described first is the primary market served, the 45 school districts and 326 private schools in the CESA #1 area. Moreover, the primary clients among this group are to be those schools and school districts and their staff in need of specific expertise for the following: analysis of instructional services; research and service development services; provision of scarce specialists at a competitive cost; technical expertise and programs too costly to be maintained by an individual school or district; specific service consultants needed for staff training; and, instructional staff/therapy services needed for high-cost, low-incidence student populations (p. 23).

The discussion of primary clients and a review of how the agency will prioritize the determination of client needs are followed by three other statements regarding positioning of services, pricing strategy, and marketing strategy. The position of services will focus on five key attributes: cost savings; ease of use; research-based services, techniques, and tools; traditional high-quality instructional/diagnostic/consultative services; and reliability of services due to an on-going relationships with the agency (p. 23).

The pricing strategy adopted by the agency for its services and products is determined on a not-for-profit basis that reflects:

> A "cost only," plus growth costs needed for continuation of the service. The financial plan uses billable hours or consultation and therapy services, and full time equivalency cost for instructional services. The pricing strategy is competitive and lower than other service providers. Through the application of grants, direct service costs to the primary clients are reduced. (p. 23)

Emphasis in the marketing strategy is to be on value-added to the client as a result of participation in a service or product provided by the agency. Attributes of value-added highlighted are: identifiable and sustainable increased pupil performance; expanded services with limited resources on the part of the district; services customized to the district's specific improvement plan; measurable results that can be used by the district for planning and budgeting purposes; direct access to current research; direct access to supplemental resources such as grants; convenience; and, reliability (pp. 23-24).

Measuring performance. Kentucky Educational Development Corporation (KEDC) (Ashland, KY), a Type C: Cooperative ESA, represents one of the finest examples of an individual service agency's commitment to voluntarily engage in efforts that would result in creating a more accountable organization. Several years ago KEDC undertook an ambitious multiyear plan to develop a design for a performance measurement system. Key steps in the planning phase included: the establishment of a planning team composed of staff members, members of the governing board, and the dean of education of a regional institution of higher education; the employment of a consultant to provide technical assistance to the planning team; conference calls with chief executive officers of service agencies across the country known to be engaged in performance measurement efforts in their own agencies; and, site visits by the planning team to service centers in several states that are widely recognized as exemplary agencies.

KEDC subsequently pilot tested its performance measurement system in 2001-02 with a new service designed to assist schools and school districts in addressing the state's new emphasis on low-performing schools. Of interest, the performance measurement system used in the pilot test is an adaptation of the Program Outcome Logic Model advocated by the United Way of America (Harmon; Riggs; Lewis and Six 2002).

SUMMARY

The development of a comprehensive state accreditation system is progressing at different levels of implementation in states maintaining a state network of Special District ESAs. The inclusion of standards is a common feature in all. However, not all accreditation plans in place in the early years of the 21st century establish performance measures to judge whether or not a standard has been met or exceeded, or has not been met. Other fairly common system components include: the required submission of a comprehensive multiyear plan and a periodic progress report, an on-site accreditation review by an external review team, and the levying of sanctions against a poorly performing agency.

An increasing number of states have begun to issue an annual report card on the work of its state network of Special Districts ESAs. The comprehensiveness of these reports varies widely. Over the years, the Texas Education Agency has clearly engaged in the most comprehensive efforts to collect and disseminate information of the 20 operating agencies in the state.

REFERENCES

AEA Governing Board Council. 1993. *Statewide AEA strategic plan* (April). Des Moines, IA: Author.

Buford, C. E. 2001. Ohio's ESC network: Best practices expectations. *Perspectives,* 7:20-24.

CELT Corporation. 2001. *The State of Ohio independent review of regional service agencies: Key findings and best practices report* (November 28). Marlborough, MA: Author.

Cooperative Education Service Agency #1. no date. *CESA #1 Agency Business Plan*

2001-04. Brookfield, WI: Author.

Georgia Department of Education. 1997. *Regional educational service agencies, Amended* (160-5-1-13). Atlanta, GA: Author.

Grant Wood Area Education Agency. 1996. *Newsline 10* 12(Winter). Cedar Rapids, IA: Author.

Harmon, H. H.; Riggs, S.; Lewis, T.; and Six, S. 2002. Measuring ESA performance in improving student achievement. *Perspectives* (September 8):61-75.

Ingham Intermediate School District. 2001-02. *Profile of services, Haslett Public Schools.* Mason, MI: Author.

Iowa Department of Education, Chapter 72, Title XII, Administrative Rule— Accreditation of area education agency program and services. Des Moines, IA: Author.

Iowa General Assembly. 1996. Chapter 273, Accreditation of area education agencies. Des Moines, IA: Author.

Kansas Association of Education Service Agencies. no date. *A-b-c-ds of the Kansas Association of Education Services Agencies.* Salina, KS: Author.

Kentucky Association of Educational Cooperatives. no date. *Kentucky's Educational Cooperative 2001 service report: A new millennium of service.* Ashland, KY: author.

Michigan Association of Intermediate School Administrators (MAISA). 1989. *Mission, role, and essential services.* Lansing, MI: Author.

Nebraska Association of Educational Service Units. 1999. *Educational service unit accountability system* (March 24) Lincoln, NE: Author.

Nebraska Department of Education. 1989. *Rule 84: Regulations governing accreditation of educational service units.* Lincoln, NE: Author.

Oregon Department of Education. *Annual report of education service districts, 1998-1999.* Salem, OR: Author.

Oregon Department of Education. 1999. *Standards for education service districts (581-024-0200).* Salem, OR: Author.

Quality Counts 2001: A better balance. *Education Week* XX(January):17.

Region IV Education Service Center. 2002 Regional Advisory Committee. Executive Committee report (April). Houston, TX: Author.

Texas Center for Educational Research. 2002. *Evaluation of education service center products and services, 2001-02* (May). Austin, TX: Author.

Texas Education Agency. 2000. *Progress report on the long-range plan for technology, 1996-2010* (December). Austin, TX: Author.

Texas Education Agency. 2000-01. *Academic excellence indicator system: ESC regional report.* Austin, TX: Author.

Texas Education Agency. 1996. *Regional and district level report: A report to the 76th Texas legislature* (December). Austin, TX: Author.

Texas Education Agency. 1998. *Regional and district level report: A report to the 76th Texas legislature* (December). Austin, TX: Author.

Texas Education Agency. no date. *Commissioner's performance standards self-assessment report.* Austin, TX: Author.

Texas Education Agency. no date. *Regional education service center (ESC) self-assessment report.* Austin, TX: Author.

Texas General Assembly Education Code, S. 1158, Chapter 8. 1997. Regional Education Service Centers. Austin, TX.

United States General Accounting Office. 1996. *Executive guide: Effectively implementing the Government performance and Results Act* (June). Washington, DC: Author.

United Way of America. 1996. *Measuring program outcomes: A practical guide.* Alexandria; VA: Author.

The University of the State of New York, The State Education Department. 2001. *Financial and statistical outcomes of boards of cooperative educational services* (January). Albany, NY: Author.

Washington Association of Educational Service Districts. no date. *Accountability report 1969-99*. Olympia, WA: Author.

West Virginia State Board of Education. 2003. Title 126 Legislative Rule, Series 72. Establishment and operation of regional education service agencies (3233) (January 12). Charleston, WV: Author.

Chapter 11

The Future of Educational Service Agencies

Predicting the future is a problematic activity and the farther one seeks to see into the future, the less likely predictions can be expected to be correct. Limning the future shape of institutions that meet basic needs and therefore do not change much over time seems less hazardous than predicting the impact on social institutions of technologies that do not yet exist. For example, though there have been significant changes in the ways groceries are sold over the past 50 years, the changes have been largely evolutionary. A supermarket of the 21st century is, in many ways, a very large local grocery store. At present most people still travel to the market, select their desired commodities, pay the bill and carry home their purchases. A different future can be predicted with likely accuracy since there are already small experiments with using newer technologies to modify the manner in which these transactions are carried out. Some companies have experimented with programs that allow customers to order products over the Internet. Others have built small businesses that will deliver purchased products to the home. One can imagine that online ordering will become a more prominent feature of purchasing groceries in the future much as many vendors of durable goods have created an online option for purchasing goods such as clothing, shoes, power tools, and so forth.

Likewise, another basic need, medical care, though enhanced in the last decade or so by new medicines and diagnostic equipment, is still delivered in much the same way it has always been—at the doctor's office for routine checkups and at the hospital for serious illnesses. Perhaps the only significant addition has been the neighborhood medical center, a cross between a doctor's office and an outpatient clinic at a hospital. The positive effects of modern medicine have been dramatic, but the configuration of the delivery system has remained essentially constant for a century or more.

This book has demonstrated that the educational service agency has been rapidly growing as a new feature of the educational delivery system. Though the origins of the contemporary service agency can be traced to county school districts in the 19th century, since the 1960s and early 1970s they have taken on new roles and functions. Whether service agencies are likely to maintain their current roles and functions into the foreseeable future, evolve into a fundamentally different entity or disappear is the question this chapter attempts to answer. The perspective for estimating the future will be modest, the next five to ten years.

FORCES SHAPING THE FUTURE
It is still essentially true that, in the aggregate, the future is significantly shaped by the past and present. Therefore, to project a probable future it is necessary to estimate the likely effect of current trends and forces. However, each service agency will need to maintain the flexibility to respond to events that are a surprise and to use these events for their best advantage. Stated in another way, though we cannot determine our future we have some ability to shape it. Healthy private organizations build their futures on two concepts: they closely watch current markets to assure that they are going where the market is going. At the same time they are creating markets, fashioning new products and/or services that consumers don't even know they need until confronted with the possibility of having them. Computers, cell phones, pagers are all recent technological innovations that today's citizens can't live without. Thirty years ago consumers never felt a need to have any of them.

When once asked what made him a great hockey player, Hall of Famer Wayne Gretsky answered that he skated to where the puck was going to be, not where it was. The need to anticipate future trends and requirements is as important for public agencies as for profit-driven corporations. Though a public organization may be able, through political strength, to maintain its existence longer than a private company when it has outlived its usefulness, it cannot do so indefinitely. The public demand for choice in education has resulted from the failure of educators to read the signs of public dissatisfaction and respond quickly and in meaningful ways. Educational vouchers, with their potential to destroy the basic structure of public education, might not be on the horizon if education leaders had been more customer-focused.

Therefore, portraying the future of educational service agencies requires a consideration of current forces and possible future events that can influence the prospects of service agencies. Some of these forces are listed below. To some extent by aggregating in this chapter the forces that seem likely to affect the future, key points that have been made throughout the book are also summarized. Here are some of these forces.

Pressures on State Education Agencies
No single trend in contemporary education is more prominent than the focus on accountability. Public school achievement began to be a national issue with the realization of dropping SAT scores in the 1970s (World Book Online 2002). This concern about school effectiveness was bought to a fever pitch by the publication of *A Nation at Risk* (1983) as well as highly unfavorable comparisons of American students on international tests of math and science achievement in the 1980s (Baker 1997).

Suddenly, concern about the quality of public education became a clear preoccupation in almost every state. Governor after governor responded to this issue with proposals to test students and sanction schools that were unable or unwilling to assure success for students. When Governor George Bush of Texas became president he initiated legislation that put the federal government squarely in the K-12 education area. Mandatory testing grades three through eight was made the law of the land (No Child Left Behind 2001). However, responsibility for these tests was delegated back to the states.

The combination of local, state, and federal pressure for better schools has increased the responsibilities of state departments of education. They have been responsible for the design of more challenging curricula, the creation of new assessment tools, and the implementation of new protocols for tracking and reporting student achievement. All of this has been an addition to their traditional duties related to monitoring state education expenditures, supervising teacher and administrative certification, and aggregating information about the demographics of education.

Ironically, these additional duties were added just after a widespread effort to shrink the size of government bureaucracies, especially state education bureaucracies. This trend was probably started by President Ronald Reagan's proposal to abolish the federal Department of Education (Babcock and Denton 1982) and his leadership in articulating a free market approach to almost all services, especially services that were delivered by or monitored by government agencies.

Inevitably state government agencies have had to look for partners where they existed or to create them where they didn't. Educational service agencies have been the partner of choice in most states. It is hard to see how state education agencies can function in light of these added responsibilities without service agency support for the foreseeable future.

School Choice

The public policy literature has been cluttered with publications calling for getting government entities out of the business of providing services for almost 20 years (Beales and O'Leary 1994; Flam and Keane 1997; Gormley 1991; Pirie 1988). Therefore, privatization of government services has been an increasing phenomenon, first in the area of civil government (Hatry 1991) and then in public education (Doyle 1994). The 1980s saw many initiatives to privatize prisons, fire departments, waste hauling and other municipal services (Ascher 1991). Private companies entered the K-12 education market in a significant manner in the 1990s, specializing in attempting to improve achievement in urban school districts. EAI, Inc., one of the largest of these firms encountered loud political opposition in its work in Baltimore, Maryland and Hartford, Connecticut before retreating from both environments and disappearing into the more hospitable climate of non-urban schools in Arizona and finally expiring (Flam and Keane 1997). Edison Schools, Inc. has plowed somewhat the same ground, though more successfully. The fact that, as of this writing, they have made a profit only once seems not to deter investors.

Given the U.S. Supreme Court decision regarding the constitutionality of vouchers, the public's apparent affection for more choice in public schools is accommodated by several options:

♦   Magnet schools within school districts

♦ Contracts between public school boards of education and private providers whereby the company operates one (Pontiac, Michigan), several
  (Philadelphia, Pennsylvania), or all (Inkster, Michigan) of a district's
  schools. These contracted schools offer the special delivery system
  featured by the company.
♦ Flexible district boundaries permitted by state law. In Michigan and
  other states, students may attend any school within a broad region.
  State aid is paid to whatever district the student's family selects. (Such
  flexibility requires the affirmative agreement of the district to accept
  such students.)
♦ Charter schools. Though technically public schools, they are able to
  operate free of many rules and regulations required of traditional
  schools.

The aggregation of these options for flexibility within the system of public
education is creating an increasing diversity within the education delivery system and therefore an increasing need for curriculum development services, staff
training, financial management, and other functions from many different agencies that need these services. As was noted in the previous chapter, in most
states service agencies are practically the only entity staffed to provide such
support.

Focus on Interorganizational Cooperation

This book has discussed the growing recognition in public policy circles
that coordination of programs and services is the most effective way to service
needy individuals and families (Bardach 1998). The service agency serves as an
ideal focus for coordination of the education sector. Regional efforts to organize
collaboratives that will avoid duplication of services, identify individuals and
families who have been missed by the service delivery system, and to synergize
the efforts of each entity can readily reach into the education sector through the
auspices of a service agency. Everywhere service agency chief executives meet
regularly, usually monthly, with local school district superintendents. To link
with the service agency is to link with the total educational system in the area.
This type of linchpin brings to the education community the type of institutional
coordination that chambers of commerce bring to business, councils of government bring to municipal government entities, and United Ways bring to nonprofit agencies. The ease and effectiveness of bringing together temporary or
permanent collaboratives to deal with such issues as child care, adjudicated
youth, employment and training for unemployed and underemployed citizens
and other social problems are enhanced when a service agency is available to be
the catalyst of marshalling education staff to join solution-developing groups
and committees.

Urban and Rural School Problems

It has been noted earlier that one of the policy foundations for the creation
of service agencies was to "serve as a conduit for the implementation of state
initiatives" (Stephens and Turner 1991, p.1). It has been noted above that the

present accountability movement flows from the conspicuous lack of success of some schools, a large number of which are located in urban and rural environments. President Bush was successful in passing the *No Child Left Behind Act* of 2001 because it spoke to a large and varied constituency. Republicans supported it because it brought responsibility and accountability to a major government service and also offered help to a natural constituency, rural schools. Democrats supported it because it offered continuing pressure on urban schools to serve their students more effectively. Bringing not just equal opportunity but equal results to these two troubled sectors of American education is therefore a state responsibility. Most state departments of education are woefully short of staff to be of great assistance to local school districts. Service agencies are currently working under the direction and support of state departments to help urban and rural schools. Virginia is one state that created a form of service agency where none existed in recognition of the need to have capable staff close to the districts in need if they are to effectively help them, though it has recently abandoned them.

The Knowledge Explosion

Knowledge is growing exponentially. It is now said that knowledge doubles every 18 months. Half of the "facts" taught to engineering students in the early years of their undergraduate education are incorrect by the time they graduate. No one can keep up with all of this new knowledge. Those who produce knowledge (do research) on a full-time basis are in the best situation to stay relatively current. Those who are practitioners (for this discussion, teachers and administrators) have no hope of staying current. They must depend on those whose full-time job is to track relevant new theories and practices and share this information with full-time practitioners. In 42 states service agency personnel provide this connection to new knowledge for school personnel.

Technology

It can be argued that the capacities of newer technologies can make school buildings obsolete structures for the transmission of discipline-based knowledge. Math, science, reading, foreign language, economics and other subjects are becoming available on CDs, through television classes taught far from the students, and by "virtual learning," Internet-based material accessible to anyone, anywhere, anytime. However, technology cannot teach everything (e.g., how to get along with others, how to develop self-discipline), and all technology-based learning is probably a supplementary tool at best with very young students for whom custodial care is a significant function of traditional schools. However, even as a supplementary tool, technology can be expensive to acquire and costly to maintain if schools must rely on private industry providers. Finding, training, and maintaining local technical expertise often requires outside assistance. Service agencies are offering this assistance throughout the United States.

Site-based Delivery

Fullan (1992), Goodlad (1992), the Consortium for Renewing Education at Vanderbilt University (1998) and other scholars have argued that the individual school must be the locus of change. Some school districts have attempted to foster the capacity of individual schools to chart their own course by transferring to building decision-makers significant responsibility for budget expenditures, staff selection, hours of operation and other elements of local control (Herman 1997; Sewall 1999). In this process central office curriculum directors and staff developers become less influential in shaping program and training teachers and administrators. Why? Because Elementary School A may have fewer needs in common with Elementary School B in the same district than it does with Elementary School I in another district. Service agencies are better situated to aggregate needs over a broad range of districts.

THREE SCENARIOS FOR THE FUTURE

Since predicting the fate of educational service agencies over the next five to ten years seems beyond the capability of anyone, the more prudent course seemed to be to project three alternative futures. To some extent each of the scenarios described below assumes that each outcome is somewhat within the control of service agencies themselves. They can encourage the forces that will lead them to their preferred future. However, each scenario also recognizes that there are political, technological, economic and other forces that can significantly determine the future regardless of what service agency personnel and staff members in the districts they serve either say or do.

It should be noted that scenario writing is not a forecasting method. It is, rather, a framework upon which an analysis of the emergence of a particular future can be based (Sage and Chobot 1975). Generally accepted guidelines for scenario writing require that they meet the following criteria: They are:

- Based on data.
- Internally consistent.
- Compatible with state and federal constitutional provisions.
- Plausible.
- Politically feasible.
- Time centered.

The following scenarios meet all of these tests. All three may also be described as "operations/analytical" forms of scenario writing rather than the type of scenario that has been called "free form" (Dunn 1994). The latter form of scenario is one that is not limited by current facts or conditions. It can be built on assumptions which are highly speculative and conceptualize new paradigms for which there are not present intimations.

The operations/analytical scenarios used here start with the present state of educational service agencies and attempt to suggest how, step-by-step, a future state might evolve in a plausible fashion out of the present.

SCENARIO #1—A WORST CASE SCENARIO

This conceptualization of the future assumes that some of the trends identified in contemporary education will accelerate and have a major impact on the education landscape. Two of these trends will be particularly significant. There will be a continuation of the move to downsize state education agencies, a phenomenon which will inevitably require a downsizing in the service and technical assistance roles of state agencies, although their compliance obligations will increase. Also, the public and political support for choice in education will increase, perhaps dramatically, if a large number of states decide to allow voucher systems as permitted by the Zeman Supreme Court decision. If there is a proliferation of charter schools and independent schools as a result of vouchers, smaller school districts, at least in suburban areas, will be required to consolidate. Larger school districts will be able to afford their own curriculum and training staffs. Thus, there will be less need for these larger districts to turn to service agencies for assistance. Charter schools, religious schools, and other independent schools may also turn to private firms contracted by the schools (Edison Schools, Sylvan Learning Centers, etc.) church-affiliated consultants, or other third parties to provide most of the services previously provided by educational service agencies

Two possible alternative futures are possible for educational service agencies should these trends dominate the educational landscape. These two results are not necessarily mutually exclusive in the short term. Longer term effects are less predictable.

1. Educational service agencies established by state law, rule, or constitutional mandate (Type A: Special District ESAs) will be drawn toward becoming technical assistance branches for the state education department. More and more state funding will come to them with tightly defined requirements to deliver specific services, especially mandates to assist low-performing and failing school districts. The performance of service agencies will be less dependent on the value of programs provided for all school districts in the constituency and more on their success in helping troubled districts improve student performance to acceptable levels. To the extent that ESAs become "enforcement" arms of the state department of education, they will lose some ability to be of assistance to local districts, especially those not under the direct gaze of the state because of poor student performance. This will occur because districts will be less willing to admit weaknesses for which they need help in fear that admitting weakness may attract the gaze of the state.

2. To the extent that ESAs do not function as the training and development as well as the compliance arms of the state in working with unsuccessful districts, they will be obligated to rely on their own entrepreneurship for continued financial health, a situation currently true for Type C: Cooperative ESAs. State support for nonmandated functions will disappear. ESAs will be viewed as only one of many possible service providers. They will therefore be forced to compete with private sector service providers such as Edison Schools, Inc. and other public sector entities (e.g., universities, voluntary cooperatives, and professional

organizations) for the opportunity to serve local districts.

SCENARIO 2—A BEST CASE SCENARIO

This scenario is predicated on the assumption that all seven identified trends in public education will continue. However, some trends will be modified.

Vouchers, though declared constitutional by the Supreme Court, will go back to state courts for determination as to the application of state constitutions to vouchers and will not be approved in most states. Therefore, the present delivery system, as modified by charter schools and parental choice in the last few years, will remain essentially the same as the current configuration.

Better public control of the local governance system of charter schools will be established. Also, private companies involved in the operation of charter schools will be subject to more complete disclosure of their profit and loss statements for each school. Should some companies be found to be making large profits, public support for charter schools will likely diminish. Over the next five to 10 years ESAs will be positively impacted in four principal ways.

1. State supported ESAs will be expanded to all 50 states as policy makers recognize the cost-effectiveness and cost-efficiency of service agencies as instruments of educational change and improvement. Perhaps the best indication that this expansion is likely to occur can be found in the most recent amendments to the federal Elementary and Secondary Education Act. Several sections of the bill refer specifically to educational service agencies and describe what a state must do if it doesn't have a service agency structure.

2. State education departments will enthusiastically call on ESAs to be their local agent for school improvement services because of their track record of working collaboratively with local school districts to identify and deliver needed programs and services in a cost-effective manner. The state will support a full range of services through the ESA so that all districts in the constituency will be able to call on the agency to assist them in school improvement. Therefore, while the ESA may be working with a low-performing district on curriculum and teaching issues focused on reading and math, it may be working with more advantaged districts in developing and delivering programs in the fine arts, advanced placement courses, and offerings for gifted and talented.

3. Disputes about whether school districts should both produce and provide programs and services or just make sure they are provided, leaving to the private sector responsibility to produce them, will largely disappear. Public policy will require collaboration to effectively meet the needs of students, families, and the public, not just encourage it. There will be a growth of public/private partnerships (e.g., collaboration between schools and business in designing and delivering vocational training that requires expensive equipment and personnel with state-of-the-art training).

4. Local school districts will increasingly recognize that they must focus on their primary mission—providing a quality program focused on high-level learning for all students. Functions such as busing and feeding students will be

recognized as activities that take away from concentrating on the main mission of schools. Therefore, these functions, and others such as finance and accounting, building maintenance and other noneducational activities, will be delegated to the service agency to perform or the service agency will contract out these functions on behalf of the constituent school districts. These functions will be supervised and monitored by the service agency.

SCENARIO # 3—MOST PROBABLE SCENARIO

The identified trends will continue. School district consolidation, if it occurs at all, will not have a major impact on the education landscape. There will be a continuing trend toward routing more decision-making authority, including expenditure decisions, to school buildings. This will happen either because of a continuing trend toward site-based management or because school funding formulas will be redesigned to have dollars follow the pupil, whether within the district or to schools in other districts or to charter schools (Solmon and Fox 1998).

The recognized value of a state system of service agencies will continue to grow. Nevertheless, each state will continuously examine its delivery system to determine the appropriate functions to assign to service agencies and to balance the competing values of capacity and geography; that is, to weigh the amount the state can afford to spend to make each agency a fully functional enterprise yet keep each agency within some proximity to its constituent school districts. States will recognize that it is financially imprudent to replicate identical full functioning ESAs throughout the state. Instead they will create a series of "centers of excellence," which will each specialize in one or more functions such as special education, fine arts, technology, gifted and talented education, and other important topics. A "center of excellence" might support a few service agencies and their local districts in a region of the state or it might offer programs and services for the whole state. Newer technologies such as distance and virtual learning would make this wide-area support possible.

All currently functioning educational service agencies will have a continuing responsibility to demonstrate their cost-effectiveness and cost-efficiency based on outcome measures, not such traditional process standards as number and variety of programs offered and positive testimonials from attendees. This will be particularly true during times of financial duress since a few local districts may challenge the value of the service agency if its own resources are being reduced by the state.

Because of an earned reputation for quality, ESAs will take on more "back room" services for local districts, charter schools, and independent schools. These functions will include business and finance operations, some personnel functions such as acquiring and training substitute teachers, and transportation coordination.

Education service agencies will collaborate with businesses and unions to develop technical training programs for constituent districts at central sites. Some of these programs will be offered at facilities equipped and staffed by

ESA staff; others will be provided at commercial and industrial sites, whether offices, factories, or research centers.

DISCUSSION

There are several issues that must be confronted if ESAs are to survive in healthy condition in the future.

Shedding Invisibility

Creating a long-term vision of almost any enterprise at the beginning of the 21st century is a difficult task since change is the only constant in these times. A few examples will illustrate the problem.

Universities are at risk when they contemplate building new dormitories to open at a time when opportunities to acquire a virtual education are expanding dramatically. Will students fill these expensive living accommodations when some may argue that the "brick and mortar" university is a relic (Stallings 2000)? Drug store company presidents struggle to determine how many new stores to build when prescriptions, medical supplies, personal care items, and other products traditionally sold at the corner drug store are now available on the Internet. In light of September 11, developers need to determine whether to build tall buildings again. How tall is too tall to be rented because of residual fear of another catastrophe?

These various forms of uncertainty illustrate the hazards of projecting the future of educational service agencies. However, trends do tell a story. Twenty years ago Stephens and Turner noted that were 23 state-wide systems of service agencies with three other states with a system of service agencies that serve three-fourths or more of the local districts, "thus giving these states a virtual statewide system" (1991, p. 1). By the year 2004 there were 42 states with full or partial service to local districts. Changes adopted in 2001 in the Elementary and Secondary Education Act refer constantly to educational service agencies and authorize state education agencies to utilize service agencies in the provision of professional development services, school improvement activities, programs designed to improve the academic achievement of disadvantaged students, and the development of partnerships to enhance education through technology. Momentum is building toward a national presence for service agencies.

It is estimated that public and private schools within the boundaries of service agencies in America spend in excess of $344 billion a year (AESA 2000). Though there is no verifiable figure about the amount spent directly by and through all the educational service agencies in American, it is significant, as was demonstrated in research conducted by the authors and summarized in the Introduction. Service agency expenditures represent funds received from state aid, state and federal dollars that flow through to local districts (for example, special education dollars), local tax revenue in those few states that authorize taxing authority for service agencies, and dollars received from the sale of programs and services to customers, largely local school districts.

Nevertheless, few citizens (and voters) know much about them. Most tax-payers have no awareness of the existence of educational service agencies. Few legislators, the people responsible for creating or eliminating them, funding them adequately or inadequately, know very much about them. Much of this invisibility can be traced to an attitude among leaders of these agencies in the early years of their existence that the work they did should bring about success for local districts; it was the local districts that should be publicly recognized for their successes. Competition for public accolades could produce negative feelings toward the service agency and its leaders.

Since constituent voters know so little about service agencies, legislators are not subject to the push and pull of policy options developed through public debate that usually produce effective government. There are no books in general circulation devoted to the role and function of educational service agencies to inform policy-making about service agencies, a vacuum this publication is intended to remedy.

The visibility problem is not limited to the general public or legislators. Few educators, even those who use their programs and services frequently, understand why educational service agencies were initially created, how they are funded, how they are governed, or where they are headed. No university programs are devoted to training the next generation of service agency leaders. Most chief executives are selected from subordinate administrators within the agency or from among local school superintendents, who are often, necessarily, chosen for their successful leadership of a local district rather than a service agency. These are not very similar positions, and the skills needed for service agency leadership can be quite different than those needed to direct a local school district. More important, because there are no organized training programs, new service agency leaders need to spend a year, perhaps several years, learning about the characteristics of successful service agency programming around the state and country before becoming completely competent to provide the type of proactive leadership and vision that will enable a service agency to reach its full potential. Many local residents consider the local superintendent as the most important educator in the local district. A local superintendent who is selected to lead a service agency must quickly learn to submerge his/her own ego in order to work with the leaders of constituent districts, usually the most important persons in advising and evaluating the agency itself. Successful local superintendents do not automatically become effective service agency leaders.

The names by which service agencies are known differ from state to state (See Chapter 3) so it is understandable if citizens, and legislators, in Cedar Rapids, Iowa, are unaware that the Intermediate School District in Michigan and the Board of Cooperative Educational Services in New York are essentially the same type of entity as the Area Education Agency in their own state. In fact, service agencies in Michigan are known by three different names: Intermediate School Districts, Regional Educational Service Agencies, and Regional Educational Service Districts. It seems clear that service agencies need to build on the success they have had by being subsumed under the rubric of "educational service agencies" in federal legislation and adopt some kind of similarity of name in all states. The proliferation of names in Michigan has been caused by a halting effort to reach that goal in this state.

Data for Policy Decision-Making

Perhaps the issue regarding ESAs that dominates deliberations in state policy circles more than any other is the concern regarding the costs and benefits of the system of service agencies operating in the state. Concerns of this type appear to be especially prevalent in those states that sponsor a state network of Type A: Special District ESAs. Both state interests and the educational service agency community share responsibility for the frequent absence of timely, policy-relevant cost-analysis studies on the operations of the service agencies. The apparent reluctance of state interests to undertake more assessments of this type is difficult to understand, given the demonstrably key role that many statewide networks play in strengthening the infrastructure of the state system of elementary-secondary education. Equally difficult to understand is the apparent apathy in many service agency communities to advocate for such initiatives when, in all likelihood, they have so much to gain.

State commissioners of education need to do a far better job of collecting data about the work of service agencies and making this data available to legislators. Only in the presence of sound data can legislators make enlightened policy decisions. Educational service agency leaders in each state should be proactive in insisting on the collection of such data and in taking a leading role in gathering it. This will not be an easy task, as the authors have found out. Some agency leaders may not be very helpful in gathering this data. There are many reasons for this. Many agencies are very small and see data collection not required by law as a task that can safely be ignored in relation to other priorities. Other agencies may fear the conclusions that may arise from viewing their data: that they are ineffective, inefficient, or unfocused, especially when compared with other agencies within the same state. Insistence on the availability of comprehensive data about service agencies by state departments of education and state legislators can overcome these natural tendencies to avoid sharing information.

More Cost-Analysis Studies Needed

We argue here for the widespread use of cost-efficiency studies of programs and services designed to enhance the infrastructure requirements of schools and school districts. We support the use of cost-efficiency analysis as a first, relatively easy, design that could then serve as the forerunners for other cost-analysis probes, such as cost-effectiveness analysis and cost-benefit analysis. Completion of this type of cost-analyses for both Type A: Special District ESAs and Type C: Cooperative ESAs can then serve as building blocks for the conduct of more rigorous approaches. For example, there appears to be progress in addressing one of the major obstacles in the application of cost-benefit analysis in education, the requirement that both inputs and outputs be measured in monetary units (Hummell-Rossi and Ashdown 2002). Our advocacy for the widespread initial use of cost-efficiency analysis is in part also based on the fact that the term "efficiency" is regularly used in the official pronouncements of both the states' expectations for the programs and services of service agencies, where these have been propagated, as well as consistently used in the mission statements of individual service agencies.

For these reasons, then, what would be of immediate value in bringing more discipline to many of the debates that occur in state policy circles would be a straightforward analysis of whether the programs and services can be provided at least cost by the educational services agencies, by other service providers in the region, state, or nation, or duplicated by schools and school districts.

A cost-efficiency study, while addressing the high-interest issue of whether or not the services of an ESA is the least-cost provider, does not answer other high-interest questions. For example, a study of this type cannot assess other effects of a service, nor can it assess whether or not there are other ways a service agency or a school and school district should expend its resources. However, not to be minimized are other potential benefits that should be examined in cost-efficiency studies, such as the leverage gained through participation in ESA-sponsored programs and the resultant ability to use any savings for other purposes; the ability to multiply initial dollar investment in a program; the differences between the ESA and competitor costs to produce a program or service; and the total costs for the participating school and school district after fees or membership costs are included.

Recommended design features of cost-efficiency studies. A recommended design for the conduct of a cost-efficiency study is described below. Stephens and Harmon (1995) argue that the design guidelines "would enjoy acceptance in the policy and professional communities as a valid approach for documenting the economic benefits of the work of service agencies" (p. 2). Note that the design is directed at statewide studies of state networks of service agencies. This focus was used in part because it is here where such studies are likely to have the greatest political impact. A statewide focus can be easily modified for use by an individual agency.

It should also be noted that while the recommended design is introduced in the context of a discussion of the role of service agencies in infrastructure issues, the approach certainly has equal utility in assessing the cost-efficiency of programming more directly related to the instructional program of schools and school districts.

The recommended design of cost-efficiency studies is presented in Table 11.1.

Eleven major sequential steps are established. While all steps are important to the successful completion of a cost-efficiency study, several warrant additional comment.

1. The computation by each service agency of the total operating costs (Step 2) in the four categories used in the design (i.e., personnel, facilities,

Table 11.1

Recommended Design Features of Statewide Cost-Efficiency Studies

1. Revenue and expenditure structures are identified.
2. Coverage of report is determined.
   a. Selected, high-interest programs/services or comprehensive coverage of most or all programs/services.
   b. Selection rationale is established.
3. Total operating costs for each program/service are established.
   a. Personnel
   b. Facilities
   c. Equipment and supplies
   d. Other costs
4. Costs to clients/customers to obtain each program/service are established.
   a. Direct costs to participants
   b. Other costs for participants
5. Costs are established for clients/customers if each program/service is obtained from a source other than the ESA.
   a. Cost of program/service from another provider
   b. Cost of program/service if duplicated by client
6. Dollar benefits or dollar savings to clients/customers for each program/service is established.
7. Dollar benefits or dollar savings to clients/customers for all program service is established.
8. Cost-efficiency of each program/service is established.
9. Cost-efficiency of all program/service is established.
10. Quantifiable results are established.
    a. Aggregate for state
    b. Disaggregate for individual ESA
11. Nonquantifiable benefits are identified.

equipment and supplies, other costs) must be consistent. Moreover, and importantly, as recommended by Levin and McEwan (2001) "the degree of specificity and accuracy in listing ingredients should depend upon their overall contributions to the total costs." (p. 53). That is, there are ordinarily personnel costs in most service agency programming, and these usually represent a significant percent of the total cost. These must be accurate. On the other hand, facility and equipment costs may be minor for some programs and services, and in these cases an estimate may be sufficient, absent actual costs.

2. Equally important is the need to accurately establish all direct and indirect costs incurred by schools and school districts (Step 4) as a result of participation in a program or service. Here, again, the degree of specificity and accuracy in listing the costs of ingredients should depend upon their significance in computing the total cost.

3. The computation required to complete Step 5, costs to clients if a program were to be obtained from a service provider other than the educational ser-

vice agency, is critical to the entire exercise. And this step is generally one of the most neglected. As is often the case, there may not be another service provider offering the same program or service, particularly in the rural areas of most states. Here, an acceptable alternative to establish the value of a program or service, an estimate of the dollar value, called shadow pricing, can be used.

4. Step 11 calls for the inclusion in a cost-efficiency study of nonquantifiable benefits as a result of a program or service provided by an educational service agency that is designed to enhance the infrastructure requirements of schools and school districts. These types of benefits, though difficult to ascertain, can nonetheless be valued highly by participants in a program or service and efforts should be made to uncover the nature of these. Cited below are examples of nonquantifiable benefits given prominence in an earlier examination of five statewide cost analyses undertaken by third parties of the operations of state networks of service agencies (Stephens and Harmon 1996). The third party research reports were conducted either by a state legislative research bureau or a for-profit management consultant firm. Nonquantifiable benefits identified by school and school district staff that are related to the provision of management support services quoted in the five reports include: "provides leverage to limited resources," "promotes administrative efficiency," "personal face-to-face services is an important aspect of access and quality," "assists in compliance with federal and state regulations," "saves time for staff in development of plans and policies," "saves time for staff in development of specifications for supplies and equipment," and "improves morale of staff" (p. 12).

Special design issues in statewide studies. A number of major issues must be addressed in a statewide cost-efficiency study of organizational and management support services that are not present when the focus is on an individual service agency. These include the following:

1. The choice of organizational and management support services to be included in the study must be limited to those offered by all agencies in the state network.

2. There is a need to account for regional differences in the computation of service agency operating costs to deliver a program or service. The use of a statewide dollar value ignores variations ordinarily present among service agencies that can affect operating costs. It is especially critical that this be done for what Levin and McEwan (2001) would likely refer to as the "big ticket" costs, those associated with personnel, facilities, equipment and material. Other differences among service agencies in a single state that can affect the production and delivery of a program or service include: the size of a region with respect to number of schools, school district, and enrollment, and geographic characteristics.

Wallerstein's (1997) study of the cost-efficiency of a single program offered by the six service centers in the Connecticut network stands as a good illustration of the difficulties faced in the design of statewide studies. One focus of her study was out-of-district special education transportation. One of her conclusions was that the significant differences in the way the agencies compute costs, as well as differences in the ways that third party vendors do so, make it very difficult to implement any kind of cost-analysis study.

Benefits to be realized. Numerous benefits will result from the conduct of cost-efficiency studies, whether by an individual service agency or a state network, and whether voluntary or prescribed by the state. In proposing the use of a biennial cost-efficiency study of the Iowa Area Education Agencies (Stephens 2000) four principal benefits were cited:

1. It should provide data that will document whether or not the ESAs are achieving the state and local expectations that they improve the efficiency and economy of school and school district programming and management support practices.

2. It should simultaneously provide data that will document whether or not the programming and organizational practices of the ESAs are efficient.

3. It should facilitate the reporting of data that will document the performance of the statewide network (aggregated data) as well as that of individual ESAs (disaggregated data) while always honoring the "fairness test" in the comparison of the data on individual ESAs.

4. It should help build, over time, a systematic process for benchmarking ESAs' programming and organizational practices, and the eventual establishment of benchmarks, or performance targets (p. 54).

SURVIVING COMPETITION AND THRIVING

There are no certitudes in the workplace of the 21st century. In a global economy knowledge work can be done anywhere for instant delivery anywhere else around the globe. Manufactured items can be and are being produced in one country for just-in-time delivery to another nation.

The certitudes of another generation about the role of government in the delivery of services have been smashed. Public education has gone from being viewed as an almost sacred responsibility of government to a hotly contested marketplace, a trend started back in the late 1950s and early 1960s (Friedman 1962; Kuttner 1997). Political battles rage in state after state about how many more charter schools, many managed by private companies, will be allowed. The impact of the Supreme Court decision finding vouchers to be constitutionally permissible has yet to be seen. Wholesale flight from public schools, at least in some states, is imaginable though not likely.

Some, but certainly not all, of the policy assumptions, discussed at length in this book and which led to the formation of a system of educational service agencies in many states, no longer exist in the form they did at the time of the birth of this movement. However, the world of public education is not totally different either. The growth of charter schools and magnet schools has led to more schools, rather than fewer, reversing a trend toward consolidation in the education arena that has gone on for scores of years. And though recent research suggests that there are many advantages to personalizing schools through smaller units, whether as separate schools or "schools within schools," smaller is not an unmixed blessing either. Smaller faculties mean these schools have fewer creative ideas, special knowledge and skills, and staff to bring about change and improvement. The need to reach out to an agency that can focus on capturing and sharing new concepts and methodologies may actually increase. Smaller schools have fewer dollars to leverage for larger purchases, thereby increasing the need to collaborate with other schools to get the efficiencies of bulk purchasing and the specialized knowledge that can make such joint ventures as productive as possible. Though charter and magnet schools often focus on a singular philosophy or methodology and may thereby narrow the range of student ability and interests in each classroom, they will do so only in a relative sense. There will always be children with special needs—the gifted, the disabled, and the disaffected—who can best be serviced by pooling financial and human resources. This is what educational service agencies were established to do.

As long as each state stands fast to the imperative of providing a free public education for all who want it, the publicly funded service agency will continue to be the best, though least visible, bargain available to support American public schools in their never-ending task of maintaining a thriving democracy.

SUMMARY

Educational service agencies are relatively new components of the educational delivery system in many states. In some cases they represent permutations of 19th and early 20th century county boards of education, which had been charged largely with narrow administrative duties such as verifying teacher certification and performing health and safety inspections for rural schools. As state officials and local leaders saw the opportunities for increased effectiveness and lower costs through collaboration to provide high expense programs like special education and vocational education, newer entities, called service agencies, were developed. However, their growth has been highly influenced by each state's norms and priorities. Though service agencies exist in a majority of states, their form, funding and governance differ widely from state to state. Some states (New Jersey, Virginia) create them, only to eliminate them not too many years later. Illinois recently attempted to bring coherence to three different forms of service agency by eliminating one of the three forms.

It is not yet clear how service agencies will evolve in the future. Three scenarios for this development have been presented. Enlightened national policy in this regard will only be possible if the invisible service agency is made more visible in the policy arena. Sound data about the strengths and weaknesses of service agencies are needed. A national effort to gather this data should demonstrate the incredible flexibility, efficiency, and effectiveness of service agencies and their almost essential role in making sure no child is left behind. It is the hope of the authors that the material in this book has clearly demonstrated the value of ESAs.

REFERENCES

American Association of School Administrators 2000. *"Foundation for the future"* campaign. Arlington, VA: Author.

Ascher, K. 1991. The business of local government. In R. L. Kemp (Ed.), *Privatization: The provision of public services by the private sector* (pp.297-304). Jefferson, NC: McFarland and Co.

Babcock, C. R., and Denton, H. H. 1982. New budget would slash school aid; Department may become a foundation. *Washington Post* (February 3). Retrieved February 26, 2002, from http://www3.oakland.edu/oakland/frames.asp?main+http://www.kl.oakland.edu.

Baker, D. P. 1997. Surviving TIMSS. *Phi Delta Kappan* 79:295-300.

Bardach, E. 1998. *Getting agencies to work together: The practice and theory of management craftsmanship.* Washington, DC: Brookings Institution Press.

Beales, J., and O'Leary, J. 1994. *Making schools work: Contracting options for better management.* Midland, MI: Mackinac Center for Public Policy/Reason Foundation.

CORE (Consortium on Renewing Education) 1998. 20/20 vision: A strategy for doubling academic achievement in America by the year 2020. *Education Week* (December 26):24-25.

Doyle, D. 1994. The role of the private sector in the management of public education. *Phi Delta Kappan* 76:128-132.

Dunn, W. N. 1994. *Public policy analysis: An introduction.* Englewood Cliffs, NJ: Prentice Hall.

Flam, S., and Keane, W. 1997. *Public schools/private enterprise: What you should know and do about privatization.* Lancaster, PA: Technomic Press.

Friedman, M. 1962. *Capitalism and freedom.* Chicago: University of Chicago Press.

Fullan, M. 1992. Getting reform right: What works and what doesn't. *Phi Delta Kappan* 74:745-752.

Goodlad, J. (992. On taking school reform seriously. *Phi Delta Kappan* 74:232-238.

Gormly, W. T. ed. *Privatization and its alternatives.* Madison, WI: University of Wisconsin Press.

Hatry, H. 1991. Problems. In R.L. Kemp (Ed.), *The provision of pubic services by the private sector*, (pp. 262-266). Jefferson, NC: McFarland and Co.

Herman, J.J. 1997. *School-based budgets: Getting, spending, accounting.* Lancaster, PA: Technomic Publishing Co.

Kemp, R. L. ed. 1991. *Privatization: The provision of public service by the private sectors.* Jefferson, NC: McFarland and Co.

Kuttner, R. 1997. *Everything for sale: The virtues and limits of markets.* New York: Alfred A. Knopf.

Savas, E. S. 1987. *Privatization: The key to better government.* Chatham, NJ: Chatham Publishers.

Sewell, A. M. 1999. *Central office and site-based management: An educator's guide.* Lancaster, PA: Technomic Publishing Co.

Stallings, D. 2000. The virtual university: Legitimized at century's end; future uncertain for the new millennium. *Journal of Academic Librarianship* 26:3-14.

Stephens, E. R., and Turner, W. 1991. *Approaching the next millennium: Educational service agencies in the 1990's.* Arlington, VA: American Association of Educational Service Agencies.

United States National Commission on Excellence in Education. 1983. *A nation at risk: The imperative of educational reform.* Washington, D. C.: United States Government Printing Office.

World Book Online. 2002. Education 1977 (February 26). Retrieved from http://www.aolsvcworldbook.aol.com/wbol/wbAuth/na.

Index